Christianity
in the Luangwa Valley

FENZA Publications

The Faith and Encounter Centre Zambia (FENZA) was founded in 2007 as an initiative of the Missionaries of Africa (White Fathers) with the aim of empowering Christians to face in openness the challenges of traditional and contemporary cultures, and to encounter people of different Christian denominations, contemporary religious movements and religions. FENZA publications aim at provoking discussions on cultural and religious topics that affect the Christian faith.

Reflecting on situations of "the Church on the margins" and publishing from these margins (outside the established publishing platforms and on very limited budgets) comes with the need for wider peer review and further discussion. FENZA and its authors value feedback and honest reviews. The author of this book can be reached under the following email address:

bernhard@fenza.org

Bernhard Udelhoven

Christianity
in the Luangwa Valley

FENZA Publications
Faith and Encounter Centre Zambia, Lusaka
2007

(Published in this present book format: 2015)

FENZA Publications
Faith and Encounter Centre Zambia
P.O. Box 320 076, Lusaka, Zambia
www.fenza.org

Udelhoven, Bernhard.
Christianity in the Luangwa Valley
Includes bibliographical references and index.
BISAC category: Social Sciences / Anthropology / Cultural
Other categories: Religion / Christian Ministry / Missions
ISBN-13: 978-1515383512
ISBN-10: 1515383512

First publication date: June 2007 (photocopied manuscript, discussed and distributed within Chipata Diocese, Zambia).
Publication date of the present book version (FENZA): September 2015

Printed and distributed by CreateSpace Independent Publishing Platform, Charleston SC, U.S.A.
Available from (eStore): https://www.createspace.com/5661572
Distribution in Zambia: FENZA/Lusaka

Table of contents

Map 1: The Luangwa Valley.
Source: *New Basic Education Resource Atlas Zambia* 2004.

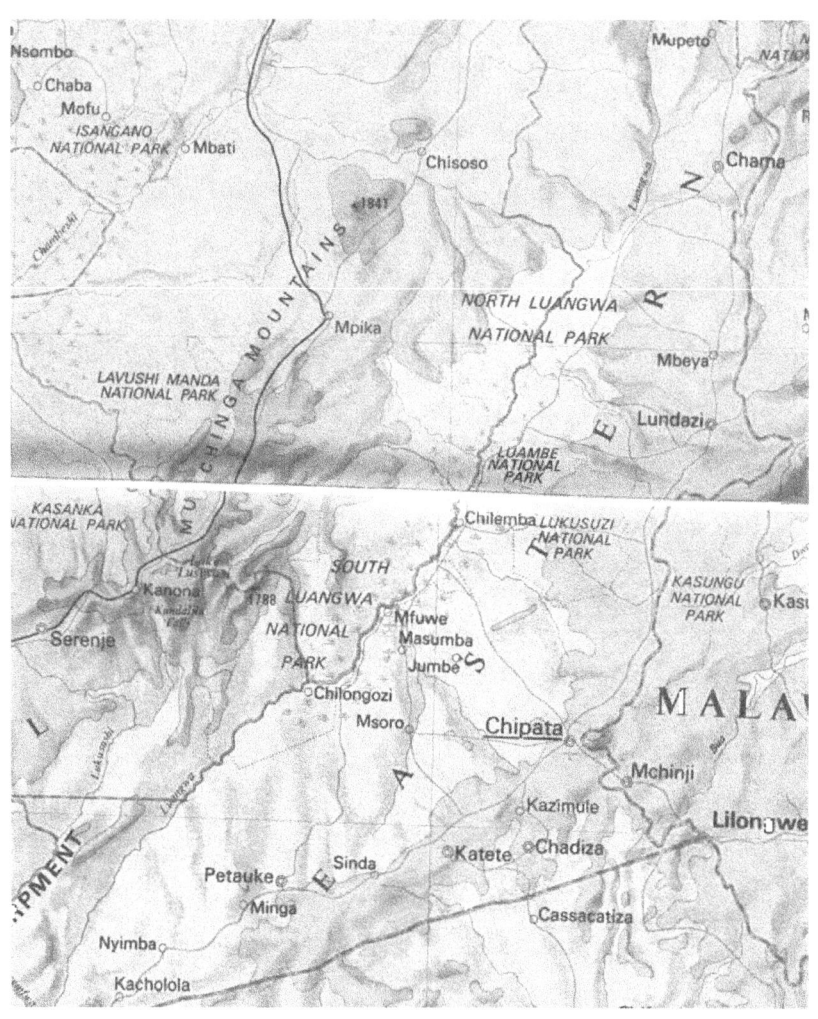

Map 2: Chieftaincies in the central valley

(Source: www.freeweb.com)

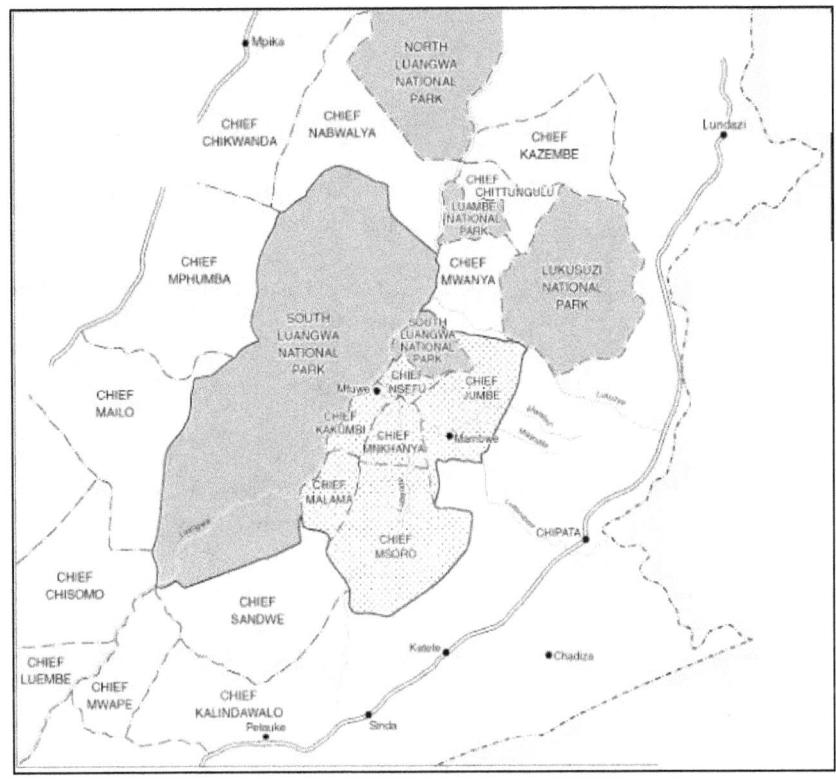

Glossary

Spellings and pronunciations of vernacular terms differ across the valley. Different, more or less equivalent words, are given in brackets.

BIGOCA	Bible Gospel Church in Africa
BSAC	British South Africa Company
CBNRM	Community Based National Resources Management
CCAP	Church of Central African Presbyterians (formerly Free Church of Scotland)
chinamwali (*chisungu*)	female initiation rites,
chiwanda (*chibanda*)	spirit of a dead person (in the southern valley usually of a non-kin or of an estranged family member)
chiwongo	"surname" (in the south inherited from a name corresponding to the matrilineal clan of the father, like Zulu from the *wene Mvula*, etc.)
chokolo (*bupyani*)	rite of inheritance (of a wife, a husband)
CRB	Community Resource Board
ganyu	piece-work
kachasu	strong distilled drink
kavimba (*kabvuwa, lufuba, mfuba*)	ancestor shrine
makolo	ancestors, parents

mashawe (ngulu, fufumi, vimbuza)	spirits (not ancestral), often linked to natural sites.
mukowa (mukoka)	clan
mwambo (lutambi)	custom, tradition
mzimu (mupashi)	spirits of the dead of the own lineage and/or other positive spiritual forces including those coming from God
namkungwi (nachimbusa)	instructor of the initiation rites (working together with the *phungu* or *anyaphungu* to instruct the girl (*ndola*)
ndola (namwali, moye, chisungu)	girl to be initiated into the puberty/marriage rites
ng'anga	traditional healer, "witchdoctor"
njala (nsala, nzala)	hunger
phungu	female instructor, tutor of the girl to be initiated during the rites
RCZ	Reformed Church in Zambia (formerly Dutch Reformed Church)
SDA	Seventh Day Adventists
ufwiti (buloshi)	witchcraft
wene Mvula (ene Mvula, bena Mfula, …), Chulu, Mbawo, Inama, Tembo, Lungu, Mumba, Ngo, Nsovu, Nkalamo, Nyendwa, Ng'oma, Miti, Ngona, Njoka, etc	matrilineal clan of the rain… (of the termite hill, the *mbawo* insect, animals, wasp, calabash, clay, leopard, elephant, lion, female sexual organ, drum, tree, mushroom, snake, etc.)
ZAWA	Zambia Wildlife Authority

1.

The background of the research and expectations

This research is about the underlying causes for the difficulties of the Catholic Church in the Luangwa valley as experienced for more than a century. It was prompted by the Centenary celebrations of the Catholic Diocese of Chipata, which were held in July 2004, in a historically significant location: in Chasera (in the past it was called Kambwiri), the spot of the first Catholic mission properly within the boundaries of today's Diocese of Chipata. The White Fathers had opened Kambwiri in 1904, but they had to close the mission and leave the valley barely seven months later. After leaving Kambwiri, the missionaries focused on greener pastures on the plateau, where their endeavours seemed to bear more fruits. Within the next 100 years of evangelisation, the valley had witnessed periods of renewed impetus, but as a whole one can say that the valley remained only an appendix to the Catholic life of Chipata Diocese. Pastoral plans focused on the plateau, and they were based mainly on the conditions of the plateau, not on the conditions of the valley. For many pastoral workers and also for many laypeople of the plateau, the valley was conceived as a difficult place, backwards, left behind; people of the valley were often labelled as stubborn, begging, living just from day to day with their fish and game meat, and not be "interested in anything pertaining to the spiritual." The oldest living missionary of Chipata diocese who had worked in the valley at the end of the 1950s (and who is well remembered) is Fr. Gundi:

> The valley was my first appointment on arrival in Northern
> Rhodesia. Bishop Courtemanche used to send young
> missionaries into the valley so that they could gain a real
> missionary experience. What concerns Christianity, there was
> nothing. Missionaries had been there for many years, but
> church-wise the level remained just at zero. We were going to
> villages to teach, and the catechist was ringing the church bell
> so many times, but people were not interested. We liked the
> people, but our approach as a Church was very much coming
> from above. We were there to teach as if we knew it all.[1]

Church structures and policies were mostly determined by the "tarmac
centres" of the plateau, far away from the valley, but actual church life
in any given village is usually more determined by the local "nitty-
gritty" of everyday life. The Church came with its own programmes,
structures, and agendas, and it was expected (in different degrees) that
the people in the valley had to fit into the structures of the plateau. But
they did not fit.

When the Catholic centenary celebrations drew near in 2004, the
Catholic Charismatic Renewal Movement conducted a small research
in Chasera about the meaning of the Christian faith for Catholics. They
found only one Catholic family with a Bible, and they concluded that
the Christian faith was largely meaningless to people in the area of the
first mission of the Diocese. At the same time they found a great desire
for a new start. An elderly Catholic of Lumimba put it this way: "We
want to be Christians, but we are left to ourselves. We have no real
leader. Give us one good leader and example and we will follow."[2]
While some areas in the valley had been given priests and missionaries
to live among the people in the valley (notably Chikowa and Chama
Parishes), other areas (like the area around Chasera) harboured a
strong feeling of being left out and of not being important to the
Church.

During the centenary celebrations in Chasera in 2004, the bishop
promised a renewed commitment for the valley, and a new pastoral
approach that would be based on the specific conditions of the valley
(historical, social, political, economic and religious). This research was

commissioned so as to understand better the conditions that mark people's lives in the valley, and that make their lives different from people on the plateau. It was financed jointly by the Diocese of Chipata and by Missio/Aachen (Germany).

THE LUANGWA VALLEY

Geographically speaking, the Luangwa valley is an extension of the East African rift valley system. The source of the Luangwa is in the Lilonda and Mafinga Hills, 1500 m high, near the border with Tanzania and Malawi. The Luangwa valley comprises an area of roughly 50,000 km^2 and starts about 150 km from the source, when the Luangwa has dropped to an elevation of about 690m. Here the Luangwa has a flood plain (often several km wide) that gives the valley its specific character. Near Mfuwe, the river has dropped to an elevation of about 520m; the valley has become 100 km wide, and is surrounded by the Muchinga escarpment in the West (with mountains 1500 m high) and a softer and more accessible slope to the East. Passing through the hilly Nyimba district, the Luangwa valley has narrowed down significantly. Eventually the Luangwa merges with the Lunsemfwa River and 720 km from its source flows into the Zambezi.[3] The valley basin is separated from the eastern and western plateaus by a 400 - 800 meter slope (in general easier accessible from the eastern side) that makes road-building very difficult. The many rivers running into the valley from the plateau cut the valley during the rainy season into tiny slices; these patches of land become cut off from the plateau and also from each other.

Since colonial times, parts of the Luangwa valley have been declared as national parks, in which people were not allowed to live any longer (North- and South Luangwa, Luambe, and Lukusuzi National Parks are in the valley). The rest of the valley is declared as Game Management Areas, where settlements of people have to follow a number of restrictions laid down and enforced by the Zambian Wildlife Authorities (ZAWA).

The part of the valley that belongs to Chipata Diocese (corresponding with Zambia's Eastern Province) is over 500 km long, and comprises different populations, cultures and tribes: Achikunda, Ambo, Nsenga, Kunda, Valley-Bisa (or Wiza), Chewa and Senga. Among people in the valley there is little unity and little centralisation, and people speak different languages: Nsenga and Kunda, Bemba dialects (Ambo and "Chiwiza", how the Bisa dialect of the valley is called), Chewa, and Senga (which is a Tumbuka dialect with a strong imprint of Bisa.) Two administrative districts of the Eastern Province are right in the valley: Mambwe in the Kunda area, and Chama in the Senga area of the North. In the 2000 population census, Chama district[4] had a population of 75,000 people, and Mambwe 47,000. Since then the population has grown significantly in Mambwe (due to the expansion of the tourist industry and the airport), but also in Chama, and the district health boards are working with higher figures. Between Chama and Mambwe Districts, we find a valley population belonging to Lundazi district of about 35,000 people.[5] In Msanzala constituency of Petauke District (west of Petauke) the census numbered 46,000 people of whom however only a part belongs strictly to the valley. The hilly southern valley has no clear demarcations, as has the central and northern valley with its wide flood plain. Thus there is no clear line of demarcation either in Nyimba District, where one would place the chieftaincies of Nyalugwe, Luwembe and Mwape as strictly belonging to the valley, with a population of around 15,000 people or more.[6] Together this brings the population in the valley of the area belonging to Chipata Diocese to around 200,000 people. Most of them live in the wider Northern part of the valley, stretching from Mambwe to Chama.

The valley population is one of the poorest in Zambia, with one of the lowest literacy levels of the whole country.[7] Schools and clinics are either missing or of very poor quality and under-staffed. Because of its isolation, the valley has since colonial times been regarded as a sanctuary for wild animals. Across the different peoples of the valley, men's culture was built in the past to a great extent on hunting and fishing, and the tough wildlife restrictions of the past 10-15 years are cutting deep into people's sense of identity. Common food crops consist mainly of maize, rice, groundnuts, and different vegetables, but floods, draughts, and crop-raiding by animals contribute to chronic food shortages (now an annual occurrence) that sometimes result in severe hunger.

The last 15 years have brought deep reaching transformations. The liberalisation of Zambia's economy has attracted a number of investors into the valley to build up the tourist industry (mainly hunting- and walking safaris). For some people this brought some chances of (mainly seasonal) employment. But the new developments also highlight and accentuate the conflict of interest in regards to wildlife: Poor farmers in many ways have to bear the real costs of the presence of wild animals near their fields. They are rarely refunded for damages done by the animals to their fields and to human life, and most would prefer to see the animals in their cooking pots, not in the fields where they destroy the crops. Another change that has taken place from around 2002 onwards is the drastic increase of commercial cotton growing in the Northern half, which has brought some money into the valley. Even in isolated villages one sees new little shops where essentials are being sold. Otherwise people live mainly from farming, fishing, seasonal work in the safari camps, ZAWA, or in one of the NGOs, or from mostly illegal hunting activities. Some people also practise some petty mining for gemstones, gold and silver. Formal employment is rare. Around the area of Lumimba, the "Luangwa Valley Project" has helped with storage facilities, where people can sell rice and maize in May/June with the option to buy it back in times of hunger at the end of the year. Food security is however a yearly problem throughout the valley, and some areas depend regularly on food aid organised by the Zambian State.

When the rains start and the rivers fill up, the valley become largely cut off and life proceeds in isolation. News of floods and draughts in the valley (sometimes in the same year following each other) hit the Zambian news year by year, and people in the valley characterise their life with the word "*njala*" (hunger).

When the rains start, also church life comes largely to an end, to be resumed again after the rains with fresh visits by the priests and pastors. During the rains, many people withdraw to their fields and in some areas whole villages become deserted. People need to live on their fields, building little huts (in Wiza called *fiteba*), to guard the crops from monkeys, elephants and other destructive animals that can destroy a whole years' crop in one unguarded day or one unguarded night. For chasing elephants away from the fields, people have to rely on banging on pots and pans, or drumming, since the possession and usage of firearms has long been outlawed. Often people's fields are located away from the villages; they have to cross fierce rivers, swollen up by the rains, to reach their fields. For many families, visits back to the village become rare in this time.

CHURCH LIFE IN THE LUANGWA VALLEY

Apart from a relatively small but growing number of Muslims in the valley, most people call themselves Christian. Like all over Zambia, churches are plentiful also in the Luangwa Valley: Catholic, Anglican (centred around Msoro), Reformed Church of Zambia (RCZ) in the middle and South, Church of Central African Presbyterians (CCAP) in the North, Chipangano (in the North), African National Church (in the North), Bible Gospel Church in Africa (BiGoCA) and a variety of other Pentecostal churches, Seventh Day Adventists (SDA), New Apostolic Church, Church of Christ, Church of God, Jehovah's Witnesses, Baptists, and a variety of small Zion churches are present in the Luangwa valley. Most congregations, however, are of a very small size when compared with the surrounding plateau.

The churches with the longest presence in the valley are the CCAP (Church of Central African Presbyterians, which emerged from the Free Church of Scotland), Catholics, Anglicans and RCZ (Reformed Church in Zambia, in the past known as the Dutch Reformed Church). All of them have a presence of more than 100 years in different parts of the valley. And all express today that in spite of 100 years of presence, they still consider the valley to be "mission territory" in the sense that they feel the churches are not yet established, have problems in finding local committed leadership, and remain financially dependent on the plateau. Especially the efforts to make the heavy structures of the Catholic and Anglican Church self-reliant proved a failure; the structures of the CCAP and RCZ are somehow lighter and remain less dependent on outside financing.

A Catholic priest coming from the plateau on a visit into the valley may sometimes attract a crowd of people for a church service (especially when people haven't seen a car for a long time); but at other times church attendance is very poor, and episodes are told of priests waiting at the church for hours, while their "flock" (including the leaders) were busy drinking beer not far away. Interest in church affairs is low even for church members. Church council meetings are held irregularly and in a number of prayer centres never take place at all. Long-term commitment of Christian leaders over several years is rather rare. Men in general are absent from church affairs (except for leadership positions), many meetings and seminars flop for lack of attendance, it is common for catechumens to give up on their way to baptism, a large percentage of those who finally reached baptism flocked to other churches, especially to new-coming churches. Very few people of the valley have trained to become catechists, priests, brothers, or religious sisters. The Catholic Church in the valley has remained financially completely dependent on outside finance throughout the 100 years of evangelisation; Catholics of the valley contribute very little in terms of money and kind. A priest may travel 200 km (one way) by four-wheel drive from Lundazi to Chasera, and as contribution for his fuel he receives from the Christian community a few Kwacha worth less than one US$ and some maize cops. Catholics usually point to their poverty as reason for failing to contribute to the Church, but pastoral workers in the valley would also question people's interest in the Church and their motivation.

One reason for the "trenched-in" situation is surely the physical condition of the valley. Most of the valley is cut off throughout the rainy season, much more so than other rural areas of the surrounding plateau. Such conditions go hand in hand with a general lack of education and an exodus of educated people. But apart from the consequences of such physical conditions, the valley poses to the church still other questions on a more uncomfortable level. Many missionaries of various congregations as well as many Diocesan priests, sisters and seminarians, and even catechists who had come from the plateau, expressed that they have serious doubts about the response of the valley population as far as evangelisation goes. Many feel a certain apathy and lack of interest in things pertaining to the spiritual. In addition, many who worked or lived in the valley for longer periods of time complain about an attitude of begging, and about a lack of initiative both in regards to issues concerning development and church-affairs. Some pastoral workers consider efforts in the valley as a sheer waste of time – not because of the physical conditions, but because of the lack of response of the population.

The valley puzzles outsiders with many contradictions. To mention but a few: Some licensed fishermen make 200,000 Kwacha (50 US$) and more in a single week of fishing when the water is warm (October), yet they will complain of *njala* (hunger) in the same month of October when it comes to Church contributions, and the state of their houses back in the village and the look of their children speak indeed for dire poverty. Fish (mainly produced by men) does not enter Church affairs and belongs to a different budget; subsistence crops in contrast are more readily given as local contribution. People call for more visits of their priests, but when a priest finally comes, only few kids turn up. Men go by bicycle deep into Malawi, to Isoka, Mpika, Chipata, Lundazi, and yet the same men complain that it is too far to the next church just three km from home.

Also discomforting for the Catholic Church is the fact that many old people in the valley today openly express that the mainstream churches (Catholic, Anglican, RCZ, and CCAP) have alienated them from their ancestors and culture. During this research a number of people expressed that God was nearer to them before the Churches came. Some missionaries expressed in the same vein that Christianity seems to have done little in the valley to diminish fear; some go further still and say that both witchcraft and fear have increased in the valley rather than decreased with the advance of Christianity. It are especially hunters and fishers whose life seem to have little affinity with the structures of the church.

Saying this, the valley has witnessed some remarkable initiatives in Christianity. In spite of many setbacks concerning the establishment of big and organised church structures, people have been open to the Christian message and also to many of its messengers. If one goes through the Catholic mission diaries, one reads little about hostilities in the valley. Exceptions were the Kambwiri adventure (chapter 3), and open clashes with the movements of the Watchtowers (from the late 1920s) and the Lumpa (middle 1950s-64). Both were linked to the independence struggle and to specific social and historical constellations. In general, however, the missionaries did not encounter open hostility in the valley. In the mission diaries of both Chilonga and Minga (the earliest missions involved in direct pastoral care of the valley) we often read about a "friendly welcome", about hospitality, and about "a good disposition" of the valley population. Throughout most of the 100 years of evangelisation, this seems to have been the rule, and the short periods of conflict the exception. Many pastoral workers in the valley also today treasure people's hospitality as much as their predecessors did. People asked throughout the time of this research for more presence and more visits of priests rather than less. Where priests stay in the valley (Chikowa and Chama parishes), people have a very friendly disposition to their priests and are visibly fond of them, beyond the Catholic boundaries. However, pastoral work, also here, comes with many challenges that are related not only to the rough physical conditions of the valley, but also to to cultural entrentchments or characteristics that make the establishment of regular church structures difficult.

EXPECTATIONS FOR THIS RESEARCH

Some expectations for this research focussed on the issue of self-reliance. People cannot be visited, because they don't contribute to the running of the Parish – and people don't contribute, because they are not visited. Some expect from this research to find ways that will improve financial contributions in the valley. Expectations of a fast track towards self-reliance in the valley are difficult to fulfil, unless maybe people will be allowed to pay in ivory, lion skins, precious stones or *fyamba* (marijuana), or the dream of an oil refinery in Chama is revived of which the church could buy some shares! This research will not open up a fast track towards self-reliance in the valley. Instead, it gives rise to the hope that local contributions to the Church will increase where the Church increases in significance for people's spiritual life.

Other expectations concerned the role of women in the Church, who are the backbone of the Church in the valley, though they may be absent from leadership positions in a number of places. What can be done to build more on their potential?

Other expectations focussed specifically on men, whose absence from the church is notorious in the valley. Why is this? Some priests encouraged me specifically to look at the place of religion in a culture of hunters and fishers to look for a religious foundation on which one can build. It is hoped that this research promotes a pastoral approach that links up with the "nitty-gritty" of daily life and with the specific conditions (cultural, religious and economic) of the valley.

THE MODALITIES OF THE RESEARCH

The time frame for this research (May 2005 – December 2006) proved to be far too limited. The research is about giving back sentiments and opinions of people in the context of their struggles and their social and religious coordinates. When, in what follows, I sometimes use formulations like: "many people in the valley said that", or "in a number of interviews, people expressed that…", or "people are aware that…", I do not claim to speak representatively for the population in the valley. I give but back the strong attitudes and ideas that a number of people, with whom I was in contact at a particular time, wanted me to bring across to the leaders of the Catholic Church in Chipata, when they were reacting to my questions and to what they perceived the research was about. The year of the research was, for example, very much marked by the conflict between the interests of farmers, whose fields and even whole villages were being harassed frequently by wild animals, and the interests of the tourism and wildlife sector, including many private investors leasing land at the Luangwa River. The people whom I interviewed may have wanted to put different points across in times marked by other events or conflicts. What I present here is a snapshot, as perceived by me during the year of research, shaped also by my own specific interests; other researchers would have asked different questions, touch different topics, interview different people, and shape the framework very differently. But I tried, as well as I could, to ground my snapshot and keep it informed by other historical and anthropological narratives that were available to me.

Another point is also very important: the Church has touched different parts of the valley in very different ways. Catholics in some areas of the valley (for example those falling under Lumimba Parish, which then had no resident priests) felt much stronger abandoned by the Church than those in areas where priests lived right amongst them during the time of the research (Chama and Chikowa Parishes), where many Catholics expressed a pride in their priests and seemed to identify also in a stronger sense with the Church. I always give back the specific locations when referring to interviews and significant statements.

As things on the ground had been well prepared, the research could bring in some results. I could benefit especially from the experience and contacts of Father Toon van Kessel, with whom I could discuss many details throughout this research. All the valley priests and sisters helped, shared and encouraged me a lot. The bulk of this research was conducted in the following Catholic prayer centres: Nyalugwe and Chitumbi (Nyimba Parish), Mwape and Chinsimbwe (Minga Parish), Kasweta, Masumba & Nsefu (Chikowa Parish), Chasera, Mwanya, and Chiweza (Lumimba Parish), Vilimukuru (Kanyanga Parish), Tembwe & Kambombo (Chama Parish), in which I spent between one and three weeks each. Shorter visits I made to Msoro, Jumbe, Chitungulu, and Lumimba and Chama. Everywhere people had been prepared by the parish team for my visit: Catechists and church councils knew about the aim the research, and had sometimes prepared meetings with chiefs, headmen and other churches in advance. In some parishes the Parish team offered me their four-wheel drive vehicles to go around, Fr. Edouard Morrison lent me his car for three months, and in Chikowa Brother Paul and Brother Oscar welded together my motorcycle which had lost a few parts on the valley roads. In the villages, in the time of hunger when many people were eating *nsima* made out of dried bananas with boiled mangoes as relish (forget about the cliché of people in the valley eating game meat every day!), I experienced great hospitality. Not rarely was I given food even four times a day, with the best people could offer.

I certainly did not have much time to become known to people, and many were surely wondering what all my questions were about. Nevertheless I found people in general very open, much more than I expected, which had surely to do with the preparations that had been going on before my coming. In each outstation in which I spent some time I met separately with women (in different groups: married, single, in polygamy: first wives, second wives, etc), men and youths, to which the Catholics were invited together with anybody else who wished to come. Discussions focused on their specific problems and on the old *miyambo* (traditions, culture), history, and issues of the youths. Then I gathered as many case histories as possible that were based roughly on the following questions: what have people been up to? Where did they live, and where are their brothers, sisters, and children? How long had they been in school? How long did they live in town or outside the valley? Why did they come back to the valley? Where did they pray in childhood and where do they pray now? What are their main problems in marriage? And so on. In some villages I could analyse the marriage- and settlement patterns. Of special help proved the interviews with chiefs, headmen, hunters, *ng'anga* (traditional healers), *alangizi* (traditional midwives), teachers, health workers, and the leaders of the different churches. In some places the chiefs themselves had organised meetings with knowledgeable persons at their palaces about the history of their chieftaincy (Mnkhanya, Chikwa, Tembwe, Nyalugwe), while others gave me names of people who proved to be very knowledgeable. In general, the chiefs were helpful in this research, and a number of them produced also written documents, like genealogies. Outside the chiefs' circles, also old people and headmen were very cooperative and surprisingly open. Finally, when staying a week or two in a village, there were usually a number of events happening that I could attend and that could be very revealing, like funerals, the visit of an incoming diviner (*ng'anga*), initiation rites, names-changing ceremonies for children, etc.

In between the meetings I was relaxing, going from house to house, asking questions about anything coming to my mind, about life-stories, history, hunting, medicines, marriage, divorce, *ziwanda* (spirits of the dead), and *ufwiti* (witchcraft). Some people were suspicious, so I went politely somewhere else, but others had actually fun answering such questions. In many places, after some days, especially women started coming (often two by two); it was their time now to ask questions: "What do women do in Germany when babies have fits? Or when they dream of the dead? How do women in Germany stop their husbands going out with other women?" The major concern for most people was sickness, which was often chronic, which is not surprising with the state of health care in the valley. People had seen me writing names of local medicines in my books and asked about the herbs that people recommended in other places. I realised that through doing this research as a Catholic priest, I was seen a little bit as a *ng'anga* myself. Many also asked for house blessings. When the sick people were just too many, in some places the catechist organised a prayer service for the sick, or for those with *mashawe* (spirits).

I was known to be a Catholic priest, but only few people asked me about issues specific to the Church, like receiving the Eucharist or how to pray. Baptism, the Eucharist, and even prayer are seen in the valley, as far as I can see, in rather legalistic framework: they may bring you to heaven (or at least help you to have a good funeral), but they have little life in themselves and little that would link up with people's daily struggles, or out of which they can live and grow. Even the Christian heaven or eternal life is seen as far away, and has little to do with people's own *makolo* (ancestors) who had given them life and brought them to the valley. Many of people's own religious experiences are rather marginal to the Catholic gate, but they are deep as three examples may show:

> In Nyalugwe brother Vinod and I were waiting at the church for a long time to little avail. People were informed of our coming, and the few kids that had come were ringing the church bells every 5 minutes, but nobody turned up for hours. At some point we gave up and went into the village. There in the afternoon we asked some women to sing some songs of the *chinamwali*. We were quickly surrounded by plenty of people

and the air was full of electricity. This was not just entertainment. It faded however when we tried to organise it and people started to become suspicious. In Kapilingisha (Kambombo), Tembwe, and especially in Mwanya, women had fewer suspicions, drummed and danced deep into the night to the tunes of the *chinamwali* songs. People (including myself) were captured by the atmosphere, and afterwards the women asked me: why is it a sin to do this?

In Malaya (Kambombo) I attracted only a very small community of Catholics in the school for mass and a meeting (the church had collapsed), but at night I followed the hypnotising sounds of the drums that led me to the house of "Doctor" Peter Mngelo, who was delivering some patients from witchcraft attacks. I was given a chair as guest of honour in the front row; the place was packed with people (including many Catholics – also among the drummers – who had not shown up for mass); the singing, the drumming and the dancing, was captivating for everybody, also for me. Some songs seemed old and traditional, but many songs were clearly inspired by Christian and Biblical themes. One song was based on the Christian creed, and in another song, with a beautiful melody, the Virgin Mary figured very highly. The drama performed by Doctor Mngelo was largely based on the symbolism of the death and resurrection of Christ. At one point, he enacted as if he himself was dying (killed by the charms) and rising again to life in order to neutralise the charms. Where Christian metaphors linked up with people's witchcraft beliefs and discourses (outside the official Christian discourse and in ways hardly acceptable to mainstream Christian morality), they received much attention and energised people who found little energy in the official church services.

In Chitumbi (Nyimba Parish), Brother Vinod, myself and the catechist had organised a prayer service for the sick and for people with *mashawe* (spirits) who had asked us for prayers. I thought it would flop, because the choir were very few and looked awfully tired at the start – they had just come back from a funeral where they had sung through the whole night. But as soon as the *mashawe* started reacting, the choirs forgot their tiredness, the pitch of the drums changed, and their songs seized the church for hours and hours; people left the church only after nightfall (having started at 14:00!), and even then people still wanted to bring more sick people the following day.

People in the valley seem strongly attuned to the spiritual life and the unseen world, but the concepts and conditions of the organised church and people's own notions and expectations rarely meet.

The Luangwa River suring dry and rainy seasons (Nyalugwe)

2.

First answers

Why has the Church encountered so many difficulties in the valley? In my interviews and in meetings, some answers focused on the different social conditions in the valley, while others focused on the churches' ways of doing things. Concerning the first point, three answers stood out:

1. "Religion of hunters". It was put to me somehow this way:

> On the plateau, in contrast to the valley, people have had a long tradition of agriculture. Long before Christianity arrived, they were very dependent on the rains. Rain came from *Chauta* (God), and dependency on rain meant dependency on God. The Chewa also had centralised rain cults, and agricultural peoples may have linked up easier with Christianity because of their long experience of centralised religion. In the valley, people were more dependent on hunting. But failure in hunting is explained rarely in reference to God. People are more inclined to look at their medicines and own skills, and there may be little thirst for looking for a God up there. Missionaries were preaching something that people were not looking for.[8]

This research confirms that Christianity, as it was presented or understood in the valley, linked up very little with what hunters expected from religion. For example, the *makolo* (ancestors) play a dominant role in hunting traditions, but Christianity is still seen or imagined as a religion that alienates people from their own ancestors and roots.

2. "Quicksand of social structure". Some priests who worked both in the valley and on the plateau experienced the social structure of the valley to be much looser. Especially in the south of the valley people come from very different places of origin. People rely more on family structures and are often only very loosely incorporated into larger village structures or even "tribal" structures, more loosely than on the Plateau. Building church structures in the valley is like building a house on sand. In the north of the valley (among the Senga) there is more cohesion than in the south, and even church structures seem to function better.

This research confirms, at least partly, this argument. Hunting people tend to disperse rather than to centralise, and this research looks into some of the forces at work. Such dispersing forces are not timeless, and in fact they have been counteracted by government policies in regards to village sizes and locations. Still, the fact of being grouped together in stable villages and the discouragement of hunting do not yet create a community. In consequence many of our structures, like for example the elected church councils, do not really have a grip on people, not for lack of elections, but for reasons that touch issues of authority and integration. All over the valley people mentioned as one of the chief reasons for failure in church matters a basic lack of cooperation. "*Sitigwirizana* – we don't cooperate together."

3. "Being left behind". Because of the physical isolation of the valley, people did not really participate in changes in the church. A Catholic women group (*Azimai a pa mtondo*) in Chama (made up mostly of women originally from the plateau) put it this way:

> Much has changed in the Church. On the Plateau, we hear for example about self-reliance from many sides, not only from priests and catechists. We meet with people from different parishes, and each week along the tarmac road there are visitors in our churches from all over Zambia, and all speak the same

message. That is why we are faster on the Plateau to believe in new issues. Here in the valley people are left to themselves for most of the year.

One can add that people of the valley were rarely consulted about the new developments of the church and pastoral issues; they had to follow the lead of the plateau and were simply overruled, which resulted in a certain alienation from the Church.

This research suggests that there is actually more movement in the valley than many assume. However, most movements happen between the valley and the towns – back in the valley one is submerged again into a very different life in which much of what was assimilated in the towns is no longer applicable.

A number of other answers were also given about cultural entrenchments:

"There is too much beer in the valley."

"There is too much polygamy."

"People always had enough meat to eat and want to be merry today – in their culture there is not much concern for tomorrow."

"People in the valley are lazy and don't know how to cultivate."

The problem with such answers is that they give very little to work on. They close an investigation instead of opening it up. This is not to deny that cultural entrenchment and habits do exist. People in the valley themselves mentioned everywhere beer and polygamy (in the north) as major setbacks to Christianity. A number of women openly spoke of the laziness of their husbands. Some Chewa immigrants settling in the valley belittled the agricultural commitment of the valley population (though some of the newcomers did not convince either with their own successes). And fishermen are often described by non-fishers as having "dry heads" and as just being difficult (*kuuma*):

"It is futile to discuss anything with a fisherman. They are just too stubborn."[9]

"They have no education, and they take their own children out of the school classes in order to go fishing. You cannot argue with them about prices of fish nor about anything else. They have only one pair of trousers and don't want a second pair. When their money for beer is finished, they just go out again fishing to make a new budget."[10]

But we don't go very far if we view cultural entrenchments as something passively inherited. It seems more fruitful to focus on the mechanisms that actively maintain the appropriation of cultural images by certain groups. What for example makes the village for the man the place of recreation and for beer rather than the place of work, and what do both men and women do to sustain this image? Or why do people today refer to *njala* (hunger) even in times of plenty? Why does the Church belong in popular image only to people with "fine clothes" (that is how many non-church goers describe their failure to attend church)? Incidentally, neither beer, nor polygamy, nor perceived laziness of men, are absent elsewhere in Zambia, and therefore can hardly attain real explanatory power for the specific failure of the Church in the valley to captivate the local population.

The second set of answers focused on the Church's pastoral approach towards the valley. Such arguments look at our side, on our own mistakes as a Church. Three points came back often:

1. Neglect. A number of priests admitted, "We concentrated on the Plateau because it was easier and we got more results". A look into history gives some nuances to this argument. There have been times of great efforts in the valley. For Bishop Martin, for example, the valley was definitely a priority. Bishop Courtemanche also appointed the young and enthusiastic to the valley. But as a whole the argument is correct and applies not only to priests and sisters: mission diaries speak of difficulties also in finding catechists and teachers willing to settle and work in the valley. In most valley parishes people mentioned the lack of being visited as the main reason for the poor state of the Church. "We want to learn, but we are left on our own."

Many pastoral workers themselves see a direct link between progress in pastoral programmes and the regularity of visits. The Lumimba/Lundazi pastoral report of 2006 states that things in Lumimba each June start from zero. In the following months, things start picking up rather satisfactory. With the rains in November pastoral visits cease and next June things start again from zero.

2. It is also the **style of pastoral work** that people complain about:

> In the past, you priests were different. We don't see priests any-
> more in our villages. In the past, Father Morrison and Father
> Gundi came into the villages, and they went from house to
> house, and asked about our families. Today we only see the
> Jehovah Witnesses at our homes. Catholic priests only come for
> mass, for meetings and seminars, and then we hear the sound
> of a leaving car [the person here imitates the racing engine].

In a way, the person said, if priests are not interested in their way of life, why should people be interested in the priests' faith and beliefs? Here a challenging comment from an ex-soldier (Kataba/Lumimba):

> We people in the valley are always blamed, even in the Church.
> It is always us with whom there is something wrong. I was in
> the army, where we were taught: "there are no bad soldiers,
> there are only bad officers." In the church it should be the same.
> If things do not go right, we should blame the ones in charge,
> but not always the people.

3. A number of priests and catechists make responsible a "**handing out mentality**" of former missionaries for the failure of self-reliance in the valley. "People have been spoiled!" This argument is pervasive for many, but not for me. Surely much has been given out in the valley, but this cannot compare with what has been given out on the plateau by the same former missionaries. This research on one hand confirms that

people in the valley see it as the task of the church to help them, and that they don't see it as their responsibility to help the church. This view is certainly entrenched. But if "handing out" and "spoiling people" is the main reason for the failure of self-reliance, then the valley should be more self-reliant than the plateau. Furthermore, the so-called begging mentality of the valley goes beyond the church, and I propose to investigate the problem in the much wider framework of political powerlessness: begging reflects a resignation into dependency.

4. Only very few priests learned a language of the valley: Chinsenga, Chikunda, or Chiwiza. Priests speak only the languages of the plateau. In general people cope well with our Chewa and Tumbuka; they themselves are used to many mixtures of languages among themselves. It were only the Anglicans in Msoro who vigorously took up Chinsenga and who published the Bible and prayer books in the language of their people. We find still today in Msoro a pride of the Anglicans in their Nsenga Bible and prayer books. In the Catholic Church, from Nyimba to Lumimba, nobody in the valley prays in his or her mother tongue. Catechists in most parishes make it a point to teach in Chichewa "so that people get used to the church language". Prayers are learned by heart in Chichewa. Not even the "Our Father" is prayed in the mother tongue. People may be speaking to you the whole day in Chinsenga; when food comes and they feel obliged to say a prayer, they say the prayer in Chichewa. God seems to speak a different language from their own. The Church language is usually well understood by people in the valley, but maybe more than anything else the use of language shows that the Church and its prayers really belong to the plateau, and not to the valley.

3.

Conceptions of the valley

Conceptions of the valley from outsiders are often very negative. Even many teachers and health workers working in the valley whom I interviewed shared this negative image and many saw their stay as a temporal episode in their lives. "People here are just difficult." To the international community, the Luangwa valley is known for its animals, not for its people. Readers of the Zambian newspapers are well acquainted with Chama and Mambwe Districts being designated as the hunger districts of Zambia, regularly struck by natural disasters. Many outsiders consider the valley as a place where people will move out and should move out in the long run. But for the valley population, the valley is a magnet that pulls people back who lived for 20 years or more in the towns. Many attempts to lure people away from the valley towards other locations have failed. Some attribute this to the presence of game and fish, but people's cooking pots today speak mostly a different language; meat was their food in the golden past times. There is more to the valley than meat.

How do people themselves describe their home? Two main metaphors came back during these inquiries all along the valley: the valley is the place of the *makolo* (ancestors) but also of *njala* (hunger), and both metaphors are very symbolic. Reading through the mission diaries and through the District notebooks, one realizes furthermore that these two metaphors have become entrenched already for many decades.

MAKOLO (ANCESTORS)

People are proud of the valley. The valley is the place of their *makolo*. One cannot speak about the valley without mentioning the *makolo*. Whenever I asked people who had stayed a long time in town why they came back, the usual answer was a reference to the *makolo*. This was so obvious that people were even surprised that I could ask a question with such an obvious answer. The image of the valley, of home, is often constructed over and against the towns. Towns are the places for jobs, to make money. But towns are also the places of AIDS and of insecurity, of high prices for food that is free in the valley. The town is the place without broad networks of kin. To speak of the *makolo* in contrast makes the valley a place of kin and family.

In the north people refer to the first ancestors who brought them into the valley, and the subsequent chain of ancestors who form the link right up to the presence. Here we find in many villages of group-headmen a *kabvuwa* or *kawimba* (spirit shrine) in which his *makolo* are remembered. This makes it rather easy to inquire about history. The *makolo* of headmen and chiefs in the north have often become synonymous with the *makolo* of everybody else. In the South we find more diversity of origins. The *makolo* of an individual family have often little to do with the *makolo* of the chief or headman. People remember their *makolo* especially if they provide the link to a previous location from which they parted, often due to marriage or war. "Remember that we are *wene Mvula* from Monde at Kasenje," a mother told her daughter. "The mother of your grandmother was so-and-so, she came here because of her marriage, but the children of her sister still live in Monde. Remember this, so that you can go back if things go bad here."[11] If this link is not important anymore, also the names of the *makolo* can be forgotten.

In spite of these differences between the north and the south, throughout the valley the *makolo* provide the vital spiritual link with the present location. People are on the right place, because their *makolo* brought them there. This makes the valley a sacred place. A number of people said that God himself had guided their ancestors into the valley. God gave them the valley as their rightful place. Such reference to God was made already 90 years ago: in a meeting of the year 1915 that is recorded in the District Notebooks. The colonial office had made a plan to remove many of the Akunda from the valley because of sleeping sickness. We read that

> Kakumbi's representative, District Messenger, and village headmen all declared that without doubt they have suffered a heavy mortality from Sleeping Sickness, and the disease is still in their villages. But they are all agreed that they do not wish to remove on any account from their present homes. Chikoko said "Kakumbi has ordered me to speak these words for him: We know that the sleeping sickness is killing us, but it is the Act of God, and we will not remove from the country where God has planted us".

In the same meeting, chiefs and headmen of Nsefu, Mnkhanya, Chiaula, Jumbe and Tindi simply denied that there was any sleeping sickness in their villages, but that people "were well off, and healthy, and would not think of moving from their present locations". A number of other attempts failed on similar grounds, including the promise of concessions (land, inputs and money) to those who would go voluntarily. People remained there where their *makolo* had brought them, on their rightful place, where God obviously wanted them to be.

Among the old people the awareness is still very strong that the blessing for one's life comes from this link with the *makolo*. Especially hunting and its religious significance is strongly linked to this notion. The metaphor of the *makolo* goes hand in hand with another metaphor: the *mwambo* (*or mudauko* in the north, or *lutambi* among the Bisa – tradition, culture). One needs to walk in the *mwambo* in order to secure the blessings of the ancestors. The *mwambo* refers often to the observance of different taboos taught in the initiation rites concerning marriage, birth and funerals, but also concerning hunting, witchcraft, authority and protection. Unfortunately, the churches are often seen in the valley as alienating people from their own ancestors and their own traditions.

NJALA (HUNGER)

As much as the valley has the connotation of being the place of the ancestors and of blessing, it has also the connotation of constant *njala,* hunger. This may look on first sight a contradiction, but it is not. Many said that God blessed them with good soil and animals. For people it is not the location which is bad, but what modern politics have made out of the valley. The blessings of the valley (animals, meat, fish, soil) are there, but politics are made outside of the valley (and by foreigners), and they have alienated people from their own home. The blessings of the *makolo* belong to the image of the past. The image of the present is one of *njala* and high risk factors in agriculture: draughts & floods during the same year, monkeys eating away their fields during the day and elephants at night, plagues of rats and birds, and the lack of markets for their products. This image is also reinforced through the negative images that outsiders paint of the valley. Even in May and June, when there is plenty to eat, people keep this image of *njala.* The person who has spent today already much money on beer and *kachasu* (locally destilled alcohol) will still complain of *njala. Njala* has become a key- metaphor with which people present themselves to the outside world. Why is this? The image of *njala* links up powerfully with the ban on game meat:

> We have tasted meat. We cannot live on vegetables. We get no strength from eating mangoes, and therefore we cannot work in our fields.[12]

The taste of meat is very symbolic. A study conducted in the 1970s suggested that people in the valley were then consuming seven times more meat than people on the Eastern plateau and more meat than in any other area studied elsewhere in the whole of Africa.[13] Meat is *their* food, is *their* culture, and meat has also many religious connotations. The distribution of meat linked kin together: your relative was the one with whom you freely shared meat. Meat gives strength. Vegetables bring weakness. The ban on hunting cuts very deep, and it can only bring *njala,* because any meal without meat means *njala.* Meat of course was also used to trade against grain and other items that were needed in the family.[14] In popular imagination there was no hunger in the past because there was always meat.

> In our houses there were hanging legs of *mbowo* (buffalos), of *mpala* (antelope), of *nguluwe* (wild pig), of *nsefu* (eland), and each day we chose what we wanted to eat. When somebody went hunting he said: 'yesterday I had a *mpombo* (duiker), today I want *mpala*', and he killed an *mpala*.[15]

From accounts in the various diaries we know that this image of the past is distorted. Much before the ban on hunting became rigorously enforced, the valley was already known for its hunger periods. Father Lukas Gundi remembers that already in the 1950s people from Nabwalya were flocking to Lumimba to look for grain, because there was real hunger. But without any doubt the enforcement of the law on hunting has aggravated the conception of *njala* and of a golden past without hunger.

Njala has come for people because of modern politics. Strickland (1998) working among the Kunda gives back a pervasive argument: In the past, Kunda hunters preferred to live in scattered villages that allowed proximity to the animals. The government said that villages were too small, that people should settle in big villages where they would build schools and clinics. People were lured out of the parks into big villages by these promises. But with higher population density, animals withdrew and hunting became more difficult: people had to go much further into the bush and kill larger animals, also because there were now more people to be fed. Living around a clinic also meant to live constantly with sick people. Larger populations and mixing of populations encouraged the spread of AIDS. It also meant to live now with game scouts as neighbours, whose work became much easier since villages regrouped. Many feel that the promises of health and education have not been fulfilled, but that government planning has brought sicknesses and hunger. In Lumimba (Temba village) I heard some people putting it this way:

> The clinics have brought us sicknesses. In the past there were
> very few sicknesses here. Now when a child is sick, when it has
> malaria, we go straight away to the clinic to get pills. Our
> children have no resistance any longer. Ask anybody here, they
> all know that we had less sicknesses before the clinics came.

In the villages of Mpamadzi (Kasweta Outstation of Chikowa Parish),
that have no clinic (the villages are located one and a half days walk
away from the nearest clinic and the nearest school), I recorded a
statement with a similar line of argument:

> We want a clinic here. But God has blessed us: we have very few
> sicknesses here, and people here are healthier than in other
> areas that we know. Here we know our sicknesses.

Both in Chitumbi (Nyimba Parish) and in Mkasanga (Lumimba
Parish), *njala* was put in direct link with increasing sickness. Here
words recorded in Chitumbi:

> Here we are all sick. You don't find anymore a healthy person
> in this area. That is because we don't eat meat any longer. Every
> day we are eating vegetables and mangoes together with the
> monkeys. Our bodies are too weak to fight any sickness, and
> therefore we are unable to do any work in the fields. That is the
> problem with *njala*.

In the metaphor of *njala* the images of insiders and outsiders of the
valley meet. While outsiders (including Church personnel) often
portray hunger as resulting from the low level of initiative of the valley
population, from backwardness, laziness, unwillingness to cultivate
properly, beer, and an attitude of not planning for the future, the valley
population takes up eagerly the same metaphor of *njala* to manifest
and even resign into their dependency on outside help. *Njala* for them
legitimises a begging mentality. It provides a frame of reference where
people today see it as their *right* to be helped, and sometimes they do
not ask for help but *demand* it. In Mkasanga somebody put it this way:

We cannot kill animals any longer. Now the animals are destroying our crops and we are not allowed to do anything about it. Farming here is impossible. The Boma has to give us food every year because we are keeping for them the animals.

Even where people separate the Zambian government from the churches as different entities (which is not always the case), they nevertheless see it as the obligation of both of them to help with food relief. The strong metaphor of *njala* reflects an attitude that the outside world (in which also the churches are situated) owes something to the valley as a kind of debt-repayment for taking away their ways of living and self-determination. It reflects also an awareness of people in the valley that they will never measure up on the present political scale of power relations with outside interests; they can only play according to rules that are made outside, that allow them little space for manoeuvring, and that are sometimes set to make them leave the valley in the long run, if they want to come to anything. In such a framework even healthy people feel like cripples: to come to something they have to surrender to outside interests, speak the language of the donors, and the best and easiest button to push is the language of *njala*.

Sonkho's Village

Chinsimbwe Village (Minga Parish)

Chigoma: women enjoying a sip

Lamek's Village (Nyimba Parish)

4.

Lessons from Kambwiri

As this research was prompted by the centenary celebrations that took place in Kambwiri (today's Chasera), the first Catholic Mission Station properly in the boundaries of today's Diocese of Chipata, it seems fitting to insert a flashback of what happened 100 years ago in the first Mission. Kambwiri (Our Lady the Intercessor) was opened on the feast of John the Baptist on the 14th of June 1904. The choice of Kambwiri seemed sound as it was right in the middle between Chilonga (opened 1899) and Kachebere (opened 1903). Kambwiri was meant to form the missing link between the earliest mission stations from Mua in Nyasaland up to Chilubula in Bemba land.

Nevertheless, hesitations about a mission within the Luangwa valley had been there from the beginning. The White Fathers had been exploring different possibilities: in May 1900 Father Boisselier and Father Louveau travelled to the Luangwa Valley to the "Senga" or "Nsenga" (the similarity of names had caused on their route some confusions), and narrated that they got lost a number of times and found many trees but only few people. In November and December of the same year another expedition was made.

> Fr Guillemé goes with Fr Molinier to the Lusenga to explore the country and see where a new mission station could be opened next year. The place they have in view to go to is Kasemba wa Nyimbo, on the left bank of the Lwangwa River. Fr Molinier, however, turned back at the administrative settlement at

Nawalia, because he was too tired to go any further. He came back to Kilonga by an easier road, via Mumpemba.[16]

They found only Nabwalya to be "reasonably populated". Father Guillemé then declared the Luangwa valley, fertile as it was, to be "unfit for European settlement".[17] But three years later he changed his mind: with the opening of Kachebere in 1903 (then called Buwa) he informed Chilubula that a mission should be opened at Kambwiri, right between Buwa and Chilonga, seven days walk from either Buwa or Chilonga (those seven days would later shrink down to five or even four, for the fast ones), and two days walk from Nabwalya, where the British had a post.[18]

What sort of place was Kambwiri at that time? Only few years earlier (in 1897) a traveller wrote that

> Caravans with goods and slaves and ivory all pass through the country of Kambwili who is the big chief of the Wa Bisa. Formerly his large stockaded villages extended north of here for ten miles and west for ten miles. The whole land was under cultivation and the settlements crowded with industrious friendly people. Slavery however has depopulated the place. The offenders are the Angoni… There are always Waswahili traders who purchase the slaves. About 3 years ago Joseph Thomson [of BSAC] and his expedition visited this village and were well received by Kambwiri although the chief was urged by an Arab [Salim ibn Nassur] living there at the time to attack the whites … The village is a central place for the interior. Two years ago Mombero's people attacked the village in hundreds, some escaped but many were killed or taken captive and taken away as slaves.[19]

Father Guillemé narrated that he found Kambwiri heavily populated. He still met the first Kambwiri, the ailing Chivunzu Mukomba, who was by then blind. Father Guillemé assisted him with medicines.[20] Chivunzu Mukomba welcomed him and seemed keen to have a mission in Kambwiri. One year later, on the 24th of June 1904, Father Davoust came to open that mission station as its superior, accompanied by Father Molinier, who was asked to give him a hand until the arrival of Father Ter Maat and Brother Sebastien. Coming to Kambwiri, however, they did not find Chivunzu Mukomba anymore; the first Kambwiri had died and had been succeeded by Salimu Mulilo, a nephew. There was a Swahili presence in Kambwiri (as before), but the White Father's diary does not give any names of the "Arabs". At first the White Fathers were well received by chief and headmen, and gifts were exchanged. But the local superior seemed from the beginning not really enthusiastic about the Kambwiri enterprise. Only one month after opening Kambwiri, the missionaries of Chilonga received a letter from the superior:

> We received a letter from Fr Davoust giving us a few pieces of information on his new mission station. Kambwili, he writes, is the Paramount Chief of a multitude of small villages, each one with its headman, strung out along both banks of the Lukuzie River and its tributary the Katondolo River. The district is thickly populated, but the population is widely scattered. It will be extremely difficult for the missionaries to reach all those people in a very near future. We are in direct contact with some three thousand people. Kambwili's capital is made up of some two hundred huts. We intend to start building just outside the Chief's headquarters. The local population has the reputation of being made of hardheaded people, and we are expected to be just as tough and unrelenting as they are to get anywhere with them. They do not seem to be hostile to our presence among them, but are they really ready to welcome the Good News? That is another cup of tea altogether. The land is desperately flat and monotonous. Water is a precious commodity, and not too good at that. All victuals are very expensive. Hens and goats are sold at a price fifty-percent higher than in the Ubemba. We are really in God's hands! (Diary entry 20th July 1904)

In July, Kambwiri was reinforced by Father Ter Maat and Brother Sebastien, and Father Molinier left for Chilonga (he then became the founder of Lubwe Mission, the first successful mission in Mansa

Diocese). Also Father Molinier expressed doubts about the new venture:

> Fr Molinier talked about what he saw at Kambwili, and we were not terribly impressed. The country is waterless, the natives are not particularly pleasant, they are even all out to exploit the missionaries, tinted as they are with Islam. We say that God's grace is all powerful, it will have to be at Kambwili if we are to get results. (Chilonga Diary, July 1904).

About a month after arrival, according to the Kambwiri diary, the Moslem faction reproached the chief for allowing the Fathers in. The diary narrates that the chief became more and more demanding; he expected more gifts than the missionaries could afford to give. The White Fathers became isolated from the local population, though they write that they had at first won their sympathies. Nobody seemed ready to enrol for work at the mission or even to sell food. The missionaries suspected that the chief had given secret orders to his subjects not to maintain contact. They overheard people speaking openly about chasing them away. By September they had built a house. With the beginning of Ramadan in October, just a month after moving into their house, the antagonism with the Muslim faction in Kambwiri grew. Even children were afraid and stopped coming to the mission. "We are completely isolated". On tour in the villages, however, the missionaries met with a better disposition.

> From time to time, we pass through villages, thus striving to get close to our people who are obstinate to keep apart. Generally during these visits, we receive a welcome that is not too bad. If taken aside, these poor people are not ill disposed. Unfortunately they are victims of some leaders to whom they obey out of fear.

In Kambwiri itself, it was the time for the Moslems. People were proud to wear the white gandourah, and the masses were enrolling to become Moslems. Non-Muslims were being despised as pagans, as *bashyenzi*. The missionaries decided to try prayers, charity and patience. "If these fail, therefore God has judged right to put later the conversion of these unobedient souls." (Kambwiri Diary, December 2004). But patience was soon to run out. The last entry of December looking back on the venture gives little hope.

> Six months passed by since our arrival at Kambwili. What have we done during this time? Humanly speaking, not much. People, excited without doubt by Moslem leaders are more than ever hostile to us...Among all this crowd that surround us, we have not yet been able to find a single sympathetic face. When we go through a village, people look at us with a defying sight and pull faces almost hateful and sometime with an insolent shift. Not one who shows us the least of interest, of confidence or attachment. Not a young man, not a kid that dares frankly come to us. We live in complete isolation. From time to time only some people...who hardly can hide their play come to see whether we can live without their flour and their chickens. No one would want to work at our place. And in a country that supplies all Fort-Jameson with workers and housekeepers, we have been obliged to plant ourselves our cabbage and to do our small cooking ourselves. This situation is really painful and in no way do we see hope in the future.

By now bishop Dupont was back after four years of absence, and he must have noticed this sharp contrast between the valley and the plateau. On the plateau missionaries were asking for more missions to be opened, to cope with the enormous demands that were bearing fruit. Passing through Kambwiri, the bishop decided on the spot to close it for good.

> His honour has judged that we should not take longer in this inhospitable land while we can find elsewhere souls more docile and better disposed,

writes the Kambwiri diarist (probably Father Davoust). Father Ter Maat was appointed to Kachebere, Brother Sebastien to Mua, and

Father Davoust to Chilonga. The Chilonga diary (January 1905) describes the closing of Kambwiri as the end of an ordeal:

> The situation in the new mission station at Kambwili must be pretty bad, since we received a letter from Bishop Dupont enjoining us to send at once 30 carriers to this location to pull out Fr Davoust and bring back all the material ... After a few days we have the pleasure to see Fr Davoust briskly coming down the mountain with all his people singing at the top of their voices. He looks fine in spite of all the privations he had to endure and the opposition he met at Kambwili. According to what he told us, the Devil is certainly very active in this part of the country. Islam is definitely very strong. The Moslems were already numerous when Fr Davoust came in, and they have strengthened their position in a few months' time. Fr Davoust will stay at Kilonga to recover from his ordeal, until he has a new appointment.

Evangelisation had met with stronger opposition than what the missionaries were able to cope with – and as the missionaries saw it, "the devil was strong in the valley!"

THE HISTORICAL BACKGROUND OF THE KAMBWIRI SAGA

The Kambwiri saga has gone down into the history of evangelisation as a marker of failure in the valley, maybe because we find already a number of issues in this early adventure that the pastoral workers of today are very familiar with: difficulties to work through the chief yet being aware that little works without the chief; people living in fear of the chief; chief and people expecting gifts and handouts; missionaries feeling exploited; entrenchments of religious and cultural concepts (the missionaries in Kambwiri called this "hard-headedness" – a term which is still used today to describe fishermen); people being scattered and "soon evading the missionaries' influence". Note also that Kambwiri mission remained dependent on gifts of food from Chilonga and Kachebere to a higher degree than anticipated. In the Kambwiri story we find already nearly the whole palette of reasons that are still used today to describe the efforts of erecting Church structures as a failure in the valley, or at least as a great challenge.

Nevertheless, the frustrations of the White Father's mission in Kambwiri were rooted in very specific historical circumstances that should caution us not to generalise from here. Father Hannecart in his historical survey (1991, 61), furthermore questioned whether the White Fathers really tried hard enough. The White Fathers gave up after only seven months (much of which must have been used for building the house) – maybe not enough time to say that they had really tried. Hannecart had heard the tale that the Superior from the beginning had little faith in the venture among the Bisa; he "was fully convinced that work among the Abemba was the only thing that mattered". Maybe if they had tried a few miles away from the Moslems and a bit longer, Hannecart asks, maybe it would have worked out very differently?

The White Fathers failed to establish a church, but the Muslims at that time managed to implant Islam. What were the particular historical circumstances that accompanied and favoured the Muslim presence in Kambwiri?

The chieftaincy of Kambwiri was only maybe twenty years old when the White Fathers appeared on the scene. Around 1880 (unsure date) the Bisa ivory trader Chivunzu Mukomba (Kambwiri I) had been able in a revolt (or a Chewa civil war) to dispose Mwase wa Minga and his loyal Chewa.[21] This revolt succeeded because of access to guns that the trader had acquired from the Arabs/Swahili.[22] Swahili traders were maintaining an important base in Kambwiri; at one time Salim ibn Nassur had been residing in Kambwiri. Throughout his life, Chivunzu Mukomba kept depending heavily on the Arabs/Swahili to protect himself against the Angoni.[23] But some incidences nevertheless show that *he* was in charge and not the Arabs. His signing of treaties with BSAC, expressly against the will of Salim ibn Nassur,[24] and also the fact that the ailing chief had welcomed Father Guillemé and seemed keen on a mission (again against the will of the Arabs) indicate strongly that he was trying in a changing world to keep different options open and not to depend alone on the Swahili. Why did his nephew and successor Salimu Mulilo fall back to a greater extend on the Muslims?

The White Fathers narrate that in 1904 the new chief was only a boy; they described him of being 15 years old.[25] Such a young chief, we may speculate, depended much on his councillors, who may have been profiting from the trade with the Swahili. Moreover, having just come into power, one of his great concerns may have been his own recognition; his Bisa people originated from a place called "Ikuza", but various families of Nabwalya, Chongo and Kopa had joined into this recent migration to settle in the new country. The White Fathers also wrote about the presence of (chiefless) Batwa of Lake Bangweulu who had become completely absorbed by the Bisa. Many Bisa thus had been only loosely connected to Chivunzu Mukomba. Chivunzo had given them villages and land; but it still had to be seen whether the diverse subjects would show the same loyalty to his young nephew. More complicated still was the position of a royal Chewa remnant left in Kambwiri. Kambwiri's revolution had been provoked by the Chewa queen Ntemba, Mwase's sister, whose descendants were now living with the Bisa but who were hardly contend to accept the role of Bisa subjects after the death of Chivunzu Mukomba. Though taking on board Bisa language and customs, the Chewa remnant remained very conscious of their origin, and considered themselves the real owners of the land. To understand this, one has to go back to the narratives of the revolt of Chivunzu Mukomba, whose meaning still today is interpreted differently by Chewa and Bisa (see Appendix I. for the narratives). All in all, Salimu Mulilo's position was surely not as strong as the one of Chivunzu. In this situation he may have clung more strongly onto his closest ally, the Muslims traders. Who knows if otherwise somebody else would have used their wealth, weapons and connections for yet another revolution?

In Kambwiri, the Muslims had a very missionary spirit and were keen to recruit new members. I have no evidence that the same had been the case in other Swahili strongholds in the valley, in Kambombo and among the other Senga chiefs, or among the Kunda, who had an equally long or even longer history of dealing with Muslims than Kambwiri. Chiefs may have adhered to Islam,[26] but little or nothing is recorded of Muslim missionary activity in these areas. This may simply be due to lack of recorded material. But one may also speculate that the

Muslim missionary activity in Kambwiri was at least partly provoked by the missionary presence of the White Fathers.

> The Moslems were already numerous when Fr Davoust came in, and they have strengthened their position in a few months' time. (Chilonga Diary January-March 1905).

The missionaries very irritated by the Muslim campaigns; they at least interpreted the "wild drumming" of the Muslims calling people to their gatherings and retreats as direct provocation to their own presence; people wanted to make them feel "excommunicated". There is a sign of relief in the diary when the Ramadan was over, but soon afterwards the time for circumcision came for new recruits; again the missionaries experienced the public rallies as direct confrontation. The feeling of being provoked may well have been reciprocal, and it would not be the first time in history that missionary activities of one faith provoked those of another.

With the two missionary faiths competing for the same souls, the White Fathers were the ones who lost out. Though the White Fathers clearly indicate that ordinary people, a step removed from the chief's influence, were sometimes sympathetic to the Christian faith, Islam was more attractive to those nearer to the capital, also for ordinary people. The missionaries wrote about the attraction of the white Muslim dress that many were proud to wear, and also of camping out and chanting during the month of Ramadan.

Maybe the Muslim faith linked up better with the developing Bisa identity of the eastern side of the Luangwa. The Bisa, having come to a new land only one generation ago and trying to define themselves over and against the surrounding Chewa culture (that was becoming more and more Christianised), may have been looking for visible signs of identity that included also a religious dimension (see next chapter). One may speculate that the Islamic faith with its distinguished dress code and religious rituals became such a marker of difference. Whatever the reason, Kambwiri is unique in that people have maintained a constant presence of Islam; sometimes this presence was fading, but it has been maintained until today and it is presently experiencing a great revival among the Bisa of Mwanya.[27]

Kambwiri (today's Chasera): the Centenary celebrations in 2004 at the spot of the first mission in the Luangwa Valley. Laying of a remembrance stone.

5.

Historical Identities

In this chapter, I describe the various historical identities of the valley as I came to understand them (rightly or wrongly) through this research; it is an ambitious chapter, but nevertheless a necessary chapter in the search for people's markers of identity.

When the BSAC took over the valley at the turn to the 20th century, peoples needed to be classified and counted, and hierarchies needed to be determined through which the new administration could work and through which taxes could be raised. The administration of people in colonial time (in the ideology of indirect rule, introduced in 1924) was based on tribal identities. Tribal law was studied so that chiefs and headmen could govern the tribe in minor matters; they were seen as the channel for the colonial government through which to govern and have orders reach even tiny villages. Population numbers were very small in the valley according to the early inventories of tax income. On the Eastern bank of the Luangwa, people were classified as Senga, Chewa, Bisa, Kunda, Nsenga, Ambo and Achikunda. Each tribe had to have a clear hierarchy of chiefs (even if a clear hierarchy did not exist as such before colonial rule), and each person had to belong to one specific tribe. But in the valley, the administrators became quickly aware that such clear tribal categories did not work here. Though there were clear maps drawn into the District Notebooks with the definitions of boundaries, one finds writings on the margins explaining that things on the ground were not as clear as on the map. Around the palace of a chief, people called themselves with a tribal name, but the further one went away from a centre, the more vague tribal identities became. Many individuals didn't seem to know (nor did they seem to bother) whether they were Chewa, Bisa, Senga or Tumbuka. The Lundazi District Notebooks, for example, refer to an occasion when headman Vunda came to the *boma* to reclaim his chieftaincy. (He is acknowledged today as a group-headman, not a chief.) His family was asked which tribe they belonged to. Some said: "We are Chewa", others "we are Bisa", and still others "we are Senga". The quest for the chieftaincy ended there. The family referred to themselves as *bene Ng'oma* by clan, but tribal identity did not play a role for them. It was difficult for the British to classify a number of important villages in the valley; they were too small to be called chieftaincies (taking into consideration also the fact that there was not enough money in the treasuries of the government to pay allowances to many chiefs), but their alliances to other chiefs had shifted over time, or people were aware of a distinctive origin, or they had been independent or semi-independent. All of this made it difficult to give them clear tribal labels.

What determined people's identities much more than the tribe was the clan (*mukoka, mukowa*). This is true especially for the matrilineal southern valley and central valley, but to an extent also for the bilineal Senga of the north. Clan relationships were inclusive, cutting across tribal markers. So the *"wene Mvula"* (or *"eni Mvula"* or *"bena Mfula"*) are found among the Nsenga, Ambo, Achikunda, Kunda, Bisa, and (though here the clans lost in importance) among the Chewa and Senga, and also among the plateau peoples; however distant, they would consider each other as relatives with specific rights and obligations. The clan determined who is a relative, an in-law, who is from the father's or grandfathers' side, with whom one has a joking relation, whom one buries, and whom one has to offer hospitality. The clans linked (and still link) people together in a network of family relationships far beyond the tribe.

The matrilineal clan-system in the valley, though it works slightly different from area to area (being for example differently influenced by the Angoni stress on the *chiwongo* through the father's side), has a long history of incorporating all kinds of strangers and refugees into its structure. Even clanless Tumbuka people coming from the north were easily absorbed: the Zimbas of Tembwe became *wene Zimba,* which sounds similar to the *bashimba* (leopards) which is the Bisa and Ambo nickname for the clan of the leopards, the *bena Ngo.* By this convention, the *wene Zimba* became blood-relatives with the *wene Ngo.* The *wene Mbawo* of Kakumbi (Kunda) have a different origin from the *wene Tembo* of Sandwe (Nsenga) or the *bena Inama* of the Bisa, but all three inherit the paternal *chiwongo* Mwale, and all the Mwales consider each other as relatives. Chief Kakumbi (a *mwine Mbawo*) considers himself a relative of chief Sandwe (a *mwine Tembo*), though he traces his ancestors from the Bangweulu while chief Sandwe traces his to the Lenje of Kabwe. (The wasp (*tembo*) feeds on the insect that is called *mbawo,* which is taken as evidence of the relationship between the two clans.) In Kakumbi all the *wene Tembo* and *wene Inama* are simply referred to as *wene Mbawo;* they are relatives, though some point as their place of origin to the west, others to the east, other to the north and still others to the south. The clan system was *the* way of incorporating them into the universe of relationships.

CHIEFLY AND TRIBAL IDENTITIES: THE NSENGA SOUTH (NSENGA, AMBO, CHIKUNDA)

Williams-Myars asserted that tribal identities in the valley are a phenomenon starting only with the late 18th century but belonging more properly only into the 19th century. In 17th century Portuguese sources describing the lower Luangwa no reference is made to the Ansenga; in the 18th century the term "Senga" of various sources (later producing many misunderstanding whether they referred actually to the Senga north or the Nsenga south) seem to refer mostly to an area / a location rather than to a specific people. The typical Nsenga clans (like the *bena Nguluwe, bena Mumba, bena Sakala, bena Lungu, bena Mwanza, bena Tembo, bena Njovu, bena Nyendwa*) were long present (some of them probably for more than a 1000 years), but the tribal identity of a people calling itself Ansenga is a 19th century phenomenon that became cemented (so Williams-Myars) in colonial times. Portuguese sources of the late 17th century of tours to the Luangwa do not mention the Nsenga; in the 18th century the term Unsenga referred to a location/ area and not to a specific people. Though several clans attained a dominant role in specific areas already more than 500 years ago, one would not speak of tribal identities in today's sense.

The first occasion of cohesion between several interlocking clans in Unsenga over a large area is today attributed to the *bena Nguluwe* (or *wene Nguluwe...*): they are acknowledged by several clans to have played at least a ritual role over other clans (maybe as an acknowledgement of their early arrival), and their widespread role is attested also by some archaeological evidence.[28] Later many lineages and clans came under the influence of the Chewa Phiri clan from the east, and the Lala/Lenje immigrants (under the *bena Nyendwa/ bena Nyangu*) from the west.[29] This was the first time that the area of Unsenga experienced chieftaincy in today's sense of a fixed political hierarchy. Chieftaincy spread also to other clans. But neither the dominance of the *Nguluwe* clan (and others), nor of the *Nyendwa*, nor of the *Phiri* clan connoted the tribal identity that we call today Nsenga. Different people had entered Unsenga for centuries from all directions; society or societies were held together by the inclusive clan structure that was partly superseded by specific clans (at least for ritual purposes) and later by chiefs.

The "Lala" invasion from the west started during the 17th century and after a number of immigrations led to the establishment of the present *bena Nyendwa* Ambo chieftaincies (Mboloma or Kankomba, Mboshya, Luwembe and Mwape) that stand in close relation to the Swaka and Lala. Several histories have been recorded and are available.[30] Chiefs Luwembe and Mwape both referred me to the works of Stefaniszyn, of which chief Luwembe even kindly lent me a copy, when I inquired about Ambo history. Apart from the *bena Nyendwa*, also other clans of the Ambo (notably *bena Tembo, bena Nyangu, bena Nswi and bena Mpande*) see the arrival of their ancestors in the valley in connection with the decent from the Lala area of the west. The Ambo language (called Chiumbo) is a Bemba-Lala dialect, but many Ambo have taken on largely a Nsenga dialect, and the valley Ambo today are often called "Ambo-Nsenga" to distinguish them from their plateau counterparts. The Chewa influence of the Phiri clan (coming then from immediately north of the Zambezi in what is today Mozambique) came about not only through conquest (as the Chewa oral narratives want to have it), but more often through marriages into influential clans and alliances.

During the 19th century, two powerful groups intruded into Unsenga from the South, mingled or raided, bringing lasting changes: the Achikunda and the Angoni. The Achikunda developed on Portuguese territory as slave-armies as a response to the rapidly expanding slave trade in the absence of effective government structures. Traders from diverse origins (often ex-slaves themselves, vaguely associated with the Portuguese by blood – traced, according to Portuguese Law, through the mother – or by alliance) built up their own armies through raiding or voluntary enslavements in times of famines and wars in return for food and protection, and such armies internalized during the latter 17th century and during the 18th century their corporate identity as "Achikunda" (*kukunda* in Shona means "to vanquish"). It was especially during the 19th century that the armies of warlords such as the infamous Kanyemba and his son-in-law Matakenya (but also a number of others) harassed the Luangwa valley. The ancestor of today's chief Nyalugwe in the valley, for example, was a Chikunda trader who depended on Matakenya.[31] Some Nsenga villages obtained guns through marriages with Achikunda leaders; others hired Achikunda mercenaries for defence purposes. Some valley chiefs (for example Luwembe) managed to resist Achikunda control.[32] Achikunda raids forced people in the Nsenga valley to unite, learn about modern warfare and the importance of alliances.

In 1835, Zwangendaba with his Ngoni army crossed the Zambezi (not far from the mouth of the Luangwa) and passed slowly through Nsenga country on their way north to Tanzania. The Nsenga were not accustomed to Ngoni warfare and resistance was limited. Zwangendaba in turn was impressed by Nsenga medicine-men (some of whom he employed) and by the *mwavi* ordeal (poison ordeal used to determine witches and for other divinations). In 1863, Mpezeni came back into Nsenga country through the Luangwa to ravage Nsenga country for a number of years before moving to Chipata area around 1870; some chiefs now were better prepared to fight, having been put on constant alert through the Achikunda raids, and could resist single

Ngoni attacks, but nevertheless few could resist repeated attacks over a long period of time.[33] Some found refuge in the Luangwa valley (chief Mwanjawanthu, for example, fled to chief Msoro – both are of the same clan – *bena Sakala* – and consider each other therefore as brothers.)[34] The Ngoni are said to have been keen on the beautiful Nsenga women and many of the incorporated Nsenga men also rose into high positions in Ngoni society; the way how Ngoni society and language became henceforth marked by the Nsenga has well been documented.[35] Incidentally, many Nsenga-Ngoni were involved in raiding other valley chiefs.[36]

Tribal identity in the Nsenga valley is to a good extend the result of the continuous Achikunda and Ngoni raids. In the later part of the 19th century, such defence depended upon access to weapons and connections. No single family or lineage could survive any longer alone; people who had been scattered before were forced to concentrate into fortified villages to defend themselves better.[37] Valley chieftaincies grew by accepting refugees from the plateau; they provided an alternative to Ngoni rule. It has been documented for the Nsenga chief Sandwe and the Kunda chief Msoro in the valley that they could, often successfully, ward off Angoni raids until the advent of colonial rule because of their increased numbers through incorporated refugees and their access to Achikunda mercenaries.[38]

When the British took over, they cemented the positions of chiefs that they found in the valley. If they did not find a chief with whom they could deal, they created one.[39] Tribal identification depended on the chief one was living with now; but for most people the network of their clans remained a more important marker of identity. Looking through history, the chiefs' positions had become cemented through a monopoly on trade, then through outside threats and raids, then through the British system of indirect rule, and today through ZAWA and the wildlife- and tourist industry (see later).

A number of people working in Nsenga area have remarked that (in general, and excluding chiefly families) people have little sense of tribal history. During this research I too found it difficult to inquire about tribal history. But I found it easy to inquire about clan- and lineage history. Indeed, many case studies revealed that the ancestors of a lineage had come (be it through marriage or as refugees) from other parts of the valley or from the plateau. Maybe one can say that in the southern valley, for most people who have no direct connection with the royal families, tribal allegiance is rather accidental and even interchangeable; clan affiliation is not.

THE KUNDA

Also the Kunda of Mambwe district have largely taken over a Nsenga dialect, and the clan relationships make them relatives with the Nsenga and Ambo[40] They share with each other largely (but with some exceptions) a supportive history, and Ambo, Nsenga and Kunda have intermarried very freely.[41] It is unlikely that there was any people calling themselves Kunda in the valley before the 1840s.[42] Still today there is a certain awareness of the "Awetwe", "Abetwa" or Batwa whom the royal lineages found on their journey down into the valley, or with whom they mixed while still on the plateau, people "who did not know what to do with elephant tusks, who were just sitting on them and who had no clothes." In return for cloth they gladly acknowledged the supremacy of Mambwe and his relatives (a story repeated in different parts of the valley) and were incorporated into the polity.[43] In chief Msoro's and Mnkhanya's area a number of scattered Chewa families were found and absorbed. There exist different (and largely conflicting) accounts about the histories of the Kunda chiefs (Nsefu, Jumbe, Malama, Mnkhanya, Msoro, and Kakumbi, and also about "deposed" chieftaincies like Tindi and Chibanda).[44]

Kunda history became very turbulent with the coming of the Angoni. Chief Mnkhanya was taken captive and died on the way into Ngoni land (his body was left to rot on a path); his successor Kawindula was killed in battle, and his nephew Mnkhanya II was taken with a good number of his people into Ngoni exile. So was chief Tindi. Mambwe III (Kavimba) lost most of his headmen who fled either to Kambwiri or still further away; his own son Chuaula allied himself with the Ngoni, and after Kavimba's death managed to kill his father's brother who was the heir to the throne. While Sefu (Nsefu), the next heir in line, and his brother Jumbe went to Lake Malawi to the Yao in Kotakota into voluntary exile (where they were to pick up their Arab names), the opportunist Chuaula filled the vacuum and became a powerful chief. Kunda consciousness is acquainted with the defeats by the Ngoni, but nevertheless people tell also of won battles in which they tricked the Ngoni, faking defeat and surrender, or revenging at night in a rather unmanly manner.

While Ambo history in the valley is closely knit with Lala and Nsenga history, the Kunda immigrants further north found a country with few people and large areas of land devoid of settlements; maybe this helped to build up a distinctive sense of identity. Nevertheless, as with the Ambo and Nsenga, also the Kunda lineages of today trace their ancestors into all different directions. To give an example, in Nsefu we find villages inherited by the *wene Ng'oma* that trace their ancestor to Vunda in the north (in the country of chief Chifunda), villages led by the *wene Lungu* with ancestors both from Luangwa in the south and from Chitungulu in the north, a *wene Mpelo* village from the Bisa west (along the Luapula, it is known as a Batwa clan), *awene Mwanza* villages from Kalindawalo in the east, *abena Ng'uni* Bisa from Mulamba-Kambwiri, etc. Furthermore, there are many Chewa from the east, some of them are newcomers, while others have been there already for some generations.[45] Once one starts looking into any specific village, one finds still much more diversification of origin than when looking at the specific lineages. What makes people "Kunda" is the allegiance to the chief of the territory in which they happen to live; many maybe would be equally happy to call themselves something else.

BISA (CHONGO, NABWALYA, KAMBWIRI) AND CHEWA (MWASE WA MINGA)

The first written reference to the Chewa of Mwase wa Minga in the central valley in the area known as Chibande (or Chiwande),[46] today's villages of Chasera, comes from the accounts of Manoel Pereira who travelled along the Luangwa in 1796.[47] Also Lacerda referred to the Chewa when he crossed the Luangwa in 1798. He was thinking of obtaining land in the country of chief Mwase wa minga for a base half way from Tete to Mwata Kazembe near Lake Mweru; Mwata Kazembe considered even the land east of the Luangwa to be dependent on him.[48] Later, in 1824, the Portuguese bought a plot along the Matizi from Mwase.[49] The Chewa along the Luangwa were an offshoot (like Mwase Lundazi) of Mwase Kasungu, who wanted access to the Luangwa in view of his expanding trade empire. But because of the turbulences and harassments during the second half of the 19th century and the ever changing alliances on the plateau, it was difficult to keep and support the Chewa chieftaincy in the valley. When Livingstone toured the Luangwa valley in 1865, he found the Chewa already harassed by the Bisa from the West and also by the Ngoni from the East. Sometime later (maybe around 1880) Mwase was overthrown by the Bisa ivory trader and nobleman, Kambwiri Chivunzo Munkomba, who himself was persuaded into the coup by Mwase's sister Ntemba in a civil revolt against her brother (see the previous chapter). At the time of the takeover, most Chewa lived in one single fortified village in Chibendame.[50] Being pushed by Ntemba, Kambwiri's soldiers killed Mwase and most of his people; the main plot happened basically in one single night (see Appendix). A number of different Bisa families from the western side of the Luangwa followed Kambwiri to take possession of their new country, and the small Chewa remnant of Ntemba was incorporated and intermarried into the new Bisa polity. When the BSAC took over, and when the White Fathers opened their mission in the valley, they were dealing with a Bisa chief supported by a number of Swahili traders. (Note that today's Chewa chieftaincies of Kazembe and Chitungulu in the valley are of later (probably 19th century) origin.

The Bisa sense of identity is special until today. The British tried to take the Luangwa as a natural boundary between its districts. The Bisa east of the Luangwa belong culturally and historically to their relatives in the west across the river, but they became incorporated into the Eastern Province that is marked by a different cultural environment and that was often hostile to them: the Chewa regarded them as intruders who should be "pushed back" across the Luangwa. The defence of distinctive Bisa customs became paramount, which provoked Kambwiri II (Salimu Mulilo) to clash with the British authorities, when he ordered the killings of *finkula* (children born with upper teeth first).[51] Salimu Mulilo in consequence was deposed in 1920 and arrested for child murder; he died in prison in Livingstone. Just three years later, according to the District Notebooks, his successor (Bulyani) ordered the killing of his own child (a *cinkula*?) and was also deposed and imprisoned.[52] Both chiefs seemed to have risked a very confrontational stance in their defence of what they considered "Bisa custom".

After the deposal of the fourth Kambwiri (note that all three Kambwiri's after Chivunzu were deposed by the British for various offences), the Chewa chieftaincy of Mwanya was reinstalled in 1946; since then the Chewa royal family (speaking Bisa, being Bisa through the fathers' lines, and having no distinctive Chewa customs like the *Nyau*) are holding onto a "minority rule".

The Bisa are far from being a coherent people. People who crossed over had come from many different families. Already on the western side of the Luangwa, so wrote Stuart Marks in his study,

> The Valley Bisa, a population in flux, have never been a homogeneous group. To be sure, the chiefs belonged to the Ngona clan, but those under them were a mixture of lineages which moved about as circumstances dictated.[53]

As said above for the Nsenga, also for the valley Bisa (the Awiza) the prime duty and obligation is to the own lineage and clan. Some lineages of different clans had been intrinsically connected with the takeover of Kambwiri (for example families of the *bena Mvula, bena Nswi,* and *bena Muti*); they have their own burial grounds until today and maintain a direct connection to the chietaincy. But other lineages have not much to do with the royal family, and some make it a point to stress that their ancestors were there already in Nabwalya area before the royal *bena Ngona* arrived, and they have their own legends and mythology, notably the *bena Nzoka* (*bena Njoka/Nsoka* of Chongo.[54]

Nevertheless, since their crossing of the Luangwa, and not stopped by the deposal of the last Kambwiri in 1946, the Bisa of Mwanya have been involved in a struggle to maintain or construct a distinctive "Bisa" identity.[55] Even what concerns the knowledge and practice of witchcraft, the Bisa are known (and feared) throughout the valley for their distinctive types. In how far the history of evangelisation has linked up or failed to link up with people's sense of identity remains to be answered. Among the Bisa majority at least I heard much discontent; mentioned was the stress (in the past) on the Tumbuka language in Catholic church services, which had been introduced with the argument that people must become incorporated into the larger deanery and Diocese. The Awiza are quite conscious of their distinctive background, and some have expressed throughout this reaearch that they their cultural background is not sufficiently valued by the Church. The Chewa of Mwanya, in contrast, would not like the Church to stress Bisa identity! The Church, operating within a polity made up of both Awiza and Achewa, risks being abused in local power plays of legitimisation.[56]

THE SENGA OF KAMBOMBO

The Senga in the north show a greater coherence and also tribal identification than the peoples of the south. Tribal history is narrated at important funerals of group headmen, at feasts, or inaugurations of chiefs; many group headmen maintain a spirit shrine (*kavuwa*) for their predecessors, which gives an awareness of history in which their authority is vested. In what follows, I look at the Kambombo narrative a bit closer (see Appendix for one full version of the narrative). It should be noted, however, that the story of Kambombo is not representative of the whole of Senga country; though he is senior chief today, the chiefs in the past were considered to be equal to each other, and the history of each Senga chief is interwoven with the people who were present before the arrival of the chiefs. However, what is said below for the encounter of the Senga with the Tumbuka of Chama, sheds also light on the encounter of the other Senga chiefs with the previous inhabitants (Tumbuka and early Bisa) in their respective locations.

In historical narratives, the term Senga is applied first to the incoming Luba aristocracy (coming from *Uluwa,* thought to be in Katanga), in search for land, placing itself above a core of (mainly) Tumbuka speaking people. In that sense it is often said that "the incoming Senga found the Tumbuka." As the narrative unfolds, the term Senga comes to describe the new polity, made up of people both of Senga and Tumbuka origin: There are no longer Sengas and Tumbukas, but all have become Sengas and are united under a common aristocracy that traces its roots to *Uluwa*. The Senga thus see themselves as having two roots: Luba and Tumbuka, which distinguishes them both from the Bisa in the west and the Tumbuka of the plateau. Chiweza's story (senior chief Kambombo) is typical for the valley: a tiny group of traders, linked to long distant trade, cloth and weapons, set itself up as chiefs over a scattered, decentralised local group of people (in this case Tumbuka), and in the process a new tribe or people was formed.

Culturally speaking (if one ignores the absence of cows in Senga culture) one could place the Senga today rather close to the Tumbuka in what concerns language, virilocality of marriages (including polygamous marriages),[57] the factual absence of the matrilineal clan system (though rudiments are still there), or the relatively high marriage payments that are more and more regarded (as in Angoni culture) as transferring to the husband rights over wives and children, and the high percentage of polygamy. Yet the narrative of Senga history deals nearly exclusively with the royal side of the incoming Luba people. When people around Chama recall their history, it is Luba history of a few incoming individuals rather than Tumbuka history. Though everybody acknowledges that the incoming Luba (or Bisa) or "Senga" found Tumbuka settlements (and in some parts, like Zaongo, little settlements of people related to the Bisa), nothing seems left in public memory of events that preceded the coming of the Senga chiefs. The arrival of Chiweza is considered the official start of Senga history; even for the descendants of the Tumbuka, historical awareness starts only with the arrival of Chiweza. Today the date 1790 appears often in the Senga's own narratives for this event. The colonial administration had given this date in the District Notebooks of Lundazi, in which they referred to an estimate of the British official Lane Poole, who in turn refers to other estimates.[58]

The Luba identity of the aristocracy is strong. The narrative stresses that Chiweza himself was born in Luba country. The Luba part in the story is very similar to the departure legends of other Luba migrants like the Bemba, Bisa, Aushi, Lala, or Ng'umbo. The reason given for Chiweza's departure from Luba-country is a resentment against weeding in his father's fields. Though it is not impossible that Chiweza came directly from Luba, the remainder of the narrative contradicts it. It says that he had stayed a long time with the Bisa, lived at Chibesa Kunda (or Kopa), that his first wife, a little girl, was given to him by chief Chibesa Kunda, and that his first-born child was only born near Chama after he had reached the valley, and that the child's mother was a Tumbuka woman. Chiweza therefore must have been quite young when he came to Chama. Notwithstanding that the term "Bisa" in the time of the migration was a very loose term and that the Bisa hardly had the tribal cohesion and identity that developed in later years, the Luba connection in the narrative goes via the Bisa connection, if we follow the view of the colonial historians. When Lane Poole inquired about Senga identity during the 1920s (or even earlier), the then oldest living headman told him that the Senga were in fact Bisa. In his version of the Kambombo narrative (which is quite different from the narratives described in this book), the dispute about the succession of Chiweza after his death was referred back to the Bisa chief Chibesa Kunda, an indication that Chiweza was considered a Bisa. That Chiweza is said to be born in Luba country indicates that Luba is an important marker of identity for the Senga aristocracy who are surrounded now by people who trace their origin to the East rather than the West. Luba has to be present in the first chapter of the migration narrative. The Senga, having adopted custom and language from the Tumbuka, would hardly consider themselves a Bisa offshoot; instead they view themselves (like the Kunda who have a similar Bisa connection) on equal footing with the Bisa, meaning originating like them directly from Luba. "We passed through Bisa country on our journey and stayed with them, but we are from Uluwa."

When Lacerda crossed the Luangwa in 1798 just a bit south of Senga location, the Senga were not known to him; he did not mention the Senga at all. Lacerda had a big interest in the area where he crossed, as he was thinking of establishing at the Matizi River a Portuguese colony (an area which belongs today to the Chewa chief Kazembe). Lacerda recorded in that area the presence of "Wizas and Botumbucas". That the Senga are not mentioned does not mean that Chiweza (or indeed Chifunda, Chikwa and Tembwe) had not yet arrived; it does mean, however, that Senga identity was not yet formed; people were known as Wizas and Tumbucas. At the beginning of the colonial administration, however, an awareness was found in the valley and also among the neighbouring people that the Senga had been there already for centuries,[59] an indicator of the interiorisation of Senga identity by that time and an acknowledgement of that identity by the neighbours (for example the Bemba).[60]

Chiweza's journey eastwards finds its parallels all along the valley (Kunda, Ambo, Bisa and some early Nsenga dynasties). Roberts (1976, 91) suggested that the end of the 18th century was not yet marked by centralisation and cohesion, but rather by fission and migration, and one migratory trend went from the West into the Luangwa valley and across the Luangwa. The movement of the Senga aristocracy (like that of the Ambo or Kunda) would have been part of this trend.

The scale of the Luba migration into Senga country was very small. The narrative of Kambombo stresses that the Luba or Bisa immigrants consisted just of a small number of men with hardly any woman. Furthermore, according to the Senga narrative of Kambombo, the country that Chiweza inherited, was sparsely populated. Chiweza found only a handful of scattered villages of decentralized Tumbuka people, who were not linked to any major trading network.[61]

The oldest settlements in the area of Kambombo are said to be the Tumbuka villages of Chili, Mpyana Kamimbe, Mungwalala, Mungulube and Chama.[62] There are still a number of other old Tumbuka villages (like Kajumba), but they are said to have come after the arrival of the Luba/Bisa aristocracy, who were nicknamed Senga. But even for the preceding Tumbuka villages, history only seems to start with the arrival of the Senga. For example, when I asked group headman Chama about the very first Chama, I was given the name of Musolomoka. But Musolomoka was the very Chama who was found by the Senga; no Tumbuka individuals are remembered in Chama from the time before the arrival of the Senga. The same happened in Mungwalala: I was given the name of Bwengu (though others say Juzi) as the very first Mungwalala, in both cases the very one who was found by the Senga on their arrival. Even in the spirit shrines (*tukafuwa*) of the Tumbuka group-headmen, the line of ancestors starts only with the leader who was encountered by the incoming Senga. And also the name of the striking landmark of the mountain called Mphala Usenga has to do with the Senga. That the Senga had the power of naming is quite a contrast to the fact that they quickly lost their own language in subsequent history.[63]

Tew, as quoted by Brelsford (1956, 93-94), gave a helpful distinction, in that she differentiated three different Tumbuka layers in the Luangwa valley as well as elsewhere: the first consisting of ancient, widely scattered, decentralised, small-scale Tumbuka settlements, not linked to the long distant trade; secondly the Tumbuka group of Mlowoka, an ivory trader from the East in contact with the Swahili, who started his dynasty in Kamanga at around 1780-1800 and who introduced many new (Arab) elements into Tumbuka culture that fell under his influence; and thirdly the wave of Tumbuka refugees that resulted from the onslaught of the Angoni on the Tumbuka of Nkananga in the 1850s. Kajumba of Kambombo for example falls into the third category, while one would place the five ancient Tumbuka villages of Kambombo mentioned above into the first category, as they were said to have been unaware of the value of elephant tusks.

With the arrival of the Senga immigrants life changed for the Tumbuka. Chiweza is said to have collected ivory tusks from the Tumbuka (considered to be without any value), sent out a caravan to look for trading partners (or went himself), which then came back with much cloth and other trading items, which he generously distributed among the leaders of the Tumbuka. But the price for these items was an acknowledgement of Chiweza's supremacy. Subsequently, the descendants of the Tumbuka came to identify themselves so strongly with the new Senga identity that there was no need any longer to narrate own Tumbuka history as a separate form of identity. The Tumbuka villages became firmly incorporated into the Senga polity; they intermarried, and Tumbuka leaders from the beginning were given Induna-ship at the palace; they merged under one new polity called Senga; the induna-ship of both Tumbuka and Senga villages became hereditary only through incorporation into the Senga-polity. Chama was called *"Mtaya calo"* ("the one who gave the country away") by his fellow Tumbuka (Chama was the first Tumbuka leader to acknowledge Chiweza's supremacy), but this must be put into perspective by the fact that Chama's grandsons became the chiefs of the new Senga tribe in Kambombo, because Chama's daughter Mulolwa, though being only second wife, constituted the main line of chiefly descend until today. The descendants of Chama therefore can hardly be called losers in the Senga affair. While the term "Senga" had once described the incoming Luba people begging for land, it was now denoting the new polity, a new tribal identity comprising both groups. Since the Tumbuka identified themselves with the Senga polity and took up political positions within the new framework, there was little need to keep genealogies reaching into pre-Senga era; their own political history in the new sense started only with the arrival of Kambombo.[64]

With the exception of Mungwalala, who was killed on Chiweza's command for refusing to accept Chiweza's supremacy, people say that the take-over of Chiweza was peaceful, and that the Tumbuka rather readily submitted under his rule. Chiweza was a political intruder, but less of a cultural intruder. The immigrants took over both language and culture from their subjects. There were compelling reasons – beyond the gifts of cloth – why the scattered Tumbuka of the valley would have accepted readily a new political and centralised identity in a rapidly changing world: the ravages of the slave trade that was wiping out isolated families and lineages; the Bemba were rapidly expanding in the west, but also Bisa, Chewa, Swahili, and later the Achikunda, Angoni and diverse warlords, were drawn into the slave trade and all were looking for elephants and slaves in the valley.[65] That the Senga escaped annihilation and even managed to resist the Angoni onslaught was due to their level of centralization and their access to guns and powder through the trade and, at least for the latter part of the 19th century, an Arab/Swahili presence, since Kambombo hosted Arab traders. Sengas became important trading partners for all the neighbouring peoples. Though at least one Kambombo was killed in warfare, the Senga present themselves today as having successfully evaded the Angoni and even leading counterattacks against them. In the latter half of the 19th century also the Achikunda coming from the Zambezi raided at times as far north as the upper Luangwa. Surviving along the Luangwa meant to be part of a larger and centralized polity, and depended on access to guns and powder through trade.

Senga aristocracy managed to set itself apart as a political class of rulers. The cruel burial rites of Senga chiefs and important Senga headmen testify to this (see the Senga narratives of the Appendix). Aristocracy was not restricted to chieftaincy but was extended to many important villages; many of today's Senga group-headmen trace their ancestry back to the royal line. The title of the Senga group-headman Kazembe, for example, goes back to a grandchild of Kasolwe (Kambombo II);[66] the titles both of Kapilingishya and Kapwanyanga (Chikhalanga) have to do with a daughter of Kacila Fitanda (Kambombo VII);[67] the title of Malama goes back to a son of a Kambombo, while the title of Ng'anjo Chibwato in Tembwe's area goes back to a grandson of Muzieba (Kambombo VI).[68]

The Kambombo narrative mentions a feature that became characteristic for the Senga in the valley: the presence of indigenous cotton. People are proud to say that this cotton was of a different and higher quality to the commercial cotton that was introduced lately. It is said that the trees were bigger and that they produced bigger cotton balls. The Senga were famous for their cotton, which they traded with the neighbouring tribes, and they used to make their own cotton clothing. Gouldsbury and Sheane (1911, 14, 24, 337) described it as high quality cotton able to fetch a high price in London. Apart from cotton, the Senga also used to sell tobacco, baskets, cloth and dried meat to several of the surrounding peoples (they in turn were dependent on salt, iron goods and other items). It was through trade that the Senga became known to their neighbours with their distinctive identity as Senga; their goods made them to be valued as trading partners, or caused them to be raided.

It was in the third generation after Chiweza that a Kambombo is reported to have been killed by the Angoni (Chimbundu, son of Muzieba, son of Mwimba, son of Chiweza). But the narrative says that, already long before Chimbundu, the Angoni had been a threat to the

Senga. Lane Poole narrated that the first ravages against the southern Senga (chief Chifunda) had started already on the northern journey of the Angoni in the late 1830s, which lead chief Chifunda to beg the Chewa chief Chinunda for protection against the Angoni. A short time of peace came when Zwangendaba moved north along the plateau, bypassing the Senga and ravaging instead the Tumbuka and Fipa. Zwangendaba died (around 1845), brothers and sons quarrelled and fought over succession, and eventually his son Mombera moved back south to trouble the Henga, Poka, Nkamanga (all related to the Tumbuka) and the Tumbuka, part of whose refugees then came to populate Kambombo's country. During the 1850s it were the Angoni of Mombera who frequently came down to the *marambo* to trouble the Senga.[69] A second catastrophe occurred for the Senga when Mperembe with his army decided to join his brother Mombera in Tumbuka country.[70] While Mpezeni later came to the southern part of the Luangwa valley to ravage the Ansenga, Kunda, Ambo and Bisa, his brothers Mombera and Mperembe were in charge of disturbing the Senga of the north.

SENGA IDENTITY

The Senga proudly distinguish themselves from the Tumbuka on the plateau, whom they regard as strongly influenced by Angoni culture, and this is not just for the absence of cows in Senga cultural life. I was told several times that prior to 1930 Senga culture was much more marked by their Luba heritage than it is now, and even today the Senga understand themselves as having kept trends of both the matrilineal and of the patrilineal systems of their founding members. Even if the marriage practice may as a matter of fact hardly differ from that of the Tumbuka, the Senga often stress that their main marriage payment, the *cimalo,* is different from the *lobola* of the Angoni.

> The children for us belong to both sides, father and mother, and if the marriage breaks up, they can go to either side, even if the *cimalo* has been fully paid. In Tumbuka and Ngoni culture, the

man buys with the *lobola* payments the rights to both wife and children. This is not the case in Senga culture.

I was told that the present marriage payments, which are rather high (today easily exceeding a million Kwacha (250 US$), though the money is not always paid), entered into the equation only during the 1930s as a result of migrant workers commodifying their bride services.

> Before that time, a man paid a ring of beads and gave a how or a chicken to the family of the wife; that was all. That was the real Senga custom.

Some add that in the past the marriage was more strongly matrilineal, and some go as far as to say that the husband in Senga custom, prior to the 1930s, was understood to be just the "*tambala*" (cock) – similar to the Nsenga culture – meaning he was there only to beget children, who did not belong to him but to the wife's family. This, however, is a memory of the distant past; things have changed with the high marriage payments. The matrilineal impact on the Senga is stronger in Tembwe, Chikwa or Chifunda than it is in Kambombo; apart from Kambombo's area, the inheritance of many other Senga villages still follows the matrilineal side: a maternal nephew inherits a headman, not a son.

The marriage payments have obtained a very legal dimension in Senga land: If something happens to the wife (death), or if divorce takes place before the *cimalo* has been fully paid to her family, then the husband will not obtain freedom of remarriage until this money has been paid, an issue which can be pressed through the local courts. Social organisation and the sense of belonging is markedly different in Senga culture from the cultures of the southern valley. At the death of a husband, for example, children remain attached to their father's plot, and it is much rarer that a widow is being chased away from this plot, as is the case in the matrilineal societies further south. This different sense of belonging has also spiritual repercussions in what concerns the understanding of death, of the *chiwanda*, and of the meaning of the *kususula* (the ritual cleansing of the remaining spouse), in which respect the Senga differentiate themselves strongly from their Bisa and Luba roots. A number of times, when I made in a meeting a comparison with the Bemba customs of inheritance and their notion of the *chiwanda*, I was told: "But we are not like the Bemba or the Bisa. Our culture is different."

Most tribes in Zambia have seen in recent history efforts to sustain (if not even to create) markers of identity. In what concerns Senga folklore and festivals, the Kwenje ceremony and Miyombe celebrations have been established during the last decades, centred on the chiefs and with organising committees based in the towns. Yet as a real spiritual marker of identity typical for the Senga one could mention the Mulenga cult (often referred to as Kamulenga). The cult is very old, and it is still alive from Kambombo to Chifunda and also on the western side of the Luangwa in Fulaza and Pondo. When the rains fail, spirit shrines for Mulenga (Kamulenga) are erected at crossroads and decorated, seeds and beer are brought and dancing takes place. These Kamulenga shrines are different from the spirit shrines for ancestors (*tukafuwa*) which can be seen throughout the Senga valley in the villages of important group-headmen. People whom I asked were proud to have kept the Kamulenga cult, yet nobody was too sure whether it was a Luba or Tumbuka custom. As the Senga are proud to stress that they successfully mixed the two, most say that it is both.

> All the Luba people had similar customs, as the Bemba also venerate Mulenga, but also the Tumbuka had their cults. The Kamulenga cult came from both sides.

THE CHEWA OF KAZEMBE

According to Lane Poole's estimate, the chieftaincy of Kazembe goes back to a Chewa hunting exhibition maybe in the middle of the 19th century sent out by Mwase Kasungu, which made itself independent on seeing the fertile lands in the valley.[71] According to the royal family,[72] the first Kazembe – the name meaning ambassador (of chief Mwase Kasungu) – who entered the valley was Nguwa, who settled at the Matizi at the same time as the first Senga chiefs arrived from the west (the end of the 18th century), [73] but many Senga say that Kazembe came only much later. The chiefs are *wene Mwanza* through the mothers' line. Nguwa found Tumbuka people in the country (the Mwina Mutondo, a Zimba) whom they kicked out. Some of the Tumbuka are said to have committed mass suicide after being robbed of their country by drowning themselves in a pond of the Lumezi River (see the appendix for the narrative). Nguwa himself was said (by some) to have been killed in a fight with the Bisa. Also his granddaughter Chitete (Kazembe IV), who moved from the Matizi to the present location, is said to have been struggling with the Bisa. The relationship between Kazembe and his Senga neighbour Chifunda is said, in contrast, to have been supportive, especially during the time of Angoni raids. The royal family of Kazembe regards the whole country up to chief Mwanya as Chewa and as historically theirs (chief Chitungulu in this Kazembe narrative is not a chief but a glorified headman). In Chitungulu also, there are narratives of hunting groups of Chewa entering the valley from the plateau (the ancestors of group-headman Mpipa) and finding chiefless people "who did not know what to do with ivory" and intermarrying with them. But the population is very mixed, coming from all sides, and people speak more Tumbuka (Senga) and Wiza than Chewa. Like in Mwanya, there is no Nyau in neither Kazembe nor Chitungulu.

CONCLUSION: THE DYNAMICS OF VALLEY TRIBAL IDENTITIES

Life in the valley was based economically mainly on hunting, and hunting peoples tend towards dispersion. Animals avoid big villages, but to kill a bigger animal far from the village implies the problem of carrying it home over long distances. Also the style of cultivation (often shifting cultivation) encouraged dispersion and living in small settlements. People in the valley had entered from all possible directions, and in any given area they were hardly unified; lineage segments were the main focus of a person's identity. Also the hunting traditions that involved excessive use of medicines (some bordering to what we may call witchcraft) increased suspicions between different lineages.

The key factor to tribal identity in the valley (Nsenga, Chikunda, Ambo, Kunda, Bisa, Chewa, and Senga) was long distance trade, the slave and ivory trade and the accompanying raids. Starting with the end of the 18th century small lineage segments could not continue to survive by themselves. In the middle of the 19th Century, the Senga, Chewa, Bisa and Kunda chiefs, themselves traders, had been firmly linked to the trade networks of Swahili traders, and the ruling classes of the valley were well aware of what was happening at the coast of Mozambique, at Lake Malawi, Lake Tanganyika and at the palace of Mwata Kazembe. The Nsenga and Ambo in turn were in contact with the Achikunda trade from whom they acquired weapons and mercenaries. Kambwiri was right on the way between Nkotakota and Mwata Kazembe, and had access both to Katanga and Lake Malawi. That is why David Livingstone, and those in his footsteps, went through Kambwiri. Kambwiri was of course chosen by the White Fathers as the first Catholic Mission station in the valley because of this central position. The map at the end of this chapter (taken from Isaakman 1971) shows how Kambombo and in fact all Senga chiefs were on the trade roots with Kilwa, Karongo, Lake Tanganyika, and with the route West that ran through Bisa and Bemba country, the way the first Kambombo Chiweza "Goma" himself had taken to establish himself as trader and chief among the Tumbuka.[74] Those in the valley who were isolated from the long distance trade or even ignorant of it were subdued: The Tumbuka of Chama "who did not know anything about the value of elephants", early Bisa migrations lead by the *bena Nzoka* of Chongo around Nabwalya, other small Bisa settlements along the east bank of the Luangwa, the "Betwa" or "Awetwe" of Nsefu "who knew nothing", and Tumbuka people encountered by the incoming Senga Chikwa Ng'uni "who were naked and used ivory to place cooking pots on the fire", all such earlier peoples shared a common fate: they had either to submit under the authority of the incoming chiefs (Chama and others did so voluntarily, while others were forced), were killed (like Mungwalala), or were driven away (like the Bene Mutondo of Kazembe)[75], or committed suicide or even mass suicide (see the narratives of the appendix). Whether such stories of suicide of earlier inhabitants recall actual happenings, or myths, may be difficult to tell, especially since some of them are contested. But they show that isolation in the valley meant powerlessness. The incoming chiefs had come as traders with connections, and the long distance trade had made them chiefs over the isolated societies. The incoming trader-chiefs depended on their outside connections to sustain their power. And many chiefs (the Senga, Bisa, and the Kunda chiefs) depended on monopolised access to the Swahili to maintain their authority.

Langworthy (1970) and also Wright and Lary (1970) suggest that Swahili influence in the valley had been of a different kind from their influence on the plateau. In the latter half of the 19th century, a chiefs' position depended on how he managed to monopolise the slave and the ivory trade. In the valley, chiefs in general succeeded better than chiefs on the plateau, where they were often bypassed by headmen or lesser chiefs closer on the routes: As long as cloth was available, headmen on the plateau were dealing directly with the slavers. When slavers bypassed the chiefs, they had a centrifugal effect, weakening the chief's position. The effects were also more disruptive and bringing more insecurity, as anybody could be kidnapped and sold off on short notice. Also in the valley we find many records of the destructive side of the slave trade. Kambwiri had been depopulated by the Angoni selling their slaves to the Swahili on the plateau. But chiefs in the valley nevertheless monopolised the trade to a much greater extend, and – according to Langworthy – somehow managed to block any direct trade of the Swahili with headmen. Swahili influence therefore had a unifying influence: though the chiefs had come into the valley only in an arbitrary fashion often ruling over very diverse and mixed "tribes", they managed through the Swahili influence to cement their position in regards to the local population. On the plateau, in the second half of the 19th century, the Arabs were engaging in own empire building, and their interests ran directly against the chiefs (e.g. against Mwase Kasungu or the Angoni). But the Swahili had little interest in overthrowing valley chiefs: elephant hunting depended on the skilled local population, and therefore it was much easier to work through the local chiefs rather than starting own empires. In consequence, the

Swahili presence stabilised the position of chiefs; in fact Swahili fire arms enabled Kambwiri and the Senga chiefs to defend themselves more or less successfully against the Angoni (and also against the Achikunda of Matakenya), though they also had to lick their wounds. Not denying the destructive side of the slave trade also within the valley, it must be said that the Arab presence brought quite a degree of security. Without the Arabs in the Eastern valley we may well speculate that there would be no traces left today of Senga, Bisa or Kunda chieftaincies.

But if long distant trade was the fuel for centralisation to function, one would expect still-stand once that trade was stopped by the British, like a car that runs out of diesel. Since it had been the raids of the slave traders (especially but not exclusively Achikunda and Ngoni) that had forced people to live in large and fortified villages, once the threats were over or a time of peace resumed, people tended to disperse again (Vail 1977). This is what had happened in the valley, a trend that was already noticed by the White Fathers in Kambwiri in 1904. Soon after the British took over, people in the valley had already scattered back into tiny settlements and farms.

The south of the Valley was never as coherent as the north. Achikunda and Ngoni raids put people more strongly on the defensive. The history of the various (small) and often recent chieftaincies within the Southern valley is one of hit and run, hide and seek, and of refugees from different corners, who sometimes set themselves up as chiefs. Tribute changed with time and alliance: be it to Lala chiefs, to the Chewa, the Angoni, or Achikunda, and rivalries between the little chieftaincies themselves could be as fierce as the attacks from outside forces, as the history of Mwape for example shows (Lane Poole 1938). History was marked by a great deal of manoeuvring: people went into different alliances to fight off different threats and were often successful to play off one enemy against the other.

Looking at the subsequent history of Christianity and the different churches, we may not be surprised to find that people were also successful in playing off one church against the other as much as possible to their advantage, when the Dutch Reformed, the Free Church of Scotland, Catholics, Anglicans and Watchtowers were at one and the same time trying to make alliances during the first decades of colonisation. Valley chiefs, confirmed and supervised by the colonial office, remained in need of legitimisation before their own people. Some churches made strong alliances with valley chiefs (for example the CCAP with some Senga chiefs, sometimes even mediating succession disputes on behalf of the colonial office); they may have profited by the good will of the chiefs, but there was also the danger that the Church could be seen as a spiritual legitimisation of the chiefs and their aristocratic families over and against the rest of the population that had few connections to the chiefs; the Church was being indirectly used or abused in the chief's powerplays. The White Fathers' method of evangelisation was to pass through chiefs (in Kambwiri they had decided to build right next to the palace) so as to gain easier access to labour and porters. In many ways, the White Fathers were seen as little chiefs themselves. Also the Christian message was largely presented in chiefly terminology. But people in the valley maybe were not looking for new chiefs. Their lineages and clans remained main point of reference, but that system of relationships was not entered by the priests.[76]

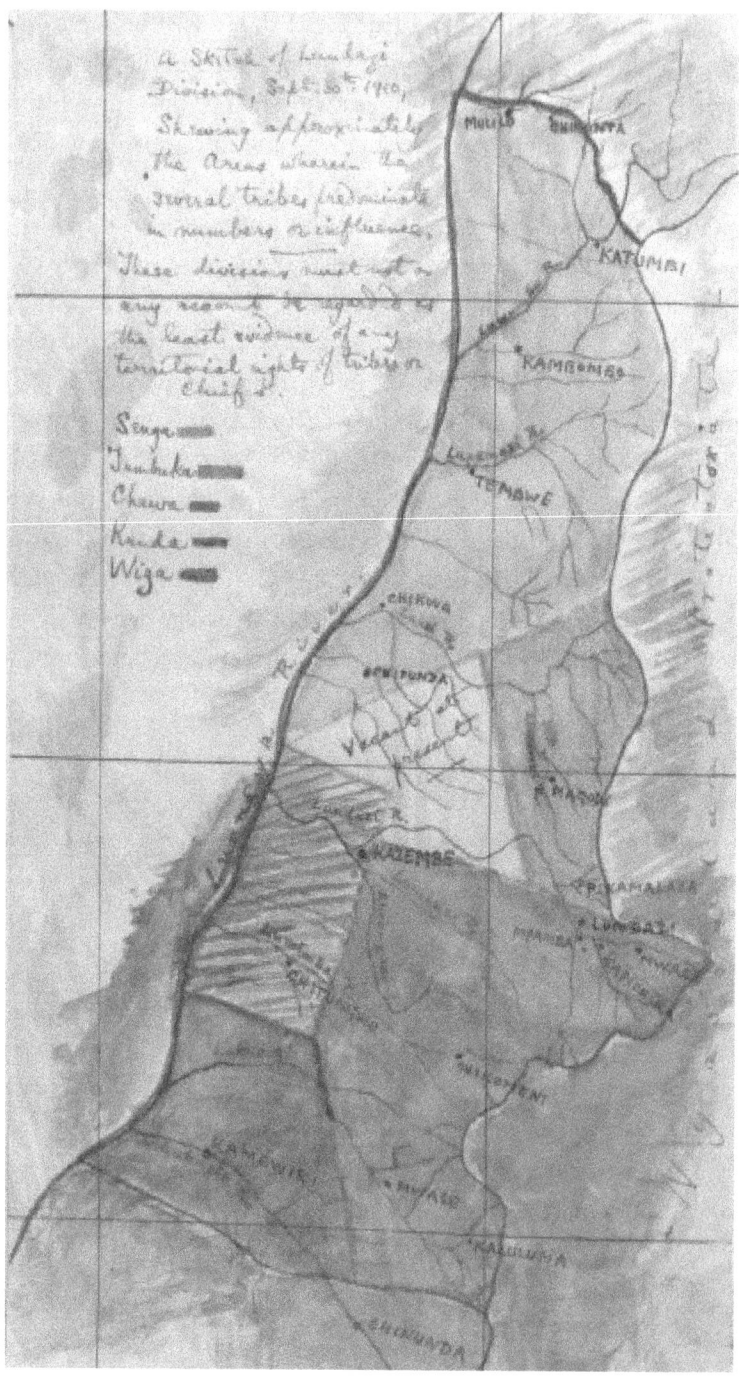

Map 4. NAZ, Lundazi District Notebook Vol II, p.449

Trade routes through the Northern Valley (Isaakman 1971)

MAP OF SWAHILI INFLUENCE IN THE AREA BETWEEN LAKE MALAWI
AND THE LUANGWA RIVER

From the drawings of Fr. Foulon among the Babemba at around the time of the opening of Kambwiri. (Archives of the Missionaries of Africa): A blacksmith, two ancestor shrines, a kalubi drum, and a scene of mourning (next page).

6.

A Century of Isolation

The isolation of the valley may be more ambivalent than it seems at first. On one hand, the valley is isolated in terms of its difficult topography. Rivers coming down from the plateau cut the valley into tiny slices at the onset of the rains, and life proceeds now in splendid isolation for up to six months each year. There is very little communication between different parts of the valley, even within a single Parish. Many people leave their villages to reside in their fields, often across a river that has, of course, no bridges. Most lines of communication run outside. Goods don't circulate much within the valley but they go in and out. In consequence, what we do in one part of the valley may have little impact on other parts. The physical conditions, and its lack of basic infrastructures (roads, schools, clinics, etc.) make the valley a different and surely more difficult place to work in. But this isolation has to be put into perspective. The Luangwa valley occupies a very central position within the Southern African region between two of Zambia's triangles of growth: Eastern Province/ Malawi/ Mozambique and Nakonde/ Tanzania/ Lubumbashi. Because of this central geographical position, until the time of colonisation, major trade routes ran right through the valley (more precisely through the centre and the north of the valley). Prior to colonisation topographic conditions did not prevent the valley to play an active role in the economics and politics of Central Africa. Therefore the early colonial administrative centres, the *bomas*, were built right inside the valley (Nabwalya and the old Petauke), the Catholics started in Kambwiri, the Free Church of Scotland in Kazembe (in a village also called Kambwiri), the Anglicans in Msoro, and the Dutch Reformed Church came to Kamoto; all early churches considered the valley as prime area for starting their missionary endeavours because of its central position. The topography of the valley has not changed since then, but the political framework has, together with the means of transport. The isolation of the valley has to be seen in relation to such changing frameworks.

FACTORS OF ISOLATION

Today, the absence of good roads or a railway in the valley has become *the* symbol for the valley's isolation. But it must be stressed that this isolation is better described in terms of lack of political motivation. Early colonial times had seen great efforts in road building in and right through the valley: the Ford Jameson – Serenje road via Msoro was completed in 1919, other roads followed,[77] and communication between the early *bomas* continued to run through the valley. Nevertheless, as infrastructures for motorised vehicles were difficult to build and to maintain, the valley came to be seen in colonial times as a territory too difficult to be enriched at large with basic structures. People would have to move out in the long run. First attempts of isolation were prompted by the fears of sleeping sickness (a colonial panic):[78] the valley was closed for all Europeans, barriers were erected and segregation camps created at Nabwalya, Mpika and Lundazi; passes were introduced, but for lack of manpower such laws of isolation could not be strictly enforced.

Any such isolation of the valley could only be partial. It was offset for example by the colonial overriding concern for male labour. Taxes were needed, and men from the valley soon started to flock to "Harare", to South Africa, to the Copperbelt, to Tanganyika. In 1938, a colonial officer noted that

In the Luangwa valley, whence men go to work in all directions ranging for Tanganyika Territory to Southern Rhodesia, an extraordinary admixture of tongues can sometimes be heard.[79]

This does not look like isolation. But the exodus of men left the valley like many other rural areas depleted of men, which at the same time also diminished opportunities for balanced structural change. Chief Jumbe for example complained to the colonial office in 1924 that the absence of men had led to the disappearance of the local cotton weaving industry.[80] Prior to colonisation, people from all over came into the valley or passed through the valley for business. After colonisation, people from the valley went everywhere else for business. The valley itself was cut-off. A dichotomy developed between life in the valley and life outside.

THE RULE OF WILDLIFE CONSERVATION

A crucial factor for the isolation of the valley during this century was the (ever changing) vision for wildlife. The creation of game-parks in the valley and the colonial visions towards wildlife have been examined and re-examined,[81] and the colonial policies entailed many complexities. The establishment of the game parks and the policies applied to Game Management Areas had been the results of continuous debates between quite different stakeholders (colonial administration, chiefs and headmen, park administration and conversationalists). Wildlife parks along the Luangwa were created in colonial times (the first but short lived park already in 1904, the Luangwa Lukusuzi Game Reserve in1942, Nsefu Game Reserve in 1949, Luambe early 1950s. Today the national parks are North- and South Luangwa, Luambe and Lukusuzi).

The creation of parks in the valley seemed to the colonial office the best solution of making use of the valley with its difficult topography and giving it a purpose.[82] As a whole, colonial policies of protecting wildlife were guided by a vision to preserve for people access to subsistence hunting. In oral testimonies of today the colonial government is often praised in regards to such issues as protecting fields, cropping animals and paying compensation for crop damage. Funds from wildlife revenues were redistributed to the local authorities from 1946 onwards (though the stakeholders within the wildlife authorities of today claim this to be their invention of the 1990s.)[83] But with the creation of parks (in the national and international interest) the foundations were laid that forced the population of the Luangwa valley to submit to national and especially international interests of wildlife protection, whatever the human costs.

The valley was not free from clashes of the local population with the colonial government, and such clashes were often based on policies towards hunting and crop protection from raiding animals. Many chiefs in the valley were sacked when they disrespected the rules on elephant hunting. But the colonial administration is often positively evaluated by the valley population when contrasted with the wildlife rules of the present administration. Often I was told that real slavery started with national independence. "We thought we were entering freedom, but instead we entered slavery." Some go as far as calling Independence Day "*ukapolo* day" (slavery day) "We were looking for freedom. Yet in colonial times the government was listening more to us than our Zambian government does."

Colonial rule had laid the foundations to see in the Luangwa valley a sanctuary for animals that needed protection. Hunting was restricted, but at the same time agricultural development and production was hardly emphasised or promoted (Astle 1999). Even though the colonial administration realised the importance of hunting in the life of people, people's connection with hunting turned them more and more into "poachers". But "poachers" in official wildlife discourse are a liability for game protection, not an asset. Official policies came to alienate people from their own home-grounds; at the same time very few viable alternatives to hunting were given.

After Independence, Game Management Areas and open areas were created, and guns of people were more strictly licensed. But many people suspect that the UNIP government (at least during the late 1970s) was itself profiting from the benefits of poaching. Many government officials were rumoured to be much involved in the trade with ivory and game meat. Statistics relate the extent of poaching clearly to changing political frameworks: still in the 1970s the elephant population of the valley was estimated to run to 90,000, the rhino population to 8,000. By the middle of the 1980s the elephants numbered fewer than 15,000 and the rhinos had disappeared.[84] People in the valley had been living with wildlife for hundreds of years; but it was within one single decade, during the reign of UNIP, that it nearly all got butchered. It was not the local population that was suddenly consuming much more meat than ever before, but the fact that Zambia's wildlife, ivory and horns were now on large scale feeding the towns and international markets. Many in the UNIP government were either themselves deeply involved in this trade, or unable (and unwilling?) to stop the butchering that was performed with heavy weapons (some say with weapons of the Zambian army). Game meat was (and still is) much wanted on the urban markets, and nobody has much confidence in the working of game barriers, and the political will to make them work was (and still is?) largely lacking. Blamed for poaching was, of course, the local population.

This brought a radical shift in how people came to look at their own location. In contrast to the official laws of game management, poaching had become heavily commercialised. From now onwards the suspicion and the conviction started to go around that the valley was being isolated and that they were forbidden to hunt so that other people could make money with the animals. National and international markets had placed their eyes on the Luangwa Valley. People's attitudes to animals also changed, as a former game guard told me,

> Before independence we were killing only one animal at a time. But then we started to realize that animals were business. We used to see white people coming every year from July onwards to kill animals, elephants and rhinos, and we were told '*anagula nyama*' ('they have bought the animals'). Now we also came to know that animals were good business, and from then onwards people butchered and finished elephants and rhinos.[85]

People in Chiweza speak about much confusion in the 1970s and 1980s. "Big white Americans were coming to hunt and other white Americans were coming to prevent us from hunting, and both groups were very rough with us." People in the area of Chiweza today especially accuse the "Save the Rhinos Trust" of itself finishing off the remaining rhinos.[86] People became aware that there were many contradictions in official policies towards the valley.

Towards the end of the second Republic, "national interests" came to merge with the interests of international wildlife protection: The insight came to prevail that revenues can only flow in the long run, if animals are protected from extinction. Yet the logic, that the Luangwa Valley and its animals had become commercially attractive to outsiders (no longer through poaching, but now through tourism and legalised hunting safaris) remained intact; people's activities for making a living (farming, fishing and hunting) had to be sacrificed in order to safeguards the commercial interests of the outside world.

With the Third Republic and increasing privatisation of wildlife resorts, a much stronger presence of international interests is felt. Tourism within the Luangwa Valley has grown very strongly, and the valley is known and actively portrayed as an area of untouched wilderness left on the globe. With such shifts in "national interests" and greater control through international agents, the pendulum went into the opposite direction: the law today criminalises a person not only for poaching, but also for shooting an elephant that has destroyed his/her crop, eats from his granary, and that may have even killed a family member.

> Touch an animal on your own field, and the game guards will travel 100 km to catch you, beat you, and put you to prison. They may even kill you. But if you call a game guard to help you drive out the elephant from your field, you can call and call, nobody will answer.

This is not an isolated comment, but a perception throughout the valley.

> ZAWA anaika nyama pa mwamba munthu pansi. ("ZAWA – the Zambian Wildlife Authority – put the animals on top, human beings down")

People are alienated from the politics that shape their lives.

> Before independence they made game parks, but we were living together with the guards and they were understanding us. When independence came our slavery started, but we could still receive sometimes compensation when animals destroyed our fields. With Chiluba things got worse, and we started to be sold out to ZAWA. Our chiefs love sugar, so what can we do? The elephants now have independence and we are their slaves.[87]

In 2004 alone, 18 deaths of people killed by elephants and other wild animals were reported.[88] Today, all across the valley, there is a deep dissatisfaction of people with the post-colonial wildlife policies (funded often by international stakeholders), with the way ZAWA operates and with the power that foreign investors wield today in the valley. One business man, who owns a chain of little shops, asked me:

> People come from Germany, France and Ireland to protect wildlife in Zambia. Why do they not protect the wildlife in Europe? We hear that the wild animals are not allowed to harass people in Europe or destroy their fields and kill their children, men and women. But here in Africa, they are allowed and even protected!

ZAWA (ZAMBIAN WILDLIFE AUTHORITY), CBNRM (COMMUNITY BASED NATIONAL RESOURCES MANAGEMENT) AND PRIVATE INVESTORS

ZAWA was established in 1999; it is the successor of the former Department of National Parks and Wildlife Service (NPWS) which was transformed by an act of parliament into an autonomous body. ZAWA is governed by the Zambia Wildlife Act, No. 12 of 1998 and has its own Board of Directors under the policy guidance of the Ministry of Tourism, Environment and Natural Resources.

ZAWA is an institution whose power people can hardly evade in the valley. But the reputation of ZAWA in the valley (during the time of this research) was bad. It may be that the negative opinion about

ZAWA that I encountered during the year of research was a result of individual misbehaviour of some members at that specific time. While I was in Nsefu in October 2005, a local man was shot dead in the Game Management Area by a guard with an AK47; he had no gun with him, no game meat, just an axe and a (hunting?) dog that was barking at the guards. Not the dog was shot dead, but its owner. When I was in Tembwe in October 2006, two youths (described by people as children) were shot dead from a tree in which they were hiding by ZAWA officers, which caused people to riot and destroy the ZAWA camp. Chief Tembwe promised to bring the rioters to book. Many people saw in the chief's reaction an expression that the chief himself, as a beneficiary of the incomes secured through tourism, was defending the cause of foreign investors over and against the security of his own people. Chiefs gain large shares of the funds that are supposed to be "redistributed" to the local community. People all over the valley speak widely of beatings by ZAWA. "They beat us until we make false confessions so that the beatings stop." I asked one ZAWA officer in Kazembe about official policies towards beatings. He replied:

> We are not given instructions from above to beat. When we beat people, they themselves have given us permission to beat them, because they are not truthful and hide things from us.

Torture of suspected poachers is quasi tolerated and condoned, maybe even encouraged, as an unofficial way to have more results in the fight against poaching. A number of catechists told me that people in the valley have few rights, because they cannot defend themselves, for lack of education and organisation, and also as direct consequence of the valley's isolation. "Who in the valley can check the dealings of ZAWA? Here in the valley they can get away with things that would be punished elsewhere in Zambia."[89]

Most people in the Luangwa valley live in Game Management Areas (GMAs) that are outlined as puffer zones to the game parks: Munyamadzi, Musalangu, Lupande, Lumimba, Sandwe, Mukungule, and Chisomo GMAs. Here the CBNRM programmes are advocated with the view to co-manage the wildlife resources.[90] Community

Resource Boards (CRBs) are established that are supposed to function as the link between ZAWA and the local community. Through them, parts of the hunting concessions are fed back into the community to help with the buildings of schools, infrastructures, the drilling of boreholes, buying of hammer mills, sponsorships in school or financial help to "women clubs".[91] They are composed of elected members and representatives of the local authorities and chiefs; chiefs are the patrons of the CRBs. No doubt, the national and international wildlife authorities are making many efforts to advocate that wildlife protection will benefit the people of the valley in the long run by bringing in resources and by feeding back these resources into the local community. This vision is enshrined also in the constitution of ZAWA. But people often experience it the other way round: that wildlife protection first and foremost has taken their own resources away. Many people whom I interviewed were aware that the benefits that trickle through to them through these institutions have been paid for by the fact that "the country has been sold out", first and foremost to wildlife protection. Then they also experience a lot of corruption in the trickle down process of benefits. People are well aware that money generated through hunting licenses enters the CRBs, but only very few people know where the money goes. As somebody put in Chasera:

> Those of us whose crops are destroyed, family members killed, those who can no longer fish in the Luangwa, see nothing of that money. But we see the leaders of the CRBs eating very well, buying mattresses, and marrying many wives, because they have suddenly become rich.[92]

Whenever money is redistributed within a community, there are by nature many complains; negative views about the CRBs should therefore not surprise. Also few people, even within the valley, would contest the idea that wildlife in today's world need protection. Any form of protection is linked to measures of force. But the present outright negative image of ZAWA and its policies through the CBNRM in the valley sheds doubts on the promises that the benefits of wildlife protection are broadly fed back into the community, and especially to those who have to carry its real costs (farmers whose crops are raided, fishers whose licences are revoked, people whose houses are destroyed, etc.) The people who bear the hidden costs of wildlife protection see little of the benefits. Here a revealing opinion from Kalasa about ZAWA and a private investor running a hunting safari just across the river:

> We always had animals around our village, but now it has become worse. At 5 o clock in the afternoon we don't go out any more. The lions enter our villages. Nobody goes at night to the toilet. In the past the animals stayed on the other side of the Luangwa. But now P.J. (a Zimbabwean investor running a hunting safari) has bought the place. Whenever somebody goes to the Luangwa he is beaten by ZAWA, because P.J. says: "you are chasing away the animals!" P.J. says he has bought the place with much money from the chief. But when the animals eat our gardens and when the lions eat our children in our own village, whose animals are they?[93]

Many people see clearly that they have to carry the hidden costs of wildlife protection, while others reap the benefits. Some safari enterprises, much in contrast to the above case, are praised for actively helping the local population with education, water, health services and employment with generous salaries, far beyond paying their taxes to the government. Much of such help, however, happens outside the official channels that were set up to involve the local population in wildlife management; they rest on the private, personal initiatives of the managers of individual safari camps. Wildlife protection can bring and does bring benefits to many people (employment and infrastructural resources). On the other hand, many people also recognize in the care for the animals the main cause for their isolation and difficult life.

ISOLATION AND THE PRESENCE AND ABSENCE OF
CHITUKUKO ("DEVELOPMENT")

The "new ways" of wildlife conservation, starting with the 1990s in
Zambia's liberalised economy, are a result of new coalitions between
the private sector (based in the valley mainly on tourism), the Zambian
government (with ZAWA) and the donor community. Having been
alienated from their own hunting culture, development agents now
wish to show to the local population how to cultivate in "harmony"
with wildlife protection. Conservation farming advocates land
preparation during the dry season, using so-called "minimum tillage
methods", a complete stop of burning and a stress on retention of crop
residue from the previous harvest, and nitrogen-fixing crop rotations.
Conservation farming has been accepted by the donor community as
the future oriented way of cultivation and comes with precisely laid out
grids and schemes for cultivation. The isolation of the valley means
that, in the absence of viable alternatives (that would secure richer
harvests than conservation farming), many people feel coerced into
forms of living and farming that are determined by the outside world
far beyond Zambia.

What has really changed the valley, more than many projects of
NGOs, is the recent massive expansion of the cotton industry in the
wake of the liberalisation of the cotton market. Cotton is not new to
the valley: it had been grown on and off since colonial times, and even
before colonial times the Senga of the North and other valley peoples
were known for their local cotton. The cotton revolution of the last
years comes largely from the operations of two international
companies in the valley: Dunavant (USA based) and Clark Cotton
(South Africa based), who give out seeds, fertilizer and bags on a loan
system. Cotton grown in the Luangwa valley is known to be of high
quality. Though the average price fetched per kg is very low, cotton
grows well in the valley and in the absence of other forms of income it
has brought a seasonal cash flow. It is true that many experience new
hardships through cotton: more hunger if the money is not well kept,
more beer and also more polygamy after rapid cash incomes, more
power to the husband over the crop than is the case with other crops.

Yet it is felt by many that cotton has brought real development. "Since Dunavant and Clark cotton companies are here, we have also more shops in the village, because there is money now. More children go to school than before, and people dress better."[94] A number of grade 12 students of Kambombo said they would not leave the valley after school. "With cotton there are more chances for us in the valley than elsewhere." Cotton somehow transcends the valley's isolation: in spite of the bad roads the lorries are rolling. The companies have received criticism due to the low prices that they pay out to farmers (according to the figures I received from farmers in Kazembe, Chikwa, Tembwe and Kambombo areas, in 2004 people were still paid 1440 Kwacha/kg; in 2005 it had dropped to 1200, but in 2006 it were only 850 Kwacha for grade A cotton). But in spite of the low prices, the cotton production in the valley has economically transformed the valley in a short time, a powerful indicator how much development in the valley depends on wider integration and transport rather than on individual projects.

The rapid expansion of cotton farming (possible only through the road link) shows what people really associate with *chitukuko* (development). People often mention schools, hospitals, and water, but roads are usually given priority: "We will never have proper teachers and doctors as long as we have no road." It is only a road that puts people on the map. The road has become a metaphor for linking up the valley with the promises of development, and the bad state of the roads are seen as a reflection that the valley is sidelined. Tarmac (the few km from Mfuwe airport to the park) and the bridge over the Luangwa at Mfuwe are for tourists.

STRETCHING TO TOWN

The word isolation does not describe properly the reality of the valley. Many families living in the valley have either relatives in town (brother, sisters, children) with whom they try to keep contact, or they have lived themselves for some, if not many years, in town. In the south of the valley I randomly chose 11 villages to look at migration patterns: 149 out of 367 adult people now living in these villages had lived more than one year in Lusaka or in the Copperbelt (58 out of a total of 152 men, and 91 out of a total of 215 women). This are 40% out of the adult population, who have lived in town for more than one year.[95] In this number are not included those others who do visit their relatives in town from time to time. The 11 villages I chose may not be representative for the whole of the valley, and we see great differences between the villages themselves (see appendix), but it shows that people in the valley are in fact less isolated from the rest of Zambia than many think. Most people try to keep open the option to live somewhere else for some time so as to look for better opportunities. Not to stretch out means to end up in poverty. The poorest people in the villages are those with no outside contacts. They are more likely to be women, and especially women without education and especially with broken family connections.

As people in the valley try to stretch out, also valley-people in the towns try to keep contact with their home: many encourage strongly their children to marry somebody from their home village. I was surprised to find quite a few men born and brought up in town who had come back to the valley to marry. Some of them had settled permanently back to the valley, while others were thinking of taking their wives eventually back to town. Most of them had been encouraged by their parents or grandparents to marry in the valley, while others justified their choice by saying that "women in town don't listen and don't obey their husbands". Many people mentioned the insecurities of urban life; they wanted to keep the option open to go back to the valley if they lose their job or if things in town turn out really badly. Many parents came back to the village after many years in town when their children, but more specifically their daughters, reached marriageable age. "Marriages in towns don't last, and our daughters will have nothing to fall back on." For most people with town experience it was normal and beyond discussion that their children would come back to the valley, though in fact a number of them did marry elsewhere, especially sons. And there are many others, of course, who have lost contact with the valley up to the point of no return.

Stretching out to town proceeds on different lines from family to family. For many people the home village, despite its location in the valley, gives in the long run much greater securities than any other location could give. Life may be easier in town or outside the valley in terms of education, health, transport, and money, but if someone is sick or if the wife or husband dies, there will be no relatives around. At home, labour for the fields can be found more easily with the many types of relationships, while outside people are more dependent on *ganyu* (piece-work). But the main reason given by many for staying in the village was that problems can be sorted out more easily: problems in marriage, *milandu* (cases, court-cases) caused by husbands and children. Especially sons bring *milandu* into the house by impregnating girls, which calls for high amounts of compensation ("damage") outside the valley, but which is often settled without payments and much more easily within the valley. "If you have many children, then you have also many *milandu*". Also disputes about fields, about village fights, about divorces, or about witchcraft can be sorted out better when many relatives are around. To live without much family makes people very vulnerable in *milandu* but also to witchcraft attacks. This makes it also difficult for outsiders to settle within the valley. Two teachers who have been in the valley for many years told me: "We never go to court. We know if we take somebody to court we will eventually die in some mysterious way."[96] The same fears people of the valley have when they think about settling somewhere else outside the valley. If one only evaluates the valley in terms of education, healthcare, and transport, then one will never understand why people stay. In Kamwendo (Chikowa parish) where the last teacher left in 1990 and where the next school is 1½ walking days away (there is not even a bicycle path), somebody said: "What can we do outside? Our children will become thieves as soon as they leave the valley!"

In spite of the stretching going on, there remains much mistrust within the population between returnees and those who never went out; their worlds are very different.

THE VALLEY, THE OUTSIDE WORLD, AND THE CHURCHES

Marks (1976) wrote that Christianity was brought to Nabwalya by people who came from the towns. Also in our own church councils today we find a large percentage of people who spent many years in the towns. This was for me most striking in Chama: when I conducted my interviews, basically all active church members came from outside (workers in the Boma) or had spent half their lives outside the valley. In general we find not much participation in the Church of those who never left the valley for a longer time. The Catholic Church is more relevant to people who have experienced life outside the valley for a lengthy period of time.

This fact may help us to understand better the contradictions with which people approach it. The churches remain associated with the ambivalent outside world. Looking at the valley's long history of being exploited for outside interests, it is not surprising that it is difficult for people to build up a basic trust. The churches of course are also evaluated in reference to the jungle of *chitukuko*. The Catholic Church in particular is seen as a rich church, as a church with plenty of means at its disposal. In a number of places people want to see more involvement of the Catholic Church, "because we want a better school and a hospital". There are many different churches in the valley with different programmes and possibilities, and people try to gain the most from all. As they learnt how to adapt to the language of the different development discourses, they have also learnt the language of the churches. At the same time, the churches play a major role in overcoming people's isolation; apart from kinship it is often through church membership that people of the valley become integrated on their journeys into town structures and into the wider world. In theory, the churches could link up with the metaphor of the "ancestors" described above (chapter 2) and rescue that powerful metaphor from the past into the present. People want the churches and they want more of them, and yet find it difficult to be committed to one.

The clinic of Mwanya without transport. The next referral hospital (Lundazi) is 200 km away, and accessible only in the dry season

Crossing the Luangwa by car (pontoon) at Mushalila, Nyimba Parish

A full granary but no market to sell the crops and make money

The road through the Lukusuzi River, passible only in the dry season
with a 4x4 vehicle.

The little school of Kamwendo: it has been without teacher for the last 15 years.
Several teachers appointed to Kamwendo from Mpika had run away after only a
few months residing in Kamwendo. The village is accessible from the Great
North Road only on foot (1½ days walk), or through Nabwalya crossing the
whole of the South Luangwa National Park.

The valley and its modes of transport

7.

The Gendered Valley

Men are notoriously absent from church activities throughout the valley; many feel that the church is not their place. Women, in contrast, are more plentiful. However, upon marriage, also many young women stop going to church. They may again reappear in church after many years, once their position within their new family is strengthened, or after having gone through a painful story of divorce. During the most difficult part of their lives, the early years of their marriage, the Church has little or no significance for them. Many are even stigmatised by the Church for agreeing to get married outside the sacramental provisions of the Church, for which they may have a number of reasons.

Among the women who do come to Church, a large proportion are no longer married: in a number of prayer centres that I visited, nearly half of the church-going women were no longer married at that time (meaning either divorced or widowed), a percentage that was much higher than among the general population in the surrounding villages. Putting it bluntly: the church in the valley is a place for unmarried boys and girls, and for middle-aged and elderly women, many of them no longer married, plus the occasional man in a leadership position.

The majority of the church-going women, furthermore, have difficulties, to form a coherent community; "*sitimagwirizana*" – "we women are not united amongst ourselves and there is a lot of jealousy." This poses the question about the sociological and demographical circumstances that accelerate this situation, the subject matter of this chapter.

GENDER ROLES

In the past, according to the cultural norms, it was the man to go out, the woman to stay behind, or eventually be fetched and accompany her husband to town. In the early 1970s, a study of Nabwalya's Bisa suggested that 90% of men knew life outside the valley compared with only 30% of the women.[97] Gendered conceptions in the valley were sometimes strongly defended. In 1945, for example, when it was a criminal act for the woman to go out to town without a pass, or without being accompanied by either father or husband, a number of chiefs and headmen appealed to the colonial office to enforce this law more rigorously.[98] A young woman without either a father or a husband was seen as a threat to the social system. The village in the valley became the place for the waiting woman, a female domain, and in spite of very many cultural changes, it still is, especially in the south.

The *chinamwali* or *chisungu* (girls' initiation rites) described the woman's place mainly in reference to the domestic sphere: the household, family, parents, husband, in-laws, the village, the garden. In contrast, real initiation for the boy may be his first visit to town. The man goes out: hunting in the bush, commercially fishing at the river, out in town, out for piece-work. Gendered patterns are reinforced also through the job-opportunities within the valley. Most jobs in the safari camps centre on men (yearly building of the camps, safaris, etc.); there are hardly any female teachers or nurses in the valley (lack of educated role-models for women), and more men than women are in charge of the income from growing cotton.

Recent efforts, supported by the government, by a number of NGOs (in few areas where they operate), and also by various Churches (including the Catholic Church), try to counterbalance this trend by offering specific opportunities to women. These efforts are often described with the English word "*gender*", a word that has come to mean the enhancement of women's social and economic position and the vision of increasing the percentage of women in positions of authority. A number of women clubs, operating in various parts of the valley, have received a positive reception by many women, who are offered skills and also, at times, access to micro finances for starting off small businesses. Women's increasing activities in business ventures have also brought them out of the valley on many business trips, of which they, not their husbands, take charge. Many men expressed to me that they saw in this a threat to the social system and to their marriages; cultural norms are clearly in the process of change and renegotiation.

Due to the irregular nature of most jobs (much is but piece-work), life for men, in general, is very unstable. Men's economic life for a great deal takes place outside the village, if not outside the valley. Many men in my interviews mentioned this irregularity as one of the main reasons why they find it difficult to develop much attachment to a church. When they are in the village it is for recreation, which means mainly beer. The matrilineal systems of the south does not help the man to develop strong links to the village affairs if he lives in the village of his father (who always belongs to a different clan than one's own) or of his wife and children (again of a clan not his own).

The virilocal north of the Senga gives a different picture. The woman nearly always follows the husband and lives in the village of her husband and his brothers.[99] Among the Senga, the man's interests and stakes in his village are higher than in the south. Also the rapid growth of the cotton industry in the north gives the man higher involvement in his village. The Senga stress their bi-lineal descent and have retained matrilineal aspects in some respects (villages and offices, except for Kambombo, are still inherited matrilineal in Tembwe, Chikwa and Chifunda). However, by accepting *lobola*, from the 1930s onwards, they have *de facto* become patrilineal in regards to the understanding of marriage. *Lobola* payments (bride wealth) are understood by many in popular discourse to mean that the woman and children are bought (*kugula*) and become quasi property of the husband. The Senga have no cows, but as *lobola* is measured in cows, some women described their domestic situation to me as one of "cows":

> I work daily on the cotton fields of my husband, but I know nothing about the money that was raised by the sales. When he gets his millions, he gives me 10 pin (2.50 US$) or buys me a *chitenge* (cloth). I am the ox that ploughs his fields.

Some women in contrast expressed that they received a fair share in the produce and said that decisions about the money were done in common. Many women come to identify very strongly with the husband's location. I met in Tembwe and Kambombo some widows who chose to stay with their late husbands' families even though they did not want to become remarried to one of his relatives. "This is my home now, and my children are here. My husband's family looks after me." Such a strong identification with the husband's family I did not witness in the matrilineal south.

As a rule of thumb, women's lives are, across the valley, much more regular and centred on the village and often also to a certain extent locked-up within the village, at least if we look away from the increasing number of independent businesswomen in the valley. The church belongs into the village, so the women belong into the church. But the church is not the sphere of which the women take charge. First of all, they are in their husband's church, not in their own. In the north basically all women, and in the south most women, take on board upon marriage the religion of their husbands and leave the church of their youth. The multitude of different churches makes it very difficult for most girls to become married within their own church. "If you want us to get married within the Catholic Church, then bring us a lorry with Catholic men!" choir girls told me in Chinsimbwe. "But if our husbands are not Catholic, we will have to go to their church."

Secondly, also in church, many people are of the opinion that men are needed to lead the women, especially where very few women are literate. Women may do the work in church (as also on their husbands' fields), but they remain under legal tutelage until the time when they assume a new role as grandmothers, when they gain much more autonomy. In that sense, the church is a place for women, but not a place they can control. Nevertheless it can be a strong and often the only means for women that facilitates wider contacts and opportunities, and that gives moral support while stressing the husband's family duties in an age where the modern economy, more than the traditional values, dominate also domestic life.

SURPLUS OF WOMEN

While gender roles are renegotiated today, the demographic situation has not changed that is responsible for creating a high surplus of marriageable women and a high demand for marriageable men, who seem to be very scarce in the valley: men therefore find, at any age, another marriage partner, if they want to walk out of their old marriage. Women do not.

People have the memory that, in colonial times, there were few men left in the valley. Men were out in the towns and in the mines, and often had left their wives behind. It was common for a man to marry a wife, and leave her in the village to disappear for many years into the towns in search for work. The woman waited and waited for the day that her husband would come back and fetch her to go to town; some waited all their life. Still in the 1970s, the valley was marked by a sharp absence of men.

Today this gap has closed down. Various statistics of the valley (clinic counts, counts of wildlife authorities and of the statistical office) confirm that there are basically as many men as there are women in the valley (see the Appendix for the 2000 population counts). What has not changed, however, is the sharp surplus of marriageable women resulting in many women not finding a husband.

I chose randomly 23 villages (see appendix), in which I found a total of 339 adult men and 480 adult women; "adult" here means those married, divorced or widowed. Out of the adult women, 126 were without husbands, which is more than 25%. 72 of them were widows, and 54 were divorced. Some did not want to remarry, but most were not able to remarry for lack of men. Among the men basically all were married; those few ones who were single remained single not for lack of women but out of free choice; they were old. Distribution is very diverse and unequal: in the isolated villages for example of Kasweta, Sonko or Mushalila one finds hardly any women surplus. Nor do we find much polygamy here. In other villages one finds double as many adult women (with experience of marriage) than men, or even more.

At the end of the 1990s, chief Kazembe is said to have made an open appeal on the radio to men outside his kingdom to come and marry the many unmarried women in his chieftaincy. This appeal was received very badly by women of chief Chikwa: "How can they ask for our men to marry their women! We need men ourselves!" Chief Tembwe is said to have made a similar appeal a decade earlier in Kambombo, an appeal which was equally bad received. "For each boy, we give birth to two girls", women explained. Others said that "men die earlier; whenever they are a little bit sick, they die. We women don't die so easily." Or again: "most men leave the valley." Statistics, of course, speak a different language. There are as many men as there are women in the valley today, but there are many more marriageable women, women who either have a husband or seek a husband, than there are marriageable men. This creates for people the image of a high surplus of women, which also legitimises for them the widespread practice of polygamy in the north: "There are not enough men for every woman to have one alone."

The reason for the surplus of marriageable women is simple: Girls are married before the age of 15, while many boys only marry with 25. Girls marry men who are older than they, while men always marry younger women, often much younger ones. With this trend, marriageable men are found in a much smaller pool than marriageable women:

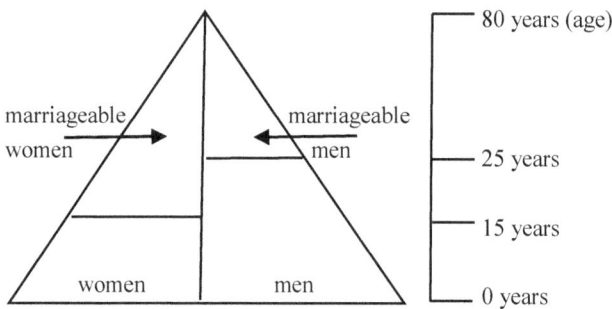

Young women (girls) find a husband, when they want to marry. Most girls whom I interviewed got married within two years of the *chinamwali* ceremony, if not at the *chinamwali* itself, and many in the south became engaged already before the *chinamwali*. But if the marriage does not work out, or if the husband dies, many have great difficulties to find another partner.

Given that as many boys are born as girls, the total surplus of marriageable women equals the number of girls aged 14-24, and this is a very large number. Equally, in the age group between 15 and 20 years of age we find many unmarried boys, but few unmarried girls. Chigoma Primary School has presently 34 boys in grade 7, but only 1 girl. "In grades one to four we have as many girls as boys", explained the headmaster, "but from grade 5 onwards they all get married or pregnant." Chikwasha just started a Basic School with 34 boys in grade 8 but only one single girl. "We wanted more girls, but they were all married", explained a teacher. In all schools I visited I found a similar pattern, though slightly less dramatically. A boy may make a girl pregnant at school, but he rarely marries her; if he is forced to, or if he marries so as to escape the payments of high fines for "damage", he often disappears to town after the birth of the child. In fact boys up to the age of 20 are not counted as marriageable boys, and most marry much later. The surplus of marriageable women in the valley is compensated to a great extent by the surplus of not-yet-ready-to marry boys.

Why do we find in the valley such a pressure on girls for early marriages? Parents in the valley are often ill-at-ease with girls between the age of their *chinamwali* and their marriage. A young woman is seen as belonging under legal tutelage: either under the parents or under the husband. But after the *namwali* they are somehow betwixt and between. Parents try to have their daughters married before they develop too many own initiatives. "The youths today don't listen anymore." They have also different role-models. Parents try to keep this period as small as possible, so as to win more authority over the following marriage matters. They have good reasons for this. In the South, people know no *lobola* payments and are very well aware that marriages have little chances to last if they take place between families who don't know each other well. Still today one comes across quite a good number of young marriages that were arranged by the parents. The longer they wait, the more independence and initiative comes to the girl, and the further she may want to marry away from the home village. Pregnancy outside marriage means that chances go down to find a suitable husband. As jobs centre on men, schooling for girls is often still seen as waste of time and money. One man put it much more bluntly: "Girls who go to school are prostitutes and it is just a question of time that they will be pregnant or have AIDS."

Unfortunately, statistics prove that the parents' worries are not unfounded. The headmaster of Chinsimbwe who was once a teacher in Chama Secondary School shared with me his experience of school life in the Secondary School in Chama:

> When a girl from the village manages to go to Grade 8 or Grade 10, and starts to live at school, then she needs a "protector" to whom she has to give sexual favours. Most girls at Grade 10 are taken at the beginning of school by older boys of Grades 11 and 12 in "protection". You will see that elder boys are always in time for the first term when new girls arrive, to make their picks. That is also how the girls earn a few clothes here and there or a packet of vanilla biscuits.

In popular talk, both among youths themselves and among the elder generation commenting on the morals of the youths, "vanilla" has become synonymous with the payment for sleeping with a boy – "though often we only get a bubble gum!", girls complained in one village. A number of girls who got a "vanilla child" at school explained to me simply: "*ndinalibe nzeru*" ("I had no brains yet"). Another woman explained that she didn't have sex in school, because her grandmother told her that both of her parents would die if she slept with a boy. But then her friends started to laugh at her: "you are stupid; we all sleep with boys, and come home with *vitenge* and soap, and our parents are still alive!" She went out with a boy and became pregnant. Then her school results came out and she had passed to go to grade 8 with the best marks of the whole school, "and I cried bitterly", she explained. Many early marriages are the result of pregnancy. A pregnant woman needs a husband. Parents cannot keep her; the state of pregnancy is too precarious, too dangerous, and intrinsically connected to the conduct of the husband.

The moral reputation but also the reputation for quality education of many schools in the valley is low. Mwanya Basic School needs 14 teachers, but during my visit they had only 4, two of them untrained. Out of the four, some are always out; if somebody goes for his salary to Chipata, it means he is away for some weeks. When I visited the school in June 2006, I found only two teachers (one trained and one untrained) for a total of 409 students from grade 1-9. An impossible task! In Chingozi Basic School the head-teacher complained to me about many voluntary teachers.

> They are only interested in the girls. Some bluntly refuse to teach grades 1-4, and want to teach only the higher grades where the girls have developed breasts. That is why the lower grades are much neglected and students here have a bad foundation.

During the school assembly that I attended, two girls asked me publicly what to do:

> Since we have breasts, it is every single day that we are stopped by boys on our way home from school, asking for sex. We are seen as being free for all. What can we do so as not to die of AIDS?

In this context one can understand the mothers when they want their daughters to marry as early as possible. Marriage payments are very different in the valley, ranging from over a million (250 US$) in the north (though the money is often not paid or paid only partly), and a plate of flour among the Bisa in times of *njala*.

As said above, girls and young women find a husband rather easily. But most women have troubles finding another husband when their marriage has broken. Men in contrast know that they will always find another wife, also a young one, if they but want. Many women complain that "*azimuna saika nzeru mu ukwati*" (husbands don't put their minds anymore into their marriages). The man can easily walk out and often threatens to walk out, or marries from time to time another girl "to teach my wife a lesson." Domestic problems are plenty, and women groups filled up pages about the asymmetry in marriage: in the work load, in the care for children, the access to cash, the compassion given in times of sickness, and in the direction of domestic violence. (Though I also came across two men who had been severely beaten up by their wives, and women in the valley in general do not appear to be just silent victims...)

The high surplus of marriageable women brings many tensions also between women. "*Sitimagwirizana*" – "we don't cooperate with each other". A woman below the menopause without a husband is not respected. Her image is that of a woman free for all for sex. She is feared by married women. A still youngish widow in Masumba put it this way: "Whenever I greet a man on the road, his wife thinks that I am sleeping with him. Many married women think that I want to take their husbands."

It is not surprising that medicines and *vikondi* (love charms) are sought after by many if not by most women. *Chimwemwe, chikoka, mwito, mphetu, kumbukira, mwanjani, nkhaka, ndilile, chiselu, muchemani, sioni, ntheuntheu, nyasalande, lumphangala, kabeleka,* and *kalunguti* are all used in various combinations in ointments, incisions, bathing water, or smoked, to find a husband, or inserted into the vagina, or eaten, to have "sweeter" sex. (Boys in turn know that demand his high for their male powers, and they try to keep in form by eating plenty of raw *nshawa* and digging out *bwazi, mthothotho, nyang'nya, chibvukuzera, kankhande, mwanya or bvubwe.*) That the girl keeps her husband is important not only for the girl but for the whole family, because access to cash in the valley is very gendered. Husbands also bring a certain authority into the family that commands respect, also in court cases.

The need for a husband can be demonstrated on the example of cotton growing, the crop that has dramatically increased the cash flow to the valley. Most unmarried women whom I interviewed did not grow cotton at all. Cotton is very labour intensive and calls for tough management and regularity, and women without husbands and without ready cash for *ganyu* (piece work) rarely get much out of their cotton fields, for lack of access to labour at the right moments, or being sick at the wrong moments. The little they can cultivate they invest usually in food crops rather than cotton. In Chikwa, I interviewed 29 married and 12 unmarried women who grew cotton in 2005. The following table shows a comparison between the productivity of the two groups of cotton growers:

	Average lima per household	Average number of bags harvested per household	Average estimated cash sale per household	Profit per lima per household	Average Number of older children helping per household	Number of households asked
Married women	2.5	9	900,000	360,000	1.8	29
Widowed or divorced women	1.5	4.3	430,000	287,000	1.3	12

There was no significant difference between women in monogamous unions (22 out of the 29) and polygamous union (7 out of the 29). They had the same average results. But unmarried women grew a lesser acreage and got also less results per "Lima" (50 x 50 meters). However, unlike the married women, they can keep all the profits from their sales (if they have any at all). The cash sale that year was calculated to be 100,000 Kwacha (250 US$) per 100 kg bag, which was a rough average. I used this average in my calculations, as many women whom I interviewed had not been involved in the sale of the cotton and did not know how much the husband had raised. Out of the 22 married women of monogamous unions, 10 got nothing from the money and did not even know how it was spent (except for the obvious fact that their husbands had plenty of money available for beer); the other 12 said that they had either shared the money or, in most cases, had gone together to town to buy what was needed for the house, like a mattress, cooking pots, or clothes. Two out of the 7 polygamous households did not see any money from their sales.

Here a comparison with Chikowa Parish (an average from villages in Ncheka and Masumba):

	Average lima per household	Average number of bags harvested per household	Average estimated cash sale per household	Profit per lima per household	Average Number of older children helping per household	Number of households asked
Married women	2.55	8.1	810,000	317,000	2.5	20
Widowed or divorced women	1.4	3.6	360,000	257,000	2.7	8

Results of Chikowa were more erratic; many had lost their crops in floods. All over the valley people tend to cultivate near the rivers because of the fertility of the soil, which increases the risk factor of having floods ruining the harvest. One farmer got 9 bags per Lima, a number of farmers got 5-8 bags/Lima, while others lost everything, which brought the average down to only 3 bags per Lima for the married women and 2.5 bags for the widows. In Ncheka there was also an acknowledged difference between Chewa immigrants from Chikungu and the Kunda population: The Chewa tended to have bigger fields and also a better harvest per Lima. But nearly all of them had to pay quite high inputs for *ganyu* (piece-work), needing the availability of cash, which the Akunda were more reluctant or more unable to pay. Also among the Achewa there were some with a total loss because of flooding. There was nobody who made a significant income with cotton without investment in *ganyu,* some up to 600,000 Kwacha (150 US$).

POLYGAMY

Economically speaking, women in polygamous unions were faring better than women who were alone. But also polygamy has changed in the valley:

In the past it were elderly men who had several wives, but nowadays it are the young men. They have more money now than the old and don't listen to anyone anymore.[100]

Others explained that in the past the first wife had some authority to refuse the second wife by refusing to take the *chiselo* (gift taken in recognition of the second marriage). Nowadays there is often no *chiselo* given anymore, and even if the husband pays only a *nkhuku* (chicken), it is often impossible for the first wife to refuse it. In the past traditions, there were also a number of occasions that affirmed the privileged position of the first wife and when the first wife was shown ritual respect by the second: she paid her, for example, a *nkhuku* for the *kutoshya nyumba* (mutual shaving of private parts). "Nowadays this is all gone", a woman explained:

> There is no *mwambo* (tradition) left for the first wife. The husband may even come home and you see he was shaven by the second wife. Today everything just depends on how the husband feels like.[101]

During the research I met a number of co-wives who found it very difficult to share a husband. "We cannot eat together, and we show our hostilities openly towards each other."

Some find fights between co-wives unbearable. I met a number of first wives who left their husbands when they tried to bring another woman into the house. Others however expressed that polygamy is the only way to find a husband, because there are simply not enough marriageable men in the valley. Many became second and third wives because they could not live a life without *ulemu* ("respect") – said of a life without a husband.

But I also met quiet a number of women (including first wives, but more often second wives) who said that they went on well along with their co-wives; some I found sitting and laughing together, when I visited them at their homes, regarding each other as sisters. Here the advice I heard from a first wife in Masumba:

At the beginning it was very tough for me when my husband
came with another wife, but after one year I thought it better to
make the best out of it. Polygamy brings easily quarrels. The
secret is to speak things out straight away with your co-wife and
your husband, and not to hide things in your heart. Ourselves
we work together, we go together to the choir, and we care for
each other's children and even breastfeed each other's children.
We help each other every day.

Since many women marry elderly men, the presence of another wife
can be a help in the daily chores and also provide a measure of freedom
and spare time.

MARRIAGE AND CHURCH

In this chapters I have shown some of the reasons why the concern of
a woman to find and keep a husband, and thus be recognised as a
woman who has *ulemu* (respect), detaches the young, married woman
from the church. It is not only because she almost always has to join
the church of her husband, which is still foreign to her upon marriage
and often attached to the ambivalent sphere of her in-laws. Even if both
partners as youths had prayed Catholic before their marriage, they are
rarely seen any more in the church after getting married. In a number
of outstations I found that half of the adult women coming to church
were not married (meaning they were widowed or divorced), while the
surrounding villages had a surplus of unmarried women only of 25%.
Many married couples don't go to church. "The husband will always
mistrust the wife if she goes for a church seminar or in the choir." Some
men said they mistrust the church: "You may think that you find
friends in church, but the very friend will be the one who sleeps with
you wife."

It is often only after many years of marriage that a basic trust
develops, but up to this time there is little from the church which helps
to support the most difficult stages of the marriage. Many cannot
understand the legalistic stance of the Church. When in Lumimba the
parish council, after their meeting, announced in church the
reinforcement of a strict Deanary policy that parents should be barred

from the sacraments if they receive marriage payments for a union of their baptised child outside the blessings of the Catholic Church, the whole church burst into laughter. The secretary of the church council stood her ground, and in public defended the rule, but each additional explanation was answered by further outbursts of laughter, until she gave up and laughed herself. The more she explained, the more it became clear to the people and to herself how little sense the rule made for the situation in the valley. Not only because marriage payments among the Bisa (especially in times of hunger) can be very little. Not only because a girl will always follow the religion of her husband, wherever he prays, and there are too few Catholics to get married to. Not only because the majority of Catholics in the valley are already barred from the sacraments for marital reasons or never reached baptism. But also because people – and this point was made all along the valley – consider the church to be imprudent with marriages. "Why do you priests want to bless marriages of couples before they are ready?" was a question I was sometimes asked, most forcefully in a big meeting with the Catholic chief Mnkhanya. In the valley girls marry early, and parents want their girls to be married early, for reasons discussed above. But that does not mean that they consider their children to be ready for marriage in Church and for life. Marriages in the valley proceed in stages, and are fully recognised only when several children are born and when the marriage has been tested by both families concerned. Marriages in the valley are often unstable, and for the Church to press for a blessing of a marriage before that final stage is reached, is met with little understanding.

But also the unmarried feel neglected by the church. Here a quote of a widow from Masumba:

> In the village we are only second class people. We have no *ulemu*. But even in the church we feel second class. The properly married have their own *vipani* (church groups), exclusively for married women. There is no *chipani* which is specific for our situation. Is it not also a vocation to lead an unmarried life? There is nothing that is designed for us *aziche* (unmarried women) which recognises our specific position.

The question arises about ways of increasing the significance for the young man, and linking up with his own spiritual needs (see chapter 9), but also for the young, married woman. The Catholic stance has shown a very firm commitment against polygamy and early marriages. Less visible in the valley is the Church's inclusiveness that gives a home also to people who have failed to have their marriages blessed (often for a variety of very different reasons), or who find themselves in polygamous situations, again for a variety of reasons. Stiffness of rules has often blended out a basic attitude of compassion, of listening, and of respect shown towards persons who made their decisions in a mind-frame that was determined by various cultural values, family pressures and economic considerations, not all of them evangelised by the Gospel, and most of them not even addressed in the catechumenate. While people have heard the Church saying a firm "no" to polygamy and unblessed marriages, they have seen less emphasis on the spiritual dimension of their married life. Many feel left alone in a relationship, where marriage has become something that needs to be endured in the presence of beer, other women, domestic violence and uncountable quarrels day by day, not something that gives life and opens a meaningful spiritual path. Many priests have spent much more time explaining why certain people cannot receive the sacraments, because of their marital status, than drawing out a spiritual path of married life (and of no longer married life) in a way that could be understood by people and be meaningful to them.

Religious movements, in contrast, that managed to develop a meaningful spirituality of marriage (building on actual experiences of marriage, and on cultural and mystical values) have seen a surprising success in the valley; unfortunately, they unfolded often outside the Catholic gates (see chapter 10, especially the example of the Lumpa church). The lack of a meaningful, spiritual path of married life also draws attention to the need to engage much more positively with the cultural initiation rites that prepare women, but also men, for their marriages (see chapter 9).

Men drinking. Important for the Church are the questions about the social conditions that make the village a place of recreation and drinking for the men, and about possibilities for the Church to become more significant for men and link up with their aspirations in life.

Church life in Masumba (Chikowa): all Catholics were called to make bricks; twelve women turned up and two men.

Chibale, a popular game played with beads for the women

Women (Mpamadzi) spending each day many hours grinding

Fishing activities of the men

The pride of many men is found in (largely illegal)
hunting activities

8.

Alliances of power

Power has to do with influence over people. Lines of power like nerves in our bodies run through all sections of society, through relationships including the cultural and religious spheres. There are many dimensions of power; we identify with some, capture and appropriate them, and allow them to shape our actions and even our dispositions, while we may oppose others, or try to evade them if they come on unfavourable terms. Different power relations often conflict with one another. In this chapter, I look at some of the conflicting focal points of power in the valley that arise from its isolation: the government, the chiefs, investors (the private sector), NGOs, churches, and the lineage. People have to find their way within the possibilities that are open to them. None of the focal points of power is subscribed to completely, but none can be avoided either completely. Alliances therefore are often situational and partial. This applies also to the alliance of people to a specific church. The main reference point of orientation for most people in the valley remains the family and lineage; where other focal points of power, including the churches, stand in conflict to the demands of the family/lineage, diffuse commitments can be the result.

VOTING PATTERNS

During the 2006 elections, most people in the valley voted for the ruling MMD. In the constituencies of Eastern Province that reach into the valley (Chama North, Chama South, Lumezi, Malambo, Msanzala, and Nyimba), the ruling MMD got in average around 10% more votes than the national average and also than the Eastern province average (see appendix). I happened to be in Chasera on the day of the elections, and a number of headmen firmly told people who approached the voting cabins to vote for the ruling party, since they had received food relief. "If you vote for somebody else we will not receive food relief any longer." But beyond the issue of food relief the vote may also indicate a desire for more integration into national schemes from which people feel isolated.

Five years earlier, in the 2001 elections, the ruling MMD received only very few votes in the Luangwa valley (with the only exception of Msanzala), much in line with the pattern of the rest of the Eastern Province that voted mainly for UNIP and in second place for FDD. Note however that in the valley MMD got an average of 10% more votes than in the rest of the Eastern Province, while UNIP got an average of 5% less. MMD won the elections on the national level under the suspicions and accusations of rigging the results, and the poor results in the valley reflects the level of disillusionment people had at that time with the ruling party. Before that, in the 1996 elections (that had been boycotted by UNIP), the valley voted for the ruling MMD with a high majority, significantly higher (nearly 10% on average) than the average of the Eastern Province. In the 1991 elections the voting pattern of the valley had followed very closely the pattern of the Eastern Province: people had voted for the then ruling UNIP rather than the MMD which won a three quarter majority on the national level.

The voting pattern of the valley in the 3rd Republic then is a vote for the ruling party, except for the 2001 elections, but even then the ruling party got more votes in the valley than it got in the rest of Eastern province. The tendency in the voting pattern for the ruling party (sometimes in contrast to the rest of the Eastern Province) may indicate a fear of being sidelined in gaining a fair share of national resources (food relief, etc., if people elect a member of parliament who is not part of the ruling party), and a desire for national integration to break the isolation of the valley.

RELATING TO NATIONAL POLITICS AND THE LAW

The political landscape of the valley is different from other parts of Zambia since it mostly falls under the policies of the Game Management Areas that have been described in chapter 6. Through the CBNRM programmes a local elite has been built up that controls the benefits of wildlife protection, working in close collaboration with the chiefs. I have already mentioned the factor of isolation, which makes it difficult to appeal against abuses of power, and the grave lack of education and a resulting resignation. The law that determined life in the valley (game parks, game management areas with the ban on hunting, the renting of huge junks of land to outside investors, licensing of fishing) was not made by the valley population; it was imposed on them against their will. The elected members of parliament (MPs) are hardly seen, except maybe for some major festivals or for a good rest in some safari lodge. Chiefs expect much money from the tourist and wildlife sector and have thereby become more independent of the structures linking them to their own people (headmen, *indunas*).

The law, made outside of the valley, creates a legal and an illegal sphere. Much of life in the valley proceeds within the illegal, especially hunting, but also the growing of drugs (*fyamba*) and popular methods of fishing (with fish poisons – *buba* – or indeed any fishing without licence). Because of the law, a hunter has become a poacher, and a fisherman without a license a criminal whose nets (and livelihood) can be taken away from him as if he had stolen it; indeed the valley population is known across Zambia as a population of "poachers" and "criminals". A young, unmarried female teacher, freshly appointed to Lumimba, cried upon arrival and asked: "What shall I do here? Get married to a poacher?" She was trying her best to get a different appointment.

The people enforcing the law (game guards, etc.), may not see the poachers as criminals in a moral perspective; they themselves like meat and eat much game meat, and their own job is hardly a job done out of moral conviction for animal protection. Many, however, consider the poachers to be unreasonable; game guards surely sympathise with the poachers, yet they hardly understand that someone risks many years in prison just for a good meal.[102] But from the other side of the coin the continuation of poaching in the face of very stiff punishments indicates how much hunting is a style of life and a second nature to many people; it is not an issue that becomes object of rational reflection weighing advantages against disadvantages.

The government has the power of making laws, but to convince people to identify with the laws is a different matter. Values of people are often linked up to the lineage/family to whom they belong. Boys learn especially through hunting the values that count in their families: courage, solidarity and the level of skills. Hunting, in spite of the total ban, remains a high value and a reference to manhood. Stuart Marks put the finger on this point when he wrote:

> Comparatively few individuals are recognized as "hunters" (*bachibinda*) in the local idiom. These men may appear as "poachers" or "criminals" in various government reports, yet they possess more tenaciousness and local charisma among their dependents than these outsider reporters know.[103]

The "criminals" and "poachers" of the official discourse are often highly esteemed in their own communities. Their adventures are the material for storytelling. In Kasweta (Chikowa), many men have spent some years of their lives in prison "eating beans", because they had been caught by the game guards, but they are nevertheless the local heroes. Hunting remains a powerful marker of identity in the valley, and this has not been changed yet by the re-education programmes of the wildlife sector. In consequence people hunt now much more with traps and snares to avoid alerting the game guards with gunshots and to avoid confiscation of the few guns they still have. Here a revealing quote collected by Stuart Marks among the Bisa of Nabwalya in 1997:

> In nowadays, every man here is a trapper. Snaring is the only way of getting or killing animals. Even children aged ten years are good trappers. Even people of 70 or 82 years are setting wire snares. Guns are seldom used. Very shortly, we will be using bow and arrows putting poison on them. In the past years, snaring was mostly used during the dry season, but now snaring

is used throughout the year. Some ones can kill many animals by snares, more than with a gun. Very soon young women will begin setting snares.[104]

But it is not only that many of people's activities proceed in the realm of the illegal: they themselves are becoming illegal. Powerful investors have bought up the prime pieces of land near the river. Teachers working in Chinsimbwe, for example, told me that they don't think the local people will have a chance to stay there in the long run.

> How can people still cultivate with so many elephants around? The new laws are just made to get people out of this place. In future, all this land will belong to Sable Company. People get beaten up and tortured by private security guards when they seek access to the river.

People's relationship with the government is therefore ambivalent: people look strongly towards effective integration, but are also aware that such integration has too often come on unfavourable terms: They could not be agents who participate in official channels and many people feel that the valley population has been sold out to foreign interests.

THE STATE AND THE CHURCHES

We take it for granted that government and churches are different entities in their own rights; they may merge in some aspects and differ in others. Yet this distinction may not be as clear to people in the valley. Church and government may come together in the broader category of outside forces that try to gain influence over people in the valley. The government presents itself as Christian, and on public functions churches, government and its institutions merge and are seen together. Most public meetings open with a prayer of a church representative. The following voice of a fisherman in Kalasa describes why he does not pray:

> For us to pray in a church, the Boma first has to come and
> explain things to us. We are still waiting for the Boma to explain
> [the ban on hunting, the selling of land to a Zimbabwean
> investor who banned fishing along the Luangwa near Kalasa].
> We will not pray before the Boma explains. Boma and church
> are one and the same. The Boma receive their *malamulo* (laws)
> from the church and from the Bible.

The history of the church in the valley should not be seen in isolation
from people's relationship with the government of the day. For
example, ten years before independence, in Chikowa the White Fathers
wrote that

> The Akunda are pretty apathetic and show little interest in
> religious matters, they seem to be more concerned about
> national independence and material development.[105]

The apathy of people and the "little interest in religious matters" maybe
was not geared solely towards the Catholic Church in itself, but in its
perceived association with the colonial regime that was alienating
people from their own land. The Watchtower movement/ Jehovah's
Witnesses that presented itself in a radical break from the state did gain
adherents in Chikowa (see chapter 9). Another example is the role of
the UCZ in Chikwa. I was told there that the UCZ in the past had been
perceived as a national church.

After Independence, people saw it spreading fast on the
surrounding plateaus, but they gave it, at first, no chance in the valley.
In a large meeting held in Chikwa, people mentioned to me that the
UCZ had been associated for a long time with the nationalism of
Kaunda and that it had been boycotted because of that.[106] It was only
after the Kaunda era that the UCZ gained a foothold in Chikwa area,
starting with the 1990s. The church then grew rapidly and attracted
especially returnees from the Copperbelt. Today it is one of the liveliest
churches in the area, with attractive and strong choirs; many people see
today in the UCZ a means towards wider integration into Zambia –
maybe as an alternative to (rather than an instrument of) government
structures, or at least as a complementary structure in its own right.

The distinction between Church and government becomes clearer for people where they see the church getting involved in issues of justice and peace, especially regarding the abuses of the wildlife authorities.

RELATING TO DEVELOPMENT PROJECTS

Wildlife protection needs in the long run some legitimisation through development projects. Everywhere now there are clubs for *chitukuko* (development), here a meeting, there yet another workshop where sitting allowances are paid for those attending, over there a new club for bee keepers. Internet web pages and safari brochures convince tourists that the local population is benefiting from wildlife protection, that they find jobs, learn crafts, benefit from sold licences, have more schools and clinics available, that many water wells have been dug with good drinking water, and that much of this has been paid with funds raised from the wildlife industry fed back into the community. Apart from regulated redistribution of funds through the Community Resource Boards (CRB) (if they are really working....), one finds in the valley also a number of private initiatives from safari enterprises engaged in local education and healthcare. Many combine their concern for animals with concern for the local population. Yet, it remains a fact that in spite of all the development initiates the Luangwa Valley remains marked by one of the highest poverty levels of the whole country, and the poverty is chronic. This contrasts with the fact that the valley forms one of the greatest tourist attractions of Zambia, and provides the country with a steady income. Local initiatives of a number of safari camps bring development; at the same time, the policies of isolation, the failure to link the valley to a solid road network (maybe in view of wildlife protection), and the fact that people have to bear the real cost of wildlife protection when the animals ravage their fields, are the structural cause for people's poverty and dependency.

The new wildlife policies that are applied to the Game Management Areas have a strong stress on community participation in policies and in profits. However, new words such as "community based natural resource programmes" or the "Luangwa Integrated Resource Development Project" together with the new "Village Action Groups",

"Area Development Committees", or "Chiefs and Local leaders Committees" have not dispelled the popular conception that the wildlife protection programmes have created a new elite and cemented also the position of traditional authorities within that elite, who share amongst themselves most of the profits from the new "community based" principles; the people whose crops are destroyed and who have to sleep inside their fields are too often left with nothing. The isolation from the plateau has made people powerless to seek official redress in the face of corruption and nepotism; isolation from the plateau and the rest of Zambia and a gross lack of communication structures has made people very dependent on the valley elite (ZAWA, chiefs and close associates, private investors).

When I asked in meetings people's opinions about development programmes, they didn't fail to enumerate what had improved in recent years: water supply (boreholes), clinics, more schools (though of poor quality). But most participants contrasted the present situation negatively with the past when they could hunt and eat (see chapter 3). "We were healthier in the past, we ate better, and there were also fewer sicknesses, and fewer deaths."[107] Concerning a number of development projects that we find in the valley, people were ambivalent: they wanted such projects, but I hardly came across anybody who was really convinced that projects will lift the area out of poverty. The key metaphor of poverty in the valley was not the absence of development projects, but the absence of a proper road. Projects in general are seen as a source for allowances and meals, here and there a bit of piece-work; the ideology of conservation farming is subscribed to because with each step done on their own fields, people receive handouts of maize. "I do it because of the maize, but I can't see how this sort of farming can really bring results," said one of the catechists of Chikowa parish. In fact, many people in the valley tend to evaluate projects not for their communal benefits but for the personal profits that they may bring. Many individuals look at a project of road building, or a clinic, or a school, in terms of piecework opportunities and employment rather than for what it does for the community. In turn, many outsiders find people in the valley ungrateful and very demanding, criticising them for a lack of own inputs and initiatives in the development projects.

People have learned how to play the game: how to adapt to the new world of *chitukuko* (development) that is now going through the valley, how to use the right language, so as to receive some short-term gain. Obviously, the educated can adapt best to this new language and they can best discern the right channels. The uneducated become more dependent. For them, the world becomes smaller and smaller, as more and more spheres of life are removed from their competence. The low level of internal cooperation together with the low level of education reinforces a sense of hopelessness in regards to having effective political power. A response is often not to confront an outsider, not to fight, but to get as much as possible out of him/her, and for the rest to ignore the person. Another response is seeking access to alternative but illegitimate means of power, especially to witchcraft (see the next chapter). At the same time, many chiefs and headmen refuse to be sidelined by an upcoming elite: they make sure they are part in development deals and get their share, which brings a certain heaviness to many programmes.

THE CHIEFS

When the church calls for a meeting or a seminar, people are late or more likely don't come at all. A church programme is sent out well in advance, a priest comes down 200 km on bad roads all the way from Lundazi to Chasera, but finds only four or five people and a few kids looking at the car, and he gets the reply: *"bantu bali ku minda"* ("the people are in the fields - though you may suspect that a number of church councillors are just drinking around the corner). Chief Mwanya calls for a meeting, further away, and earlier in the morning, and though the Awiza may tell you in private that they don't consider him to be their chief, they will be there at call without delay. How does the chief, even an unpopular chief, maintain his grip on people in the valley, and how does the church lose it?

The tradition of chiefdoms in the valley has been very ambiguous (see chapter 5), and the present chiefdoms are the result of a rather arbitrary history; their position became cemented and sometimes even invented (like chief Nyalugwe) under colonial rule. The state today affirms appointments, provides chiefs with a salary and chief retainers, and regulates the chief's authority through the legal framework. But the chiefs in the valley are greatly feared and they form powerful political coordinates that by far surpass the legal framework. Many chiefs profit from the wildlife sector. They see themselves as the owners of the land, and any safari enterprise looking for land has to pass through the chief. The assumption is still shared by some outsiders that if the chief consents to give away land, then also the local people have consented.

Equally surprising is the fact that chiefs in the valley have managed, despite shallow historical traditions, to become national focal points of folklore. The Senga have their Kwenje ceremony and the Miyombe celebrations, the Kunda the Malaila, and the Nsenga the Tuwimba. Two reasons seem obvious: there is support from the tourist sector (the chiefs incidentally become again focal point for the cultural scene), and secondly people of the valley are travelling a lot, many live in Lusaka and in the Copperbelt, and they are looking for markers of their identity. The festivals are fundraised and organised much in the folklore societies of the towns.

Under the chief's authority, a variety of other local interests merge in a structure of dependencies and patronages. The Chiefs Act (chapter 479 of the Laws of Zambia) provides the chief with the authority to

> discharge ... the traditional functions of his office under African customary law in so far as the discharge of such functions is not contrary to the Constitution or any written law and is not repugnant to natural justice or morality. (§10a).

The focal point is the word 'tradition'. In rural Zambia, the chiefs' authority depends much on how they have managed to reinvent themselves as guarantors of tradition, of the *miyambo*. Some of the issues they deal with can also be dealt with in the local courts: adultery, divorces, "damage" of a girl, village fights, insults and thefts, but other issues are seen as belonging properly to the palace: anything to do with the land and people's gardens, village affairs and appointments of headmen, but also dealings with witchcraft (*ufwiti*). Witchcraft cannot be dealt with anywhere else (as witchcraft accusations are outlawed by the official courts), and dealing with witchcraft has been successfully monopolised in the valley by the chiefs, falling under their 'traditional functions', even if against the official law as outlined in the Witchcraft Act. People depend on the chief for land, settlement, gardens and certain offices, but moreover they depend on the chief for certain types of security. Despite historical arbitrariness, the chiefs have become the guarantors of the values of the valley over and against the official courts and authorities, and even the Churches.

Witchcraft disputes are examples of how chiefs manage to become focal points of the *mwambo* far beyond what is acknowledged by the law. There are accusers and there are those accused of witchcraft. It is easy to see why the accusers should go to the chief: only in the chiefs' courts can they press for compensation from the accused, and they can have their suspicions publicly acknowledged. (In the official courts, the accused would turn the accusation around and sue the accuser for defamation of character, as the official witchcraft act, Cap 90 of the Laws of Zambia, makes it an offense to accuse a person to be a witch.) But also the accused go willingly to the chief's court, however much we may try in our churches to make them go to the police or the magistrate court. In a climate where everybody believes in and experiences the presence of witchcraft, people accused of witchcraft need to be vindicated from the witchcraft accusations if they want to receive protection against the accusing lineages. Official courts that don't recognise witchcraft cannot vindicate. I have heard about the practice among many chiefs in the valley to refer the accused together with the accuser to three different but approved *ng'anga,* which usually leads to a certain dilution of the case and buys time for the accused. Without the chief, the accused would have to face alone the wrath of the accuser's lineage, which can be very powerful; someone who seeks revenge may know about poisons and witchcraft. Only the chief's court can control the accusing lineage, and the presence of independent councillors and headmen can also mean a certain amount of objectivity beyond personal opinions. Not to go to the chief can mean to put one's own life into jeopardy and also the life of family.

Witchcraft accusations are a family affair. Some individuals may be more vocal than others in witchcraft affairs, but they too are dependent on the support of their lineages or families, and on the support of headmen, chief, and broader sections of the community. Any witchcraft accusation or refutation is dependent on how much support from different sides this claim can rally behind itself. Unsupported claims can and do backfire. At the chief's court a variety of voices participate, the different lineages involved in the dispute, the councillors, indunas, headmen who are called to be present at the hearing. Witnesses are heard, letters written by the different *ng'anga* and their verdicts are read out, and in this process many views are expressed but also a certain "objectivity" (in the sense of "facts" believed to be true by everybody present) is established that recognises witchcraft and that becomes binding. Witchcraft beliefs of course become reinforced through this process. All are made to participate in the discourse on the *mwambo*, of which the chief has become the centre. Chiefs, furthermore, are themselves seen as being in close contact with the occult world in ways that can come quite close to the concepts of witchcraft. In inheritance disputes contestants are often accusing each other of witchcraft and feel threatened by each other. "Chiefs can kill" was a comment I often heard in the valley.

Two situations can be contrasted. When I was in Tembwe in August, a sick man (rather young) who lived in a poor hut and obviously did not have much money, managed to raise 340,000 Kwacha (80 US\$) in cash to book a *ng'anga* (healer, diviner, witchfinder) called "Tonde Kamulukolo Gonera Lwande" from Kambombo plus organise some chickens to feed the *ng'anga* for the days he was at his home. Three family members (two of them were "fathers" of the sick) stood accused to have caused the sickness, and the *ng'anga's* task was to point out the real culprit. In the evenings a number of young people came to help with the drumming and dancing, or just to be there. I also came, and my impression was that in this particular incident they had come for entertainment rather than for some deep commitment to the case. I spoke with some of his neighbours, but also here did not sense much involvement. Yes, maybe there was witchcraft, but nobody seemed really to care too much about this case at that particular moment. Others carefully phrased their sentences to me: "some say that… "– "This is what we hear but we have not been there…" – "ask somebody in the family, they must know ..." it seemed to me that many did not want to become dragged, at that moment of time, into the affair of somebody else. This was not their business nor their family. The sick man had raised a lot of money, but had little communal support. In the valley it is very difficult to raise public support beyond the own lineage due to the "quicksand" of the social structure, described in chapter 2. Such cases are easy to deal with for the chief, as they remain contained within small segments and can thereby be easier controlled, maybe even manipulated to some extent.

In contrast, other cases raise an enormous communal support. A whole village can get involved in the struggle to find the witches that are responsible for the misfortunes falling in the village, affecting many different families. In Chitumbi (Nyimba Parish), I was told that in 1980 a certain "Doctor" Chenda Bwamba cleansed the whole village and killed publicly more than ten "witches" with his *mwavi* within a single week. One year later "Doctor" Kasensela alias "*Kapula mu nthambo*" killed the remaining "witches" that were still left in another proper cleansing (1981). "After that we had peace for some years", the elders told me in a meeting, but then they added:

> But it is time that another *mcapi* (witch-finder and witch-cleanser) comes, because nowadays things are worse than ever: people just kill randomly (*kupayepaye*) to have a better harvest or just out of jealousy. The *ng'anga* also don't know anymore their business and don't have any longer the proper *mwavi* (poison to identify and kill witches) as in the past. Last year a certain Elias came, but he didn't do a proper cleansing. Today the youths just go to a *ng'anga* to buy a *bwanga* (charm used for sorcery) – this was not like that in the past. Even the chiefs today are afraid to give a *ng'anga* proper papers to cleanse our villages.

These people evidently called for more witchfinding activities and felt that the chiefs have become too fearful of the government and of the Zambian Law, and that they can no longer help effectively to contain the presence of witches. Chiefs can be afraid. In a situation where whole villages call for the *mcapi* and where a case has gathered public support from different sections of the community, it is very difficult for the chief to control the events. The chiefs may welcome witchcraft cases to build up their own authority, but it is always a game with fire.

People's relationship with their chiefs in the valley is ambivalent and contains many contradictions. In some respects they are proud of their chiefs. Chiefs have become markers of their identity, and guarantors of their *mwambo* against foreign encroachment. For people their relationship with the chief is often the only option to attain some security in their lives. At the same time they fear their chiefs, consider them to be corrupt, "they love sugar", and people see them selling off the country of their ancestors to foreign investors and consider themselves to be powerless against their arbitrariness; a number of Catholics compared their chief with the Biblical Pharaoh, and others called their chief "Yuda" for selling off their land. The chiefs powers far extends what has been granted to them by official law, but the power of the state limits itself in the valley to wildlife protection (and even that is privatised to a large extend), and cannot guarantee the protection of people. The old chief Kazembe, for example, just before his death publicly expelled several people accused of witchcraft, together with their families, from his country in a meeting attended not only by senior chief Mwase but also by the D.S., who just remained quiet, refusing to intervene in a situation that was evidently against the Zambia Law.[108] The families in question did not go, and in consequence their houses were burnt down on command of the chief. The authority of the chiefs in the valley can be put into direct link with the absence of effective state authority. In the valley people have few alternatives to the chiefs.

The chief's authority also passes right through the Church and the church councils. In many places in the valley, church council members fear direct reprisals from their chiefs should they dislike their decisions. The only Church known to evade chiefly powers to a greater degree are the Jehovah Witnesses. The reputation of the Jehovah Witnesses goes so far that in many places they are uniquely exempt from taxation for incoming witchfinders, because they don't pay anyway. As much as possible, they deal with disputes in their own internal courts. This also includes matters of cleansing of their widows and widowers.

THE LINEAGE

In the valley we find a multitude of lineages who immigrated from all possible directions into the valley, have a long history of co-existence, but may have little to do with each other. Political coordinates that are relevant for people remain largely inside the lineage, as many never developed a strong identification with the wider "tribe" or a chief. In the past, young hunters depended on their fathers and relatives for access to medicines: hunting and medicines were intrinsically connected, and much knowledge was passed on only inside the family. Access to medicines also meant access to occult forces and witchcraft, another reason why many people preferred to live away from each other.

All villages that I analysed contained a settlement pattern based on lineages, most clearly in the strictly virilocal north, where lineages are easily defined, but also in the matrilineal south, where, however, we find more variation in settlement patterns, as marriages here can be both viri- and uxorilocal, and as the father figure also in matrilineal societies is becoming more and more important. Still today, a person is as strong as his lineage. The stranger, and people with few relatives, or who have lost support of their lineages, feel very vulnerable. This is strongly felt by teachers. On the Western side of the Luangwa in Bisa country, a number of fishing banks and especially the *fyansa* (fish weirs) are in possession of lineages and inherited through the matri-lineage. An indication of control of the lineage was (and sometimes still is) the pre-arrangement of marriages in the Southern part of the valley, or marriages at close range. People in the south (Ambo & Kunda & Wiza) still show a preference for cross-cousin marriage.[109] One young couple (in Mkasanga) told me that their marriage had been pre-arranged by their mothers, and they were happy about it.

Authority figures within the lineage differ (fathers, maternal uncles, grandparents, etc.) But all over the valley, the power of the lineage today is steadily undermined. People mentioned especially access to money as being responsible for this trend. In some isolated parts of the valley (an example is Kasweta with its surrounding villages) there is still today hardly any circulation of cash, and trade remains based on barter, where family members depend much more on one another than in a cash economy. But most parts of the valley have become fully penetrated by the money economy, especially since the massive expansion of the cotton industry in recent years. Tiny shops can be found today even in very remote areas, where there was not a single shop ten years ago. Through money, people have become less dependent on their lineages. All over the valley I collected sentences like:

> The youths today don't listen anymore, they do what they want.

> The youths now have more money than the adults.

> There is more witchcraft now in our families than ever before.

> *Mankhwala* is not given any more by the elders, but is bought now anywhere (and therefore also witchcraft is out of bounds).

> In the past meat was freely distributed within the family. Today nothing is distributed freely anymore. Everything is being sold. Business has entered in everything, even kin.

In spite of such experience of wide erosion, we remain much aware that ideals, values, moral codes and ethics still have the lineage as main reference, rather than say the Church. Formal education provides a certain stepping back from one's own lineage. One should therefore expect that people without formal education, which is the majority of people in the valley, have only a more limited experiences of life outside the lineage structures.

Some church policies clash with what is demanded by the family. The Church outlaws the visit to a diviner (*ng'anga*) in case of death in the family to seek out the culprit, but for a lineage to accept death with closed eyes means that either more people will be killed by the witch or others will suspect the witch in the own family, which leads to an increase of suspicion within the family at the expense of family solidarity. Christians are not allowed to divorce, and also in the lineage one goes a long way to save a marriage, but there are situations where this is not possible anymore, and in such cases the whole extended family will suffer from an impossible marriage; the strain of a redundant union, if it is not broken, can break whole lineages apart (Fields 1982). Christians are not supposed to fear the spirits of the dead (*viwanda*), say a dead spouse, but to remain with the *chiwanda* of a dead spouse can have consequences far beyond one's personal life. The decisions about cleansing ceremonies are not always personal decisions; they concern the whole family and should be taken together by the whole family. For many people in the valley, the prime reference for moral codes is not the Church but the lineage, on whom one depends to a much greater extent.

In the valley pastoral workers are aware that the Christian message is accepted on a very partial and selective level. This reflects maybe also the absence of the Church in issues that really matter for people (including, for example, the absence of the church-life for the whole of the rainy season). People may feel that the Church's commitment to them is also very selective and partial and give a corresponding response.

Calling on the ancestors: a family gathering at their ancestor shrine (*kavuwa*) in Zaongo (Chama Parish). All family members wear a stripe of the same piece of cloth; such stripes also hang down from the *kavuwa*.

A game guard, – juggling between the rules of the law and the demands and values of his community.

"The moment I wear a uniform, I am no longer a human being for people, but something else, an enemy."

Above: Chief Nsefu (of the Kunda people) is carried during the Malaila ceremony of the Kunda people.

Below: Chief Chikwa (Senga people) at the royal ancestor shrine

Illegal fishing activities: killing fish with fish poison (*buba*), a communal affair of the whole village.

9.

The God of the Valley

Many pastoral workers have made the experience that people forget about the Church and fall back on what everybody else believes in the valley once the isolation starts. "When we start touring in June after the rains, we always are starting again from zero." (Pastoral report of Lundazi/Lumimba 2006). One priest put it to me jokingly this way: "If you leave a person too long in the valley, he becomes like the valley people themselves. You better take him out before he also becomes dangerous!" The valley has a very long history of provoking such remarks. Already in 1830, when Monteiro was revisiting the Portuguese colony along the Luangwa that had been acquired some years earlier to facilitate trade with Mwata Kazembe (seemingly somewhere between Lukusuzi and Matizi rivers), he found Petro Pereira (the brother of Manuel Pereira) whom he had left behind. J. C. Monteiro then described Pedro as "living like the (Africans) not only going about clothed like them but even resembling them in their customs and superstitions ... a man who has entirely forgotten his religion." (Quoted in Astle, 1997, 5). A quote from Chilonga Mission diary of 1919 shows what can happen when good Christians go back into the valley:

> Father Superior went to visit the Kasenga (Lwangwa Valley) for
> a week. One of the villages, Kachela, is peopled of ex-Chilonga
> citizens, whose faith is almost a past memory. They do keep the
> Sunday rest, but they do not gather for the Sunday service.
> Sunday is indeed different from the other days, for in the

morning the men go hunting instead of working, in the evening they drink beer, and the whole population join in singing bawdy songs and dancing lascivious dances. As for the catechists, they are cold-shouldered by the Christians. Since the villagers have turned their backs to prayer and religious instruction, they look to the old pagan practices for comfort. One day they decreed that they had to offer a sacrifice to the spirits to ward off bad luck. They stretched their nets and caught…a hen, which they ritually obliterated with bows and arrows. Then they proclaimed very seriously that they had returned to the Old Testament!!! Father Superior gathered those poor misguided people together, and kindly endeavoured to make them see light. They at last confessed they had gone completely astray, and that they would henceforward observe the genuine Christian Sunday (religious service and rest), welcome the catechists, follow the catechism classes, etc. We shall see whether the 'Israelites' of Kachela will return to Christianity! (19th February 1919)

Christianity has many links with traditional religion in Africa, and in many societies it did not seem too difficult for people to make the transition from one to the other. In the valley, however, it was more difficult. And some people in the valley today go into the offensive: they feel that the churches did not build on what was there. The Catholic chief Mnkhanya put it this way: "Jesus said he had come to fulfil the law. But you missionaries came to abolish the law." The same phrase I also heard in interviews with young men in a number of places in the valley. Some said that the churches did not build on people's old religious foundations in which they saw nothing good. This chapter is about what is left of these old foundations today, especially what is left of publicly expressed traditional religion. What attitudes do people have towards them today, how do they shape people's understanding of God, and how are the churches seen in relation to them?

RELIGION OF HUNTERS

Men's life centred until very recently on hunting. Stuart Marks wrote a well acclaimed book (Marks 1978) on the hunting traditions and religious frameworks of the Bisa of Nabwalya which proved very helpful for my interviews all across the valley (less though for the Senga of the north). Hunting in the valley was highly ritualised and the hunters' experiences in the bush were intrinsically connected to the wives' activities in the village (adultery, plastering, even sweeping). The movements and behaviour of animals mirrored domestic life back in the village. This connection between animals and people was foremost established through the influence of deceased ancestors on animals. These ancestral spirits could lure animals into the hunters' traps, but also chase animals away from the hunters. They could make animals to copulate before the hunter (to show him what his wife was doing back in the village), entice them to charge and kill the hunter, or to confuse a charging animal. Hunting was a major form of divination (*lutembo*), which was practised at all major deaths. The sex of the animal killed determined where to look for the cause of death. Going out hunting meant for the hunter to prepare himself and be in union with the ancestors. One old hunter near Nyalugwe confirmed to me that still today he pours some flour under a tree before hunting, to call on the ancestors, and check in the morning for signs of animals around the flour. Most hunters, however, including the old, told me that this was a thing of the distant past. Today hunting is much less ritualised than what Marks still described. People in the south basically confirmed to me the observations of Marks, saying that his words describe the culture of the past, but also said, as observed by Marks, that "modern rifles know no rituals". One old man born in 1920 in Mwanya told me that he still witnessed many hunting rituals as a youth during the 1930s, but that already in the 1940s many rituals were not really followed any more. But two issues remain important also today, inclusive for many young hunters whom I interviewed, and both issues show that hunting still today cannot be isolated completely from the ancestors: Many hunters (if not most hunters) do not go hunting after bad dreams, and they abstain from sex before going hunting, "otherwise you kill nothing or you may even have an accident or be killed." Most hunters will not build some systematic explanations around these taboos, but they still show the link between the ancestors and the bush with its animals. Dreams are related to the dead, and so is the taboo on sex: sexual intercourse transfers a person into the state of being ritually hot, but the ancestors and the bush are cold; to go hunting while being hot will not work but bring disaster.

Another point made by Marks also came back in some of my interviews forty years later: To become a hunter is understood by many as a calling, as a vocation. When people described how they became hunters, it reminded me of the religious language we use when describing a vocation to the priesthood. "I dreamed of my dead grandfather who gave me a rifle. The next morning my father gave me his gun and sent me away hunting", explained a hunter of Mwanya to me. Also a number of others confirmed to me that they had become hunters through a calling in a dream. Stuart Marks found in Nabwalya that most of those who are recognised by the community to be real *bachibinda* (real *bafundi,* specialists, in contrast to occasional hunters) have had a number of *bachibinda* (professional hunters) in their family trees. To refuse such a calling to become a hunter meant to reject a duty to the family and one's ancestors.

Hunting was linked not only to human ancestors, but also to the shades of animals. Like humans, also animals (especially eland & elephant) have *viwanda* (spirits, shades) from which one needs to be protected but which can also be a source of occult powers. Hunting needs medicines, but medicines are not just given to anybody; they come from the *makolo* (ancestors) or other experienced hunters, especially those close to the own family. Hunting thus linked the men to their ancestors and incorporated them also into a network of distribution. Meat was distributed in certain ways among family, headman and chief, though such distribution patterns had also given rise to many tensions; as hunting often proceeded with much secrecy and discretion (only a fool speaks out loudly what he has caught), one would talk about big kills only with other professional hunters who know about the required medicines to be protected against the shades of these animals. Stuart Marks wrote that the Bisa also had various hunting guilds in the past.

Especially outsiders in the valley consider hunting as one of the main reasons why Christianity is only accepted half-heartedly.

> In hunting there is too much secrecy, but in the church we don't want secrecy. Hunting needs medicines, but in the church we are not allowed to use medicines (interview with men in Masumba/ St. Ignatius).

One could add that hunting has to do with ancestors, and that the church was not really at ease with people's contacts with their ancestors. In spite of the fact that a number of missionaries were hunters themselves, Christianity has not built much on the religious experiences that were found in the hunting traditions. This may be another reason why many men found it very difficult to make the Church their home.

MULUNGU ANALI PAFUPI – IN THE PAST GOD WAS NEAR

In every village I tried to gather groups of people together to speak about history, the *miyambo* and religion. It were especially the groups with men who proved very responsive and from whom I got a lot. The following question was part of many interviews: "When do you think God was nearer to you, now or in the past?" I sadly write that most people answered that God was nearer to them in the past. Some even added that God ran away with the arrival of Christianity. Here a quote from men in Mwape:

> Our parents used to pray under the *Msolo* tree; whenever there was no rain they pleaded under the *Msolo* tree and rain came. When they lacked meat they went to God (Nyamalenga), and a lion came and left an animal at the village that he had killed. When sicknesses were there, they pleaded and the sick healed. When the missionaries came they forbid all these and said, "you are praying to idols (*mafano*), and that is when we stopped to pray under the *Msolo*. God was very near to our parents in the

past because when they prayed the rain came: they were just coming back from the tree and the rain fell already. Because God was near to them. But today it does not work anymore because we are only doing bad things. We don't do good things. But in the past people were listening a lot, therefore they also knew God and what he wanted. They did not know that there was another person of his who had died for them but as soon as we heard that Jesus had died for us that was precisely when God fled from us. In the past if somebody did something bad, God reprimanded and punished him, that is why things were good in the past. But that is over, because when you go today to the *kawimba* (spirit shrine) the rain will not come because it is full of sins everywhere today. In the past people feared God, and if a person was just doing bad things they killed him. They tied those people to a tree and gave them *mwavi* to drink. And if a man committed adultery they fried his hands, that is why people in the past were afraid. When the missionaries came they forbid us our things, they forbid our *miyambo* (traditions), but they did not give us their *miyambo*.[110]

This is an interestingly rich quotation; I found such arguments in similar shades all over the valley. With the arrival of Christianity people could not deal anymore with their own issues (witchcraft, adultery), and they lost fear in God, because, after all, Jesus had died for their sins. Also on the last sentence of the above quote people commented a lot:

The missionaries did not give us everything. There cannot be a country without punishment, but the missionaries only preached about love and not punishing. They were hiding some things from us people.

A group of young men in Chikowa put it this way:

Christianity is good, but we never understood it properly because either the missionaries did not tell us everything or we misquoted them. There are many things in their countries of which they never spoke about.

Here another quote of a young adult in Chikowa:

> The churches took away our *nzeru* (brains). In the past our
> ancestors knew what to do to get good crops. When they went
> to the *kavuwa* the rains came the same day. A little cloud would
> appear in heaven, and before they had reached their homes it
> would pour rain. Just make an experiment: call all church
> leaders together, the Catholics, Anglicans, and Jehovah
> Witnesses, all of them, and put them together in a house and
> we will feed them for two weeks. Let them pray together for rain
> day and night, still you will see it will not rain! We have had bad
> rains now for more than ten years, this year we had floods and
> a draught in one and the same year. This never happened in the
> past. Our ancestors knew what to do.[111]

One of the central symbols of traditional religion in the valley today is
the evergreen *msoro* tree. Whenever I asked how people knew God in
the past, I was usually referred to the prayers under the *msoro*. It stands
also for the aspect of past religion that has been abandoned. Sometimes
it stands for the feeling that God himself has abandoned the valley.
Somebody told me that today you can go back to the *msoro* tree and
perform all the old rituals, but nevertheless God will not listen any
more.

Saying this, most people expressed that much of their past religious
traditions that concerned their ancestors have become irrelevant in
todays' world, because their time, their *nyengo* is simply finished.

Those people who complained to me about the erosion of the
mvuwa or *tuwimba* were mainly headmen and chiefs, people whose
traditional authority and social position relies to some extend on such
expression of traditional religion. Ordinary people were much less
concerned about their disappearance. Young people who do not pray
in church show even less interest in the *kavuwa*. The spirit shrines
seem to be rather easily abandoned where they have no political
significance. Young generations that did seek to break away from the
authority of headmen and linage elders may have found in the churches
a convenient means to do so. Not to go to the *mvuwa* of the group-

headman also meant to weaken his political authority which could have been convenient for the upcoming generations.

In the north of the valley (from Mwanya up to Chama) I found much more open expression of public traditional religion than in the south: spirit shrines at group-headmen, public *chinamwali* ("*ca chikunja*"), and among the Senga the Mulenga or Kamulenga cult organised by headmen and chiefs when they build a decorated hut at crossroads and sing and dance for rain. I don't think that those who dance for rain at Mulenga's shrine really strongly believe that it will not rain if they don't do so. Nor do those (I guess) who go to the spirit shrine of the group-headmen, pour out beer and exclaim *pepa* with outstretched arms. But in the north such traditional religion still constitutes to some degree political authority. One headman compared the *kavuwa* with a flag: "whenever you see a flag, you know that you are in a place of authority, and when you see a *kavuwa* you know you are at the group headman." One could say that in the north the *mvuwa* and the Mulenga cult give social capital to the headmen, as does the public *chinamwali* to the *anyapungu* and the organising family. Such expressions of traditional religion remain in the north markers of identity that still fill many people with pride, and to some degree also reinforce unity.

Chief Chifunda organised in 2005 an extraordinary event in his country: He called together (for the first time) leaders of all churches (including the Catholic catechist of Chiweza/Lumimba Parish) and asked them to pray together for rain. "In the past we all went to the *msoro*. Now since we are all Christians, let us pray together for rain, rather than each one in his own church." Nearly all churches had joined (except Jehovah Witnesses and the New Apostolic church), and I was told that heavy rain fell down only few days after the prayers, and that from then onwards proper rains were falling.

CHINAMWALI (INITIATION FOR GIRLS)

For chief Mnkhanya and his council, the disregard for the *mwambo*, especially the *chinamwali*, has much to do with the absence of God. The first ancestors came into the valley because they were guided by

God and because they were walking within the *mwambo*. The ordinary union with the sacred was not done through words but through right conduct, the walking in the *mwambo*. The *chinamwali* is not just a feast; it is a teaching that determines ordinary every-day conduct. When you break the *mwambo*, then things start going wrong. Prayers and offerings (at the *msoro* tree or at the *kawimba*) were done in times of troubles (draught, hunger, disease), when something had already gone wrong. Today, religion has become a matter of formal prayers (on Sunday), but is largely detached from ordinary affairs.

Interest in the *chinamwali* is great throughout the valley, and there is much electricity in the rites. The *chinamwali* is a protected space with guarded secrets, which gives women positions of ritual authority in which men better not meddle. Sexual activity, the house, the bush, gardens, pregnancy, the kitchen, food and salt, children: everything becomes ritually charged to be hot or cold, and thereby all important aspects of life become linked together and must not be seen in isolation from the legitimate sexual union between husband and wife. Life is a unity, and the centre of all activities must be the guarded space of the married household. We find in the *chinamwali* a counter part to the hunting traditions of the men that equally link the animals with the domestic sphere and right sexual conduct.

In the *chinamwali,* women are in charge. The man may prefer a wife who has gone through the *chinamwali;* "They are taught to be docile to the husband." But he may find out that the "docile" wife will prove very strong in the long run. The man is the official head of the household, yet in the matrilineal societies he is also the *tambala* (the cock) who begets children for a lineage not his own; the cock may crow around the house and make noise, but he may remain a stranger to the affairs of the children he begets. The submissiveness of the wife, taught in the initiation rites, can give ritual control to the woman: she cleans and guards the house and the kitchen, guards the act of procreation and the ritual state of the children; the right time and the wrong time for sexual intercourse will depend more on the rhythm of her body (and the health of the children) than on his – except for what was in the past determined by hunting, which was his sphere; she takes the initiative of the ritual shaving (in the north the *kutoshya nyumba*), one of the prime symbols of unity and love in marriage. Due to the intrinsic connection between adultery and the life of the spouse and children in a milieu where men are out for long periods of time, sometimes even years, and where everybody knows about the ravages of AIDS, it is not surprising that women don't easily give up the *chinamwali* and its guarded space, that gives them some control over their common sexual life.[112]

Many women complained to me that young men have money today but that they have lost all respect for their marriage. The economic developments in the valley have sidelined women. "*Anyamata a lero saika nzeru mu ukwati* (young men don't put their brains into their marriages)", is a comment I heard all over the valley, and "*indalama zaononga mwambo.* (Money destroys tradition)" On the side of the men, especially the male youths, I found indeed little appreciation of the *chinamwali*. The whole of the Catholic choir of Lukusuzi (Liva) was depreciating the *chinamwali* to me: "It's mere superstition of uneducated women – it's just drunk women talking (*kusabaila*) about things they don't know themselves – they only want to get some beer – the Bible forbids it anyway". In the south (Nyimba, Chikowa) even the big drums needed for a ceremony are rather rare. The *chinamwali ca chikunja* is publicly discredited and young women I interviewed (though not all) had gone through the *chinamwali ca chikristu*. But also here the ritual can create excitement among the women, even when the *chinamwali* is not done as a village feast, when drums are hardly used, when women only clap, and non-alcoholic *thobwa* is served instead of beer. The girl is taught to do what is taboo in the traditional rites: putting salt into the food of her parents. Nevertheless, many women assured me that deep down it is the same *chinamwali*: the same teaching, the same songs, and the same framework, only less lively. In Chikowa where a number of women are quite articulated, some called back for the drums and spoke that request into my tape recorder "for the bishop to hear".

Women were throughout the valley very interested in discussions on the *chiamwali*. But the Catholic *alangizi*, especially in the southern part of the valley, are often the ones who seemed most ill at ease with the old rites. When they establish their authority as members of the Catholic Church over and against the traditional *alangizi*, then anything traditional becomes bad: drums are very bad, and so is beer and any form of nakedness, and the traditional decorations are also very bad, and the taboo on putting salt is said to be extremely bad. But whenever I asked them why, the only reason I received was that it is "*chikunja*" (pagan) and that it is forbidden in the Bible. I learned much more from non-Catholic women, who proved to be more open and free in the discussions with a Catholic priest on their *mwambo*, and had no need to be defensive or feel criticised. But there is much confusion, and things are messy. Often the *maphunsiro* (teachings) of the *chinamwali* are seen to be out of touch with what the girls learn at school, and also with the modern ways of looking at life. But they touch a dimension of marital life that goes very deep and that cannot be explained in words alone. In the Christianised rites of the *chinamwali* some evaluation has gone on, but also here many *anyapungu* have not gone to school themselves, and some remain rather aloof to what is going on in terms of sex education (and sex experiences) in the schools. For the Christian theologian the question would arise, how far people feel that Christ is present at all in the so-called Christianised rites of the *chinamwali*. Discussions about the *chinamwali* are a minefield, and the Church still has some homework to do.

DEALINGS WITH WITCHCRAFT

Witchcraft has to be dealt with and a religion that cannot deal with witchcraft disqualifies itself for many people in the valley. Sometimes I asked people who don't pray whether there was a reason. Many said there was no reason, but some did give a reason. "The churches are full with witches!" A young man at the beer in Nsefu was more precise: "Were there no witches in Europe? Did you not got rid of them all? But here in Zambia you forbid us to deal with our witches." He was much applauded by his colleagues. "It is especially in the churches that the witches are hiding today, and you protect them. You put the witch on top and the victims down." The point of the churches harbouring sorcerers contains some truth: in some outstations people were afraid to remove some elderly church council members or chairmen because they were known to know about witchcraft and they exploited this fear. The Bisa mentioned people "making themselves heavy" (*kwifinya*) to stay in power, which means they allude to their knowledge of occult forces.

Witchcraft is not dealt with in some arbitrary way. What is witchcraft and what is not is established in a discerning process, and this is not an individual but a communal affair. Thereby people have to deal with issues that touch death, dreams and spirits of the dead; witchcraft is therefore a religious issue. Witchcraft in the valley (as elsewhere in much of Africa) is closely related to authority. People are afraid of witchcraft, but at the same time any headman, any person in a position of authority, and especially any chief, has to know about witchcraft. Witchcraft, authority and knowledge belong into one and the same framework. A person of authority must also have knowledge of witchcraft, which means that in a certain way he has to be a wizard himself. But his knowledge is to benefit the community, while the *mfwiti* kills own family members or other members of the community for personal gain, jealousy or hatred.

A revealing example of such legitimate witchcraft used by legitimate authorities can be given of an event that took place in Tembwe just before the Lumpa war in 1964. I quote from an interview with headman Ng'anjo Chibwato and a group of elders narrating the events:

> In Chikwa and in Kambombo everybody followed Lenshina. But here in Tembwe we were mission educated (Free Church of Scotland) and chief Tembwe (Joseph Changwe) had been educated in Chasefu. We knew that a disaster was coming up. Lenshina had a group of supporters also here in Tembwe, which was led by Kalewa. We knew that many people would die if we could not stop the group. Therefore the chief sat down with his council to look for a way to get rid of Kalewa. They sent James Mwale to Kalewa to shake hands with him. James Mwale met Kalewa on the road, greeted him, shook hands with him, and went on. The same night Kalewa died, and without his leadership the group of Lenshina collapsed. Because of this

there was no war in Tembwe, while hundreds of people died in Kambombo and in Chikwa.

Kalewa was killed through the legitimate magic (witchcraft) of the chief's council, given in the hands of Joseph Changwe. Of this sort of legitimate witchcraft people are proud. Access to occult forces is a power of the valley that is also intrinsically related to the ancestors and to God. Many mentioned that it is the wisdom (*nzeru*) that God himself gave to them. Chiefs and headmen guarded the secrets of their legitimate occult forces (legitimate witchcraft) from commoners, thereby they prevented illegitimate use of witchcraft and at the same time protected those who rallied behind them by means of these very powers. Most chiefly dynasties narrate stories about the magical powers of their founding members. One of the first Mambwes for example is known in popular stories for his ability to change himself into a Baobab tree, a stone, or a bird in times of war and thus protect himself and his followers from attacks of the Angoni or Bisa. (Unfortunately he was later betrayed by his captured wife who passed on the secrets to his enemies: according to the legent, they pierced first a needle into the baobab tree, and when blood started to flow, drove a spear into the tree and this killed the chief.) Lane Poole narrated stories he heard about the occult powers of the first woman chief Mwape. In Luwembe, the *bene Kashimu* and the *bene Nzovu* are still proud today of their historical role of guarding the magic of changing dead chiefs into royal lions and of the magic to protect an army in war. Today many people regret that such knowledge is gone. "In the past headmen knew how to prevent wild animals and elephants to come into the village. They were protecting the villages with medicines. Today nobody knows anymore how to do it."

The borderline between legitimate medicines and illegitimate witchcraft is not always very clear. Many women for example use *vikondi;* such medicines are good for a giggle and seen to be rather innocent. But they can have unintended consequences. In Mkasanga this year a woman had to flee the village while I was present, because she was known for using love charms (*vikondi*) to keep her husband. But when her husband died and she started to see him in dreams, she

was accused of having put love portions into his food, which happened
to kill him.

Legitimate medicines are especially interwoven into the hunting
traditions. One hunter in Nyalugwe told me and Brother Vinod of 72
different medicines that he knows well and that he prepared for his
sons: a number of medicines are used to call different animals, to evade
angry buffaloes or charging elephants, to get rid of the *viwanda* (spirits)
of killed animals (especially the *nsefu* - eland), protections against the
consequences of adultery of the wife while he is on a hunting trip,
medicines to wash the gun and the body to free them from the animals'
viwanda, medicines when taking out the pulp of elephant tusks less one
will be haunted by headaches, etc. Children are well protected, and just
by looking at the necks of babies, one sees not only the usual medicines
found all over Zambia against the *luwombo, lunse,* sicknesses of the
eyes and *mankowesha* of sexual pollution, but with a trained eye one
also sees whether the mother has had a previous miscarriage, whether
another child has died in the family (*katwi*), whether the father of the
child left, or whether the child has dreams or fits that are attributed to
a *chiwanda*. Many speak of protective magic in homes, though nobody
showed me a single exhibit; one Catholic elderly man in Kalasa told me
that he had protected all his children and his wife by incisions against
witchcraft – "do you think I want to remain alone? Of course I protect
my family!" Business women spoke openly to me about magic for their
businesses; some showed me even how to prepare it, "so that everybody
will buy from you". I was also shown how to cut open a *mulozi* shrub
right through from top to bottom and how to walk through it naked
(though I did not practise it) before going to court, and how to put a
piece of the root of the *palibe kanthu* shrub under my tongue when
going to the chief, in case I have made a *mlandu* (court case). I was told
about medicines to protect gardens from theft (*ikai*), and wives from
adultery, but again in this case I was shown no exhibit (it were only the
others who do it). Two women were not shy and explained under much
laughter how to protect their husbands from getting sick (*nsima*) when
they have slept with another man.

Sometimes even illegitimate medicines can fill people with pride, as long as it is used against other people far away. Here a good story that I was told in Mkasanga about a local hero, Aliele Zimba (narrated by Bana Saba).

Aliele Zimba worked with "Kalanga Chuma", his powerful magic, even more powerful than that of the Indians. Locally he was known for his dreams. Whenever a lion had caught an animal he dreamed about it and led the villagers to pick up the carcass. When he was hunting, no game guard ever saw him. But his most powerful magic was his *nkoli* (stick) with which he used to go to the towns. He entered a store and put down his *nkoli* just at the entrance of the store. Now all the goods of the store that he wanted entered his stick: bicycles, bales of cloth, haws, wheelbarrows, and blankets, anything he wanted just entered the stick. Back at home in Mkasanga he dug a big pit, put his stick inside, and everything came out again, and he covered the pit with grass. That is how he stole from all the shops of Chipata and Lundazi. Whenever something was stolen, the police heard the name of Aliele Zimba. Until they looked for him in Mkasanga. Aliele Zimba was living in Chitumbi, where he had married the sister of Chitumbi. When the police came to Mkasanga, he was out in his gardens in the *citeba*. The police finally asked headman Simoni where Aliele Zimba would be found. "I know where he is, he is my grandchild," and the headman lead the police to the *citeba* (garden hut) of Aliele. It was getting evening, and Aliele was inside. Simoni called him out, and Aliele thought that his grandfather was alone. When he came out and saw the Police with him he said: "*Owe!! Mwaiza ne fipondo!* – you came with traitors!" The police then tied him up there and then onto their bicycle with many robes and said they would take him early morning to prison. Then everybody went to sleep around him. But early morning when they woke up they found he was gone, and so was their bicycle. The robes were on the grounds and in the sand they found written the following words: "*Nebo Aliele Zimba, tamwankumanishe!* – you will never keep up with me."

The police was angry, so they arrested Aliele's wife. "You are hiding him!" Again, early morning they found a note: "I am Aliele Zimba. *Tamwankumanishe!* Leave my wife alone. If you want me, just look for me in Chipata in the prison." The police went back to Chipata, and found to their surprise that Aliele Zimba had given himself up to prison on own accords! He led the prison staff to Mkasanga to the pit he had dug, but they found out that most of the goods had been spoiled by rust and water. They kept Aliele for one year in jail. When he came out and went back to Mkasanga, only a short time passed and a *ng'anga* came to cleanse the village. He was called Kamuchimba. He took away all the *fishimba* (charms) of Aliele. The only thing left now were his dreams and hunting skills.

Such stories fill people with pride rather than disgust. Yes, Aliele Zimba was a *mfwiti*, but people were also proud that their fellow villager knew more than the Indians, Europeans and the Police together! But in spite of all his superior charms and magic, he was caught in the end because he was also enmeshed in the local net of in-laws, family, wife and headmen, and as in many stories in the end betrayed by the people he trusted, in this case his grandfather with whom he used to joke, but who could not reconcile the two roles of grandfather and headman, which had to link up with the wheels of state power. Aliele Zimba's slogan *"tamwankumanishe!"* (You cannot reach up to me, you will not get me) captures people's imagination: their strength consists of their knowledge of magic and medicines.

But it is important to note that such medicines need to be controlled, and that they are allowed only in certain categories. Different parts of the valley are known for different types of medicines, and what may be legitimate in one part may not be in another. Here a story that was much talked about in Masumba and Nsefu (I heard it in February 2006):

During the rainy season, some Wiza people were changing chicken in Nsefu against flour (*unga*). One woman took two chicken, but gave *unga* only for one chicken; the other chicken she was hiding, pretending that she got only one. An argument arose, and the Wiza people left. A week later a lightning struck the family: the husband and a child were thrown away by the lightening, yet survived, but the woman who had stolen the chicken was dead on the spot.

I heard different comments. Many people in Nsefu told me it was right to kill the woman, because she had stolen. But nevertheless it was wrong, because they did not want *tulumba* (the magic of calling lightening) in Nsefu. "We don't know how to call down lightning, but the Bisa know. We don't want lightning of the Bisa here in Nsefu." Chief Nsefu was said to have made an appeal to the Bisa to leave his country: their types of witchcraft did not belong here. Then I met Bisa from Mwanya, also selling chicken in Nsefu, and asked them about this story. "Those people were not from Mwanya, but from Nabwalya", they said. "We also fear those people from Nabwalya for their *tulumba*."

Especially with the penetration of the cash economy people fear that medicines turn more and more into witchcraft. A group of elders in Mwape put it this way: "Today there is money, and people just buy medicines anywhere. Even a child may buy a charm to kill his parents. There is no control any longer."

With a general awareness that witchcraft in the valley is growing out of hands and out of control, and with the dramatic increase of sickness and death in the valley, everybody takes part in the discernment process of witchcraft, including the Christians.

Here an example from Bisa territory in the valley: the young and active chairman of the church council fell very sick while I was there in July 2005; I brought him to the next clinic, twenty kilometres away, where he died. It was a sudden death also for me, because I had been the whole week with him, and he had been organising things very well and seemed o.k. To make things still worse, the very day after his death also his lastborn child died. They were buried together. In October I came back to the same village to visit the family. It happened to be just the day when his wife, his sister and other family members were going to the chief where they had been summoned by a neighbouring headman whom they had accused of witchcraft. Here the events as narrated by the deceased man's sister:

We did not suspect witchcraft, but when we buried Jacob[113] and
came back from the grave, the headman ... was washing himself
right there at our funeral house. Why did he wash himself at
our house if he did not kill Jacob? The next week we found
inongo (rests of clay pots) at the grave. We also saw signs at our
house that medicines had been sprinkled all around at night.
He wanted obviously that the *cibanda* [shade of the dead person
pursuing the killer] should come back to us and be quiet. Then
we heard from his family and friends that he had started to
dream every night, and even during the day whenever he was
just closing his eyes. People heard him talk in his dreams:
"Jacob, go away from me! Jacob, go away from me!" Then so-
and-so told us that he was warned by the headman, "you better
fear me! Do you not know that I kill not one by one, but two by
two?"

In the old *mwambo* of the Bisa, people washed before they reached the
village when coming from the grave, so as not to pollute the village,
because the *chiwanda* of the dead is linked to the soil of his grave.
Today the family and the *anungwe* [joking clan] involved in the burial
wash when they have come back; but there is sometimes uncertainty.
That the headman – neither a family member, nor of the *anungwe* –
removed his shirt and washed at the funeral house came to be
interpreted that he wanted the *chiwanda* to stay at the funeral house.
Why? A *chiwanda* always clings to his murderer, but leaving the soil at
the funeral house brings back the *chiwanda* to where it belongs and
"where it can go to rest" – to his own family. But it did not work, and
the *chiwanda* started haunting him, so one night he went back to the
grave with medicines and then sprinkled these medicines around the
house of Jacob's family, to return the *chiwanda* to its family and make
it rest. After some more rumours here and there the sister of Jacob
started to announce publicly that this headman had killed Jacob and
his child. The headman in turn bought a court summon to the chief
with the charge of defamation of character.

I asked other Catholics about the events. Everybody knew what was
going on, but all had different stories and different explanation, some

even gave different names of the people involved. The next day his sister came back, and I asked how the case went at the chief's court.

> We won the case. The headman was asked: "Is it true that you had a fight with Jacob at the beer, and that Jacob beat you at the beer with his fist?" – "Yes, this was true." – "Did Jacob not ask for reconciliation the following day?" – "Yes he did." – "Did you forgive him with all your heart?" – No, he had not forgiven him. Then the witnesses were called in who said that the headman had boasted to kill people two by two. The case ended that the chief reprimanded the headman: "You should have brought the case to me when Jacob beat you. But you didn't. And see what happened –you killed two people, including an innocent child!'"

"So what will happen now?" I asked.

"Nothing," his sister answered, "the chief said that Jacob was a Christian leader and that his funeral should not be dragged into pagan custom."

"You did not ask for compensation?" I asked.

"No, the case is finished now."

"But why did you go all this way?"

"Because he killed my brother."

The next day I left, and I don't know how the case went on. I knew that the grief of the family of Jacob was very, very strong, and that the family would take a long time to come over it. Jacob had been the only man to have stayed with his mother and his sister back in the village; he had been the only man of the family who was supporting them. A male child was born the very month of Jacob's death, and he was called Jacob. His children now are taken care of by his sister rather than their mother, who married again into another family.

Witchcraft touches the innermost soul, issues of death, and dreams. In the above example it also touched the alleged lack of forgiveness (the reason for the headman's alleged witchcraft) – it was said that he had publicly admitted not to have forgiven Jacob. The Pentecostal churches acknowledge actively the presence of witchcraft and offer their members prayers for protection. The Zion churches go a step further: Their leaders are *ng'anga* themselves, who combat the powers of the *afwiti* with the powers given by their *mizimu* that come from God himself. They proactively discern where a sickness comes from. The Catholic Church has little part in the discernment process that deals with death and sickness, and even with forgiveness. Priests are sometimes seen as blind referees on the football pitch.

VIWANDA (SPIRITS OF THE DEAD)

In Mwanya, one old woman and her family asked me for prayers for "*kulalika chiwanda*" (putting to rest a *chiwanda*, the shade of a dead person), and she gave me this explanation:

> Everything was normal and we were living well, until my uncle (*ba yama*) died. We knew he had died of *nsima*[114] [death of a man attributed to the adultery of his wife.] At first, everything was o.k. But then one afternoon his wife (the widow) came. She knelt down from afar and greeted me, but we did not speak to each other. Then she left. The next morning when I woke up, I found before my doorstep many roots, and I swept them away. From then onwards, the *chiwanda* came every day. It enters the house like a lightning, and first moves around until it enters me and gives me terrible pain. I cannot sleep in the house any longer. And not only I have the *chiwanda*, also four of my children have it now. It is so terrible. When I was in the Chililabombwe, I saw that the Catholics have a very powerful rite for *kulalika chiwanda* (to make a *chiwanda* rest). That is why I called for a priest.

As in the story of Jacob above, also in this story the *chiwanda* followed the causer of death (the wife), but she managed, by means of using illegitimate medicines, to bring the *chiwanda* back onto his own family, where he belongs. But, I was told, she did not manage fully. The accused woman is said to have become very restless and no longer has a home. "She is now in Lundazi, but she just moves around everywhere without rest, three months at one relative and three months at another relative. She even went to Lusaka."

Ziwanda, vibanda or *fibanda* (singular: *cibanda* or *chiwanda*) usually refer to the spirits of the dead. In the quasi patrilineal north of the valley, the *ziwanda* seemed to me less of an issue than in the south. When I asked in Chasera whether *viwanda* (*fibanda*) were an issue, somebody said: *"kuno ifibanda filatuteka"* (we here are ruled by the *fibanda,* or by the fear in *fibanda*). In Lumimba, Chikowa and Minga parishes, I was given examples of people who became mad because they had picked up a *chiwanda* by engaging in sexual intercourse with a widow/ widower before she/he had been properly cleansed by the dead spouse's family.

Nowhere in the valley is the *chiwanda* a metaphysical concept on what happens to life after death; I found nobody in the valley who could give a coherent definition (say in clear distinction to *mizimu*), nor do people look for such a definition. Verbally, the Nsenga, Kunda and Bisa distinguish *viwanda* from *mizimu/mipashi*. Many Senga, in contrast, told me that *viwanda* and *mizimu* are one and the same thing. The *mzimu* can have a very positive connotation while the *chiwanda* is always a negative phenomenon. Only some types of witches manage to make good use of the power of the *viwanda,* and tap into the unseen world through utensils taken from the realm of the dead (graveyard, places of suicide, etc.) In some meetings, people referred to the *mzimu* as the spirit of a good person, and to the *chiwanda* as the spirit of a bad person. But in practice, such a crude distinction hardly works. In all meetings people confirmed that any dead person, and be it a saint or a hero, will be a *chiwanda* to his spouse, however much they loved each other, even in the best possible of marriages. The wife even of a saint needs to be cleansed from the *chiwanda* if she does not remarry within the same family.

Instead of drawing a distinction in terms of "good and bad" (a *mzimu* can be beneficial, while a *chiwanda* is a negative and destructive power), one can also draw a distinction in terms of a person's relation towards the matri-lineage of the deceased. What is a *mzimu* to the family member of the dead is a *chiwanda* to the outsider, and the spouse always remains an outsider to the matri-lineage. It is only from here that the attributes of positive or negative, good or bad, come in: for the family the dead is often a positive force (*mzimu*), and it will be given to the next born child, and it can be appeased through offerings of beer if need be. (Exceptions are death of a witch and death through suicide: both remain of negative influence to the own family from whom they have cut themselves off through their actions.) *Viwanda* are passed on through sexual intercourse. The dead usually do not harm a relative, and therefore after death there is no cleansing of the remaining spouse if he/she remarries in the same family. But the dead clings to non-members (like the spouse) as a *chiwanda,* as a foreign object, that cannot be appeased but that must be got rid of.

But again, even such a good definition that has an inert logic finds its limits. In the example given above, the good woman was haunted seemingly by the shade of her maternal uncle. And in the past whole villages were sometimes moving away on the occasion of death "because of the *chiwanda*", which indicates that the dead were more of a negative rather than positive force even to their close relatives. The *chibanda* is not a theoretical object, but discernment takes place when things happen, when a person becomes mad, or sick. Still, the argument of relation of the dead to the matri-lineage made much sense to me. The own family remains the point of reference when dealing with the dead. At other times, the chiwanda is understood to be an abstract negative spiritual force, somehow attached to the realm of the dead, which – through magic and witchcraft – became isolated from a concrete relationship and now causes havoc at random, even to relatives.

The *viwanda* show that unions don't just break with death and that families remain bound to each other beyond death, until they all take part in some formal rite. To become married to each other was not an individual affair of a man and his beloved woman, but an affair of two families who negotiated over many months, and years, the marriage of their children. A relationship developed not only between two individuals but also between their wider respective families. This relationship becomes ambivalent after the death of one of the spouses, but it does not just fall apart. To be with a *chiwanda* means to stay in dependency of the kin of the dead; only they can make it "go to sleep". But also old *milandu* (cases) may come back on the table, and the remaining spouse has to answer for them. In the valley, cleansing can be demanded in court, but then the *milandu* that contributed to the refusal will also be brought up. The cleansing from the *chiwanda* prevents the widower/widow from walking away from the family of the spouse before clearing outstanding issues about the relationship with the in-laws, domestic disputes and how the spouse was cared for in times of sickness. "If we see the dead was not shaven, then we also know they did not go on well together." In such a case, the cleansing rites, the *kususula,* will be delayed, or fines may be asked for. Total dependency on the family of the late spouse sanctifies among the Bisa also property grabbing.

We find a different situation in the Senga north, who, though officially stressing bi-lineal descent and keeping some matrilineal succession rites, have in many ways *de-facto* become patrilineal since the introduction of high marriage payments, starting with the end of the 1930s. The *chiwanda* here can hardly remain a concern strictly of the matri-lineage. The rituals of freeing the person from the old union and from the family of the spouse (*kususula*) are performed also in the north, and also here a number of people speak explicitly of *kutaya chiwanda* (getting rid of the spirit of the dead) through these rituals, but it seems to be less of an issue. In Chikwa, during a meeting of elders, people contrasted their believes with the Bemba up the plateau and the Bisa down in the valley:

> Here they don't become mad if they sleep with a person who did not go through the *kususula,* nor do they have much fear of *viwanda,* except for issues related to the grave yards. But to marry or sleep with a person prior to the *kususula* is a big *mlandu* (case) in court that calls for high fines to be paid to the dead person's family. The *kususula* is delayed when the wife dies before the *cimalo* (bride wealth) had been paid in full.

The *cimalo* being high among the Senga is often paid only bit by bit. In a way, the courts have taken over the functions of the *chiwanda*: they prevent a person walking away from his in-laws before outstanding issues (debts) have been settled. In the north, once the wife has been fully "bought", her family remains with few tangible rights over her. This pertains also to her soul, of which the *chiwanda* is an aspect. In the south, however, the *chiwanda* shows dramatically that membership to the matri-lineage always overrides marriages, until death.

Throughout the southern valley, people confirmed in meetings that the *chiwanda* of a dead spouse can only be made to rest by his own kin. Neither Jesus, nor any church, is seen to have this power. Only outstanding witches with a lot of experience in their sinister trade can (somehow) handle and tap into the powers of the realm of the dead with the aim of making these powers work for their selfish interests against the benefits of the community. In that sense, Christianity has shaped very little the understanding of death in the valley.

MASHAWE, MIZIMU, NGULU, VIMBUZA AND FUFUMI

In Chitumbi (Nyimba parish), I asked naively after Sunday mass people with *mashawe* to stay behind to talk with me about their *mashawe*. *Mashawe* are seen as spirits with a specific personality and name, not related directly to the realm of the dead, but to natural phenomena or past (extinct) peoples, or foreign tribes. I expected two or three women to come forward which would give me an opportunity to inquire more about *mashawe*. What happened instead was that one third of all women who attended Sunday mass said they had *mashawe,* not counting those who had *mashawe* in an earlier phase of their lives. It took not only the whole afternoon to listen to their stories and also to their dreams, but also the next three days myself and Brother Vinod were kept busy listening to more and more people coming with *mashawe*. Also in other villages, I was approached to pray for people with *mashawe,* and I also met one very sick woman who went the whole way from the valley to meet archbishop Milingo when he came in September 2005 on a visit to Chipata Diocese, but she was too late because of her sickness.

Again it is futile to ask about some metaphysical and theoretical explanations of the *mashawe*. In the south, people distinguish the water spirits from those of the dry land, and *mashawe* that stay within a family from those that are picked up by anybody, but the distinctive patterns seem to be disappearing more and more. A good number of European and Indian spirits have long appeared in the valley. Through Pentecostal influence (echoed also by the Catholic Charismatic Renewal Movement) *mashawe* are identified now more and more with evil spirits, with demons or with Satan. But then we have also the Biblical *mizimu* of the Zion churches, who come straight from God. In the north, people speak of different *vimbuza*, *fufumi* and *mizimu* with their distinctive dances or types of *mangwanda* (customs and bells), and different *ng'anga*. But also here the distinctions become obscure.

It seems to be especially women who are favoured by the *mashawe* spirits. Different reasons were given for this by men: "women believe everything, men are more sceptical;" – "women spend the whole day pounding maize where they are thinking over such matters"; – "women want to attract more attention (*vilele*)". But apart from such comments, women are more often seen as the passive victims of *mashawe*, who suffer from them and want to get rid of them. Only a small percentage of women who are sick with *mashawe* come to occupy the more active role of being used by their spirits to become healers and diviners, *ng'anga*, though other women with *mashawe* had, at least for short intervals of time, embarked in the task of collecting medicines from the bush under the command of their *mashawe*, without however going the full way of becoming a *ng'anga*. The female *ng'anga* whom I interviewed were all with the Zion church. For men this is very different: few men become sick with *mashawe* or *mizimu*, but the few are then much more inclined to go the whole way and become healers and diviners. Most of the male *ng'anga* whom I interviewed said they had received their vocation through sickness; they had been in hospitals to no avail, and were finally dramatically cured by a *ng'anga* with whom they then stayed some time until they were fully cured. Their sicknesses had been attributed to *mashawe* or *mizimu* (the latter then nearly all entered a Zion church or founded one themselves), and they had learned how to deal with their *mashawe* through dancing and dreams. In contrast, two male *ng'anga* with mashawe whom I interviewed were not initiated through sickness but by their fathers. From childhood on, they were asked to collect medicines on behalf of their fathers and discovered at a later moment in life that they had *mashawe* themselves.

Most of the women suffering from *mashawe* whom I came across in the valley, however, never took the road of becoming *ng'anga*. Instead, they remained in the passive role as victims of these spirits who had come without asking permission and they wanted to get rid of them. The stories of those I interviewed in the valley (more than 50) contained many similarities: Some were not able to bear children, other *mashawe* came just at the point of marriage, or when the second or third child was born (coinciding with a loss of freedom?), or at the *chinamwali,* or in school. One may be inclined to look at situations of stress and tension as catalyst for some *mashawe,* but I would not dare to say that this applied to all the people I interviewed. For one woman, I suspected that the *mashawe* provided a convenient reason for not having sex with her husband who comes home day after day completely drunk, and she also did not seem very eager to get rid of her *mashawe* herself. But the stories throughout the valley were so many, the sicknesses and personal situations that accompanied them so diverse, that we do not do justice to the *mashawe* with any simplistic answer or just saying it is stress. People themselves go through discernment by looking at their patterns of regular dreams of snakes and animals, *azungu* (white people) in robes, or of drumming and dancing, or their reactions to cat-fish and other foods that are usually forbidden by the *mashawe.* People also distinguish fake from real *mashawe,* and for most women I interviewed I had little doubt that their experiences were genuine and not faked: they believed themselves to be befallen by *mashawe.* This is not to exclude, of course, that people's convulsions and reaction, while in trance, are also socially conditioned and that they are triggered by socially accepted standard situations (for example when laying on hands).

Every sickness needs a name if we are to cope with it. Nothing is more terrifying than a serious sickness without a name. To name a sickness is as important for the community as it is for the individual sufferer; a name of a sickness has a social function. On the medicinal level, there are serious limits to what a clinic, poorly equipped and staffed, can offer in the valley. Research furthermore has shown in other African countries that the effectivity of clinics is limited in regions with a low level of basic school education; studies suggest that a minimum of six to seven years at school is required for a person to understand somehow what the clinical understanding of sickness is about and what not; traditional and clinical ways of looking at concepts of sickness and treatment are very different from each other. There are many reason why people in the valley are looking into the traditional setup to name and approach sicknesses. Making sense out of a sickness implies that this can be communicated to and eventually be shared by the community, and therefore it has to take place within those concepts that are shared by the community. *Mashawe,* witchcraft, *mizimu, viwanda,* and the *makolo* are such shared concepts.

When a sickness is ambivalent and the clinic has failed, the families of the sick have a number of possible alternatives as explanations. Maybe the sickness is accompanied by dreams of snakes. Such dreams are common for the *mashawe* but the same dreams can also be signs of witchcraft. Or they may be caused by a *chiwanda.* Or maybe the sickness was caused by adultery of the spouse. Similar symptoms give rise to multiple possibilities of explanation. Though many people, when they are asked, affirm that these alternatives can in principle be distinguished by the specialists by differences in symptoms and histories of the sicknesses, in praxis there are no fixed borders and clear-cut distinctions, and there is room for different interpretations. Many of the people I interviewed had interpreted their sickness at different times in different terms.

Occasions of sickness become often religious experiences, for the sufferer but even for the wider community. By interviewing women with *mashawe* one finds often very deep religious experiences and spiritualities. To attribute a sickness to *mashawe* sends a very important message to the community: "This sickness did not come from witchcraft. We are not looking for a guilty party." *Mashawe* are spirits that are picked up accidentally; to have *mashawe* takes away the association with personal guilt. But *mashawe* also open up a positive understanding of sickness: *mashawe* are ambivalent; they start as foreign, unknown spirits that make people sick, but when people come to terms with them and discern their names, they achieve a positive function for the community. On one hand, the *mashawe* are intrinsically erratic and difficult to control, and we find also in our patients such elements of unpredictability and changing moods. Nevertheless many women whom I interviewed seemed to have outstanding personalities; they seemed to have gained much inner strength through their own inner struggles with the *mashawe*. In some prayer centres, I made a test: I looked out for the women in the church council and lay movements who looked active, dedicated, outspoken and courageous, and I asked them whether they had had *mashawe* at some point in their lives. It came as no surprise to me that many of them had. *Mashawe* and sickness often make people open to dimensions of life that remain closed to many of us who are healthy.

There was a time in the valley when people with *mashawe* were highly respected. "The chiefs listened to them a lot." *Mashawe* were not evil, though they were ambivalent. They could become a valuable resource for the community, when the befallen person accepted the relationship with the spirit and managed (though never fully!) to appease it. Today they are tolerated, but mostly smiled at. The wider framework of people has changed. The very people with *mashawe* themselves are often lost in regards to the meaning of their experiences and how to deal with what is going on within them. Two churches are outstanding in the valley in regards to their healing ministries: the Pentecostals and the Zion churches. They came to shape the understanding of *mashawe* in the valley, but in very different directions. As the *mashawe* are seen to be demons in the Pentecostal churches, they are evil in themselves. Many Catholics have taken over this understanding. The Zion churches distinguish *mizimu* from *mashawe*: the latter can be exorcised, the former cannot. They are not much concerned with *mashawe*, but with *mizimu* who come from God himself. They have Biblical names (Lazaro, Jobo, Luka, Mariko, Paulo, etc.) and, though they make people sick in their initial coming, this sickness is often the beginning of a vocation to become a prophet, a *ng'anga,* or a "searcher", and it is a vocation that in the Zion church must be exercised for the benefit of the community and not for personal gain. During the services in the Zion churches that I attended, those possessed with *mizimu* were consulted by a number of outsiders like ordinary *ng'anga* would do, but they used the Bible (scattered verses) in their divinations. Catholics with *mashawe* in general do go to the Pentecostals or the Zion churches to get answers that they can relate to. But they are also brought closer to our own church, when they find someone with a listening ear.

BASIC CHRISTIAN THEOLOGY OF PEOPLE IN THE VALLEY

The mainstream Churches (CCAP, Catholics, Anglican, and RCZ) have now a presence in the valley of over a hundred years. All of them have experienced great difficulties in the valley, and contrast the *malambo* (valley) with the *mtunda* (plateau), where things are easier and where they had more tangible successes. However it is important to stress that all the four mainstream Churches, in spite of these difficulties, have maintained their presence in the valley, built up spheres of influence, and became Churches into which many people have been born; they have developed roots. As such, people contrast them with the new Churches that came only *manje manje* (recently): They attract many people, but, when the initial enthusiasm has faded or when a marriage has broken, people may go back to their old Churches in which they grew up. In spite of the difficulties that the mainstream churches have met in the valley, they have become part of the valley, part of its landmarks, physically and spiritually. When the Lumpa church swept through the valley, many switched sides (whole villages), but nevertheless many others kept their Church alliances throughout the difficulties, which entailed many personal sacrifices. When the enthusiasm of Lumpa weaned, already some years before the final clashes, many came back to their old religion.

Nevertheless, to be a church member is not necessarily a sign of deep faith. People may refer often to the Bible without ever having read a page in it. Christianity today is the respected suit that one wears for official life. Church membership may provide a good funeral at the time of death in the family: plenty of people, a choir, many people sleeping at one's home, and maybe somebody respectable saying some words. Many mentioned to me that they had left the Church because of feeling neglected in times of death; too few people from the church had turned up or none at all, and their expectations had not been fulfilled. Another pull factor is the advantage of church membership when travelling. When going to the towns, such membership helps to find hospitality and to link into an existing network. A number of women have established their trading networks through women church groups. Traditional religion cannot really play this role for people in the valley. Their *makolo* are too local and of no relevance in Lusaka. In that sense, today you "have to" be a Christian. Christianity is the religion today that is taken for granted. In a meeting with elders in Mwape (Minga Parish), somebody put it this way:

> There is a time for everything. Our ancestors prayed under the *msoro*, and there were other times when they went to people with *mashawe*. Today we are all Christians. Everything comes with its own *nyengo* (season).

Now is the season of Christianity. And tomorrow? It could be anything else, because there is a season for everything; but today, Zambia happens to be a Christian nation, that is how it is. To which specific Church one goes may for many people be of little importance; one is as good as the other. In Sonkho (Nyimba Parish), I and Brother Vinod gathered in the Baptist church which was full with former Catholics. "Why did you leave us and go to the Baptists?" I asked, expecting some profound answers. "Because it was new!" they said. That was all. In Chasera (Lumimba Parish), a headman summarised the attitude of many when he explained his religious affiliation:

> I was in the RCZ, but now I am a Muslim, because I did not agree with what the RCZ were saying. And if I will not agree anymore with what the Muslims are saying, I will go to another Church. There is only one God.

Catholic, Anglican, Reformed Church of Zambia, Church of Central African Prebyterians, Chipangano, African National Church, BiGoCA, Seventh Day Adventists, DTM, New Apostolic Church, Church of Christ, Church of God, the various Pentecostals, Jehovah's Witnesses, Baptists, Zion, and even Islam, they are all there in the valley and they are by many people seen as more or less one and the same, as there is only one God. On the question why there were so many churches in the valley, people mentioned a strife for leadership positions (more churches means more *mipando,* more leadership positions), local quarrels and different styles of singing. Competition between the churches has contributed towards a certain relativism. People embrace Christianity as the official religion of today, but at the same time there is a certain apprehension to commit oneself fully to any single church. One person in Kalasa (Lumimba Parish) put it this way:

> In the CCAP people are not allowed to drink, but they do drink because the Catholics are allowed. The Catholics also marry a second wife, because the Chipangano are allowed. The Chipangano also have *mizimu* because the Zion are allowed to have *mizimu.*

What are the main tenants of Christian theology in the valley? How is Christianity envisaged? Much centres on very few issues: Adam, Satan, and the last judgement. To put it in a nutshell: God made the earth with many astonishing and wondrous things and he did a very good job, and people praise him for that in their songs. But Adam messed it all up, with the help of the devil, and he was expelled from the presence of God and from paradise. God then cursed the soil, and since then we have the draughts and the floods, sicknesses, death, and hunger, a condition that is enhanced also by our own sins. But not only the soil has been cursed; some people add that God must also have cursed us humans. "If we are not cursed, then why do we die?" All our misery is because of Adam.

A second cluster has to do with Satan. This world has fallen prey to the rule of Satan. We drink, smoke marijuana, and sleep with women not our wives, because of Satan. Satan especially is in charge of all the witchcraft going on. And for many, when speaking from within the Christian rhetoric, anything that has to do with *chikunja* (paganism, traditional beliefs not incorporated in Christianity) comes also from Satan. Satan is bad, but in this present world one has somehow to accommodate with Satan. Jesus and some saints did not follow Satan, but they are far removed, and such people certainly cannot be found in the valley. People's relationship with Satan is a little bit like to a chief: they may not like their chief, but they have to accommodate with him. "Yes, we renounce Satan wholeheartedly in church, but this commitment cannot be sustained very long. As soon as we leave the church we are back in the world." A number of polygamist men told me that they married a second wife because of the way of Satan. "What can you do?"

A third cluster of theology in the valley centres on the last judgement. One of the few known Bible passages is the story of Noah, repeated at many funerals. All who follow Satan and his witchcraft, all drunkards and adulterers, and those involved in pagan or traditional (non-Christian) rites, will all be sent to hell in the last judgement. But the boat of Noah will save all those who go to church and have been baptised. This boat is in a way a foreign boat, with foreign rules and a foreign captain, but as long as you somehow catch this boat in the end, you are o.k. In fact, there are several boats around as there are many churches, and not all the rules on board need to be followed. The ship of the Roman Catholics has strong rules about marriage, but it were the "Romans" after all who killed Christ (this point is still strong in the north of the valley after Lenshina), so our rules should be taken with a pinch of salt. The entrance fee for going through the front door is the annual church tax. But why entering through the front gate? It is the last option when all other means have failed. As long as you manage to climb in the end on any boat from any side, you will be saved. And what about Christ? He does not really figure much in symbols nor in songs. God is the creator. Christ will come back and he is the final judge. In a few occasions he is also here on earth, especially when casting out some *mashawe* spirits. But he is not really overworked. In a nutshell this is what many people in the valley know of the Christian faith; it has become an official language for official occasion. It may be a male narrative; I rarely heard women spelling out theological arguments, but I heard many men, also those who don't pray, rationalising about theology and their African place in it, and also asking theological questions.

The easiness with which Christianity today is accepted as official discourse maybe shows that the valley is integrating stronger into wider Zambia than it was before. During the last ten years the valley has changed enormously; the spiritual world is also changing, and people look for orientation. Today there is definitely a chance for a new start.

A girl passing through the chinamwali ceremony (Chitungulu)

A hunter calling upon his ancestors by pouring out flour under an old tree, before embarking on a hunting expedition

A name-changing ceremony at Kalasa. The lineage of the child Emely gathered and called upon the ancestors to give her a new name (Ester).

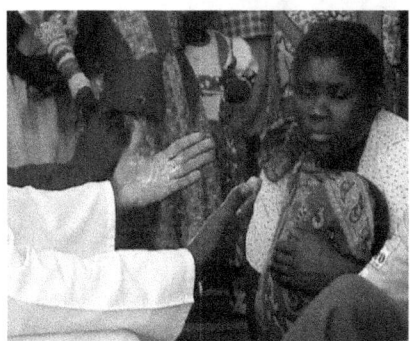

Dealing with witchcraft.
Doctor Beruka (Chitungulu) during a healing session, discerning the causes
of sickness

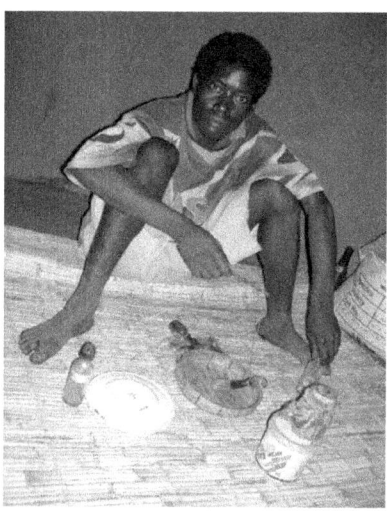

Above: Doctor Pyerani (Malama/Kambombo) shows a charm that he claims to have found in the village cleansing ceremony.

Below: Doctor Mwinko in Manga during a divination.

The need for protective medicines, especially for children

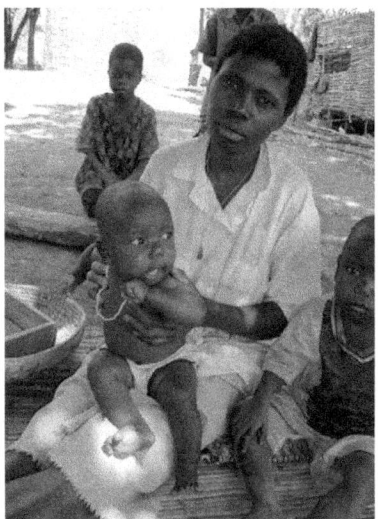

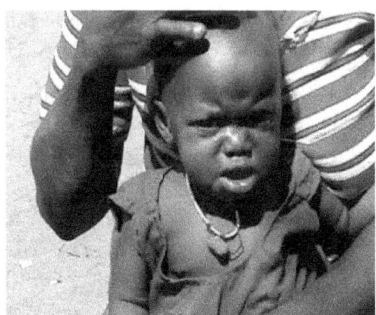

10.

Christian initiatives in the valley

The acceptance of any religion and people's identification with it depends on the agency of people in appropriating it, which is based on their own initiatives that they can take. In this chapter, I look at some exemplary initiatives, both within and outside the mainstream Churches. It is needless to say that they are not exclusive.

THE BEGINNINGS OF THE ANGLICAN CHURCH IN MSORO.

According to the narratives of Anglicans in Msoro,[115] the church started as an initiative of a local Kunda headman who had come across a school run by the Dutch Reformed Church to the West of Msoro at the beginning of the 20th century, and who approached a white settler to help him write a letter to request the coming of missionaries to his village. The British settler did not write to the Dutch Reformed Church, but requested help from the Anglicans with whom he felt more at ease. A priest from Nyasaland (one of the very first African clergy), Rev. Leonard Mattiya Kamungu, the first Chewa priest of the Anglican Diocese of Nyasaland, was entrusted with the task to look for a suitable place between the areas of the Dutch Reformed Church and the Prebyterians in the North. He arrived the beginning of 1911. Already a month later he had "crowds of people of all ages" under instruction.[116] The farm building that the British settler had put under Anglican disposal proved already too small, and Kamungu with his new converts built (with the words of bishop Hine) "a magnificent building of great length, breadth and height."[117] In 1912, nearly 200 people had been admitted into the catechumenate. Kamungu travelled a lot, and his preaching bore fruit in many places, so that it proved difficult to provide the new schools with adequate teachers from Nyasaland.[118] Kamungu saw the first baptisms during his second year. After a ministry of less than two years, he died early 1913, a saintly man (some say he was poisoned, others that he died of sickness), leaving behind a crowd of enthusiastic Christians. When Weller did his research on Rev. Kamungu more than 50 years after his death, people still remembered his instructions about brotherly love, the warnings against witchcraft, and the appeals to serve Jesus Christ;[119] his preaching was understood and made sense to many people of Msoro. I too was guided to his grave where he is buried. Rev. Kamungu is still regarded as a saint of the valley. Weller describes how the Anglican Church after Kamungu experienced difficulties, especially when decisions were imposed on the early Christians without much dialogue. Rev Kamungu, in contrast, is remembered by the local Anglican community as *their* priest who showed them that the Christian faith could have African leadership.

THE WATCHTOWER MOVEMENT AND THE JEHOVAH WITNESSES

In the 1920s, the south of the valley (Akunda, but also the Ansenga) had witnessed initiatives of the Watchtower movement, unsolicited by Western missionaries, in which adherents were even ready to die.[120] In the old mission diaries the Watchtower movement was perceived as a misguided anti-colonial revolt of fanatics, but in modern literature such endeavours are sometimes valued as the first organised initiatives of the independence struggle against foreign, colonial rule.[121] The colonial concern in repressing the Watchtower movement (merging in this regard with the concerns of the mainstream Churches) obviously was not religious but political, and the resilience of the Watchtowers has religious as well as political dimensions. But the line between religion and politics was and is not easily drawn in the valley.[122]

Today the Watchtower movement has transformed itself into an established but small Church in the valley, the Jehovah Witnesses. I did not receive much response to my questions on its beginnings in the valley, not even from Jehovah Witnesses themselves. There may be in fact little link between the independent Watchtowers of the past and modern Jehovah Witnesses. The independent Watchtower movements had been founded by returning miners from South Africa and Katanga who had been in contact abroad with local forms of the Watchtower and Bible Tract Society. They had been outlawed by the government because of their strong anti-colonial reactions and the riots which they had instigated in the Northern Province at the end of World War I. Also Tomo Nyirenda, the founder of the Mwana Lesa movement in Serenje who was later hanged for killing over a hundred "witches" with his baptisms, had started his career as an independent Watchtower.

The diary of Minga, with entries especially from 1924 onwards, contain many referents to the Watchtowers, known as the "Ethiopian sect", but especially as the *Mpatuko*; whole villages had gone over to them, and the missionaries started to experience hostility of the local population that were sympathetic to their cause. "Africa to the Africans" was a Watchtower slogan, and the religion of the White Fathers was pictured as a colonial and oppressive religion, a "foreign devil" from which the valley needed to be freed.[123] The Watchtowers advocated total disobedience to the colonial regime and its representatives which included the chiefs, and the mission schools, and called for all European missionaries to leave the country. From 1924 onwards the White Fathers of Minga made a number of requests to the government to do more to outlaw the movement, but they felt that their appeals were not given due attention. Some years later, however, the colonial regime pursued more active steps to contain Watchtower preaching; by then they had found out that the Watchtower movement especially among the Kunda was questioning the authority of the chiefs, on whom the colonial state depended during the policies of indirect rule. Already without the Watchtowers, the colonial government had had in the valley a fair share of difficulties to rule through the chiefs, and the government found it difficult to discuss issues with the valley chiefs that concerned a wider and broader level beyond village disputes and issues of gardens.[124] They saw this as a consequence of the "tribes" in the valley not forming cohesive bodies.

But now, the Watchtower preaching furthermore actively undermined the authority of the chiefs: for them, chiefs were but puppets of the colonial regime to foster colonial interests. Chief Mnkhanya and other Kunda chiefs were openly defied and disobeyed by sections of the population, and their orders were often simply ignored, while chief Sefu was praised by the administration for actively putting down the Watchtower threat.[125] In 1928 there were riots in the valley.

The Watchtowers of the 1920s were inspired by but not strictly linked to the American based Watchtower and Bible Tract Society. The groups of Watchtowers in Northern Rhodesia did not have a central leadership, and followed often very different teachings; in some parts of Northern Rhodesia, for example, they were known for their practices of wife-sharing,[126] while their American based mother-church had very strict moral codes. In the 1930s, the American Watchtower and Bible Tract Society changed its name and became known as Jehovah Witnesses. In Zambia the Watchtowers became legal only when they allowed themselves to be firmly incorporated into the structures of the Jehovah Witnesses; for this purpose the colonial government had allowed black Jehovah Witnesses from South Africa into the country. Today I found little left in public memory about the early Watchtower groups.

The valley Kunda seemed to have been a centre of the movement according to the District Notebooks, but I got only very few reactions here in my interviews. For the people I interviewed it seemed a very distant event. In Lumimba, Chitungulu, Chiweza and Kazembe, people mentioned that the Watchtower influence had come from Jumbe in the late 1920s or early 1930s. Well known figures were Makina Banda (in other villages known as Makina Nguluwe), based in Zokwe, Yobo Nguluwe, James and Mark Sakala (returnees from South Africa). There were no Watchtower church buildings; instead, wandering preachers gathered people together under mango trees. Up in the north (Chama) people mentioned little influence, though later in the 1940s some headmen (and their villages?) became Jehovah Witnesses (mentioned were Kabende and Mulumbu).

It has been said elsewhere that the Watchtowers attracted especially returning miners.[127] They were used to life of the towns, they brought new skills into the villages and sometimes also capital. It has been argued that such returning miners were often ill-at-ease with being swallowed up by their extended families and by the authority of the rural chiefs and his patrons whom they considered belonging properly to a past age. The Jehovah Witnesses strongly stress the nuclear family and a cut of ties with the extended family who are non-members; such they could provide returning miners with a support group, with an alternative ideology that positively acknowledged the skills and crafts of its members (Jehovah Witnesses according to their belief will have to build up the Paradise on earth for which such new skills are needed), and with a good reason not to be swallowed up by the rural authorities.

Today the Jehovah Witnesses have a steady presence in the valley, but it is still a small church. Their insistence on cutting ties with the extended family, and especially their policy at funerals (nobody of the extended family nor of the wider community is allowed to sleep at the funeral house; this is left to the nuclear family alone) has made it difficult for the Jehovah Witnesses to become a popular Church in the valley. To cut links with wider kin is only possible for the wealthier section of the population. But in spite of their low numbers they have a big impact in the valley due to an abundance of literature that appeals to people and due to their reputation of no compromise in regards to any issue that relates to "pagan" customs.

THE LUMPA CHURCH

In the 1950s the north of the valley became a stronghold for the Lumpa church of Alice Lenshina. Unaided by external missionaries, ten-thousands of people from the valley were flocking to Chinsali, "because we wanted to see Christ for ourselves",[128] no distances were too far, and the regular contributions for *their* church in kind, labour, and money ("one pence, one pence") made the church completely self-reliant. (Lumpa in Chinsali operated two lorries and built one of the most elaborate cathedrals in Zambia, all from local contributions). The valley population provided generous hospitality to the Lumpa members of Chinsali on their tours through the valley. Some Lumpa members from the Luangwa valley had been in key positions as treasurers of the movement in Chinsali. Within two years after the visions of Alice Lenshina, basically all the north of the valley had become Lumpa. In the final war in the year of independence many followers chose to be killed, march into exile to Congo, or starve to death rather than give up their faith. The rise of the Lumpa Church and the successive events in the valley have religious as well as political overtones. The building of separate villages and the erupting violence between Lumpa, UNIP and the chiefs show the political dimensions and implications of the movement. On the religious level, such events pose discomforting questions (asked by Oger and Hinfelaar) for the mainstream Churches about the *form* of Christianity, whether or not it resonates with people's conceptions, aspirations and life-situations. The main tenants of the church and also its attractions have been described a number of time.[129] The rise, decline and final destruction of Lumpa have been analysed by Andrew Roberts with regards to the political situation at the eve of independence, frustrations in politics at the onset of Federation and the rise of UNIP.[130] Today, the Lumpa Church is long dead in the valley, like embers drowned in water, and nobody is willing to resurrect it. But the war has left scars that are still felt.

In the meetings where I raised the question of "Elenshina", discussions were not always easy, and I felt more distrust in this topic towards me than in regards to other topics. One meeting in Chikwa, for which I had invited elders and village headmen, assisted by the Evangeliser of the CCAP, turned into a discussion between two fractions. Though the atmosphere during the meeting remained good, the evangeliser told me in the aftermath that he had been reprimanded for assisting me asking such questions. All, however, seemed in agreement that things went wrong because of politics – both the politics of the nation to be born and also the politics of the Lumpa elite.[131] About the status of Lenshina people are divided. Many today call her a *mfwiti* (witch) who had very powerful charms.

> Her in-laws wanted to kill her, but she survived – that is when she had her visions. She went to a *ng'anga* in Tanzania from whom she received very powerful magic. People then started to

flock to her, not knowing that they were carrying their own charms and *manga* along, which they handed over to Elenshina; so strong was her magic. Elenshina confused church and witch-finding, real prayers and medicines, and that is why today we still don't know what real prayers are about in the valley.[132]

In this type of narrative we also hear stories of Lenshina's people drinking their urine in the final war, that would make them invulnerable or turn bullets into water, stories which are denied by her supporters.

In the sympathetic type of narrative, in contrast, there is no doubt that Lenshina came from God. They described her Church to me as something marvellous and beautiful – something "*makora comene*", something "very good". They had gone to Chinsali to see God, to see Jesus, and at last they had found *their* Church. They don't know how things did go wrong so badly in the end. It had been something that was good and wonderful, God himself was speaking to Africans, but it got smashed in the wheels of politics and jealousy of the other Churches. Some people whom I interviewed could still sing some of Lenshina's popular songs they had been singing in the past. Some attribute the success of Lenshina in the valley to Lenshina's magic (charms and witchcraft); others interpret her success in terms of God's direct intervention; "God spoke through Lenshina a message that was meant for us." All agree it was destroyed through politics. Most people easily combine both narratives: Lenshina was a *ng'anga* who was sent by God. For a description of the war in Kambombo and Chikwa, see the appendix.

Many Lenshina people who were killed in the massacres in Chama were never buried. The places are avoided, and still today people speak about the remains of bones. The narratives about the events have been shaped by one side only. When the war was over, there were not many people left who could influence the story-telling from Lenshina's side of view. Those who had remained with Lenshina until the end had either died in the final massacres, starved to death on the way to Mokambo (Congo), or remained quiet, or maybe even changed their opinion in the aftermath, while being incorporated into the polity of the victors, Kaunda's independent Zambia. The frontiers between Lumpa and the "others" had been clear-cut; after the full defeat of Lumpa and the tragic acts of revenge and violence that did not spare women and children, there was little room for another type of narrative.[133] It has also been said (Mulenga 1998) that those returning to Chama were harassed well into the early 1970s by a procedure called "*kupelekela*" – which meant that UNIP members accompanied returnees to the bush where they assisted them to commit suicide, under supervision. The report of the official inquiry of the Republic of Zambia mentions that "villagers in Chief Kambombo's area of Lundazi district adopted a very antagonistic attitude towards Lenshina followers. They threatened to kill any strangers in the area."[134]

In our meetings in Chikwa and Chifunda we had former Lumpa members and former UNIP members present. Lumpa was the first Church with which many people in the north of the valley really identified; it was their Church. For once a religious trend was sustained by the valley population; *The Times* wrote at the heights of the conflict that

> Like a bush fire, the word swept through the valley tribes of Senga and Chewa, touching more lightly perhaps their neighbours of the plateau. For once, the valley set the trend and the plateau followed.[135]

When it ended in a disaster, it took more than a decade for people to put again some trust in any Church. "You see, those churches they speak of love, but in the end they all kill each other!" was repeated by many non-church goers. It was not a secret to anyone in the valley that the different Churches did not go on well with each other, and that other Churches did not think it possible that God could speak directly through an African. Most people stayed convinced that they were faring better without any Church. For the next ten years after the Lenshina events (the first decade of independence), no Church had real success in the northern valley; people remained suspicious about churches. "They just bring war."[136]

In the time of Lumpa, many attitudes all over Zambia were still fused together concerning the meaning of religion, politics, and the place of Africa in the Christian World, which became detangled only in subsequent years and through much time, in the Catholic Church for example through the Second Vatican Council. Outside the valley, people's expectations changed both in regards to politics and to a Church. This engagement did not take place in the northern valley. When the Churches picked up again some importance in the valley at the end of the 1970s (now the Chipangano Church multiplied throughout the Lumpa part of the valley), people on the *mtunda*, the plateau, had developed quite different attitudes and were taking things for granted that had never been heard of in the valley.

Hugo Hinfelaar (1994) studied central symbols in the teachings and hymns. He sees a central metaphor of Lenshina's songs in the symbol of light (*lubuto*), where the believers saw themselves as moving towards a wonderful light, long promised, towards God and his child. But to come into the presence of God, they needed to be purified and holy, cleansed from sin. This was done in Lenshina's baptism where witchcraft was renounced and charms handed over. But what was the most fundamental condition of sin and witchcraft? Lenshina never provided a systematic theology, but, according to Hinfelaar's interpretation, many of her symbols and references were taken from the initiation rites and concerned the proper and legitimate sexual relationship between husband and wife, and its intrinsic connection with fire, fertility and seed. Life is seen as a whole, its parts should not be separated, and the centre of life, work, food, the village, offspring, granaries and wealth was the intimate and guarded union of husband and wife, where mediation with the divine took place. Hinfelaar explained:

> Sanctity and wholesome living could only be reached through an undefiled union of husband and wife within a legal marriage.
>
> Lenshina Mulenga showed that by abolishing the taboos concerning Seed, Blood and Fire, the whole network of marital relationships had collapsed and that together with her fellow

women she believed that this was the cause of all chaos created within the families."[137]

Hinfelaar's account fits well with today's stress in the valley on initiation rites. The story of Lenshina: her death, her call from God, her presence in the wonderful light, but then being sent back with a message to preach purification, her relationship with Christ as the perfect husband and brother, expressed in her marriage with Petros her husband, this was a story that many people had taken up as their own journey towards God. It was an African journey, built on the rock of old tradition that reached far into the past, and that was transmitted primarily by the women.

But the marriage bond, central to fulfilled life and contact with the divine, had been eroded in a long process, starting with the coming of centralised chieftaincy, the slave trade, and then the advent of colonialism. In the time of Lenshina, very many young men were away from the village, and the colonial system of labour migration had made it very difficult to live a faithful marriage. In the time of Lenshina, young men tended to leave the valley in the search for work just after having married a girl. The breakdown of the marriages and the resulting chaos, jealousies, hatred, and despair were the most fertile grounds for witchcraft. Women seeking charms to keep their husbands, co-wife against co-wife, men seeking to become rich or powerful on own accords, children being killed by witchcraft to be put into granaries to make the food increase, all of such forms of witchcraft could be described as consequences of isolating the legal union between husband and wife from the other ambitions in life, in short by breaking the taboos in connection with seed, blood, fire and sex. This unity of life was not achieved by going backwards to the past; Lenshina's songs, in Hinfelaar's interpretation, were about moving forward, moving towards the light, crossing over from the old ways of sin and witchcraft to the presence of God – and the ferryman was God's son Jesus Christ, the symbol of the perfect husband – she called him in some songs the *mulongwe* (the weaver-bird), caring for and preparing the nest, a symbol that was again taken from the initiation rites. In another song the properly married were called the sparkling stars in heaven that are guiding the others (also a Bemba initiation symbol). Lenshina refused baptism to all second wives and to polygamists, unless they got rid of the unlawful wives. In this regards Lenshina's success among the Senga was mixed. A number of people commented that many men took up polygamy again after they had come back from Chinsali, but nevertheless they say that no other Church had ever had such a success against polygamy.

A number of former miners told me that, when they came back into the valley after a number of years abroad, they had to go within the very first week to Chinsali, together with their wives. They were not allowed to stay in the village if they would not make this journey. In Chinsali they had to give up their charms (though everybody explained to me that only the others had charms…), were baptised, and some of them were then also married properly; Lumpa was famous for its much embellished marriage ceremonies. The pilgrimage to Lenshina was definitely a way of being reintegrated into the valley, and Hinfelaar argues that life of the village (in contrast to life in the mines) in this new covenant was to be based on marital fidelity. Calmettes (1978) and Binsbergen (1981) showed that it was especially the peasant class (who was losing out to the returning miners) that provided the cornerstone of Lenshina's followers. Traditional networks of kin were undermined by returning miners who settled as a new middle class, and Lumpa managed to start a process of rural reconstruction based on the peasant class. Also the minutes of Lumimba Parish (Lenshina toured the Chiweza area in 1958) mention that school children and the educated in general were less interested in Lenshina.[138] This contrasts sharply with the Jehovah Witnesses who legitimised the new middle-class and its severance from the demands of peasant kin. Lenshina's strict rules on marriage were not always followed, and non-Lumpas made songs about the many unmarried women in Lenshina's following, who never found their perfect husband.

In the parts of the valley that were dominated by Lumpa during Lenshina's height, especially in the middle of the 1950s, the remaining Catholics and members of the Free Church of Scotland were ridiculed for years. "Us, who refused to be baptised in Chinsali, we were no longer seen as human beings", a number of elderly people mentioned in Kalasa. People spoke of an enormous social pressure in the villages to go and receive her baptism. Many say today that they had to go; there was no other option if one wanted to stay in the village. But some also resisted. The Catholics for example of Mukonka (Kalasa) remained Catholic and they were known over the area as the people of the *cibolya* (old and deserted village site), as the "Romans who killed Jesus", as the enemies (*balwani*) who stayed in their old ways of life of witchcraft and for whom there could be no salvation:

> *Baneni kuŵanensu – aŵa Roma e ŵaipeye Yesu – aŵa Roma ŵamuŵika pa chipandama, e ŵaipeye Yesu"* (the Romans (= the Roman Catholics) killed Jesus and hang him on the cross)

People still remember this song all over Chiweza and Chifunda, attributed locally to the Catholics of Mukonka. They were accused of displaying Jesus' corpse on rosaries around their necks, because they were following the Church of his murderers. Equally in Kazembe and in Tembwe people remained with the Free Church of Scotland when all the surrounding villages absconded.

It is not my intention to play out the sufferings on one side of the conflict against the sufferings on the other side. Lumpa suffered the far greater share of terror and torture during the final onslaught, until extinction in the valley. It is my intention, however, to ascertain that not only Lumpa members were driven by religious faith and motives. During the height of Lumpa's success in the valley, Catholics and members of the Free Church of Scotland did suffer for maintaining and professing their faith, some of them over many years, while they were cut off from the support network of their wider Church. The Catholics and the Free Church of Scotland had managed to establish at least some communities in the valley that proved themselves in a hostile environment and that made sacrifices for maintaining their faith.

Whatever the reasons for Lumpa's success, there is little doubt that Lenshina made a lot of sense to people in the valley, especially to women, and that she reached a deep level in people's hearts. Alice Lenshina herself did not have much education, like most women in the valley. Pastoral agents today go to the valley with a high level of education. Literacy provides a level of stepping back from words, concepts and meanings, but it seems that what Lenshina preached and said, and how she understood witchcraft, made more sense to people in the valley.

OTHER CHRISTIAN INITIATIVES

A decade after the Lumpa war, the Chipangano church (an offshoot of the African National church in Malawi that itself split off from the CCAP on grounds of polygamy) took root in the vacuum left in the Northern valley. Still today the northern valley is still largely dominated by the Chipangano Church that is sympathetic to polygamy, which is widespread and deeply rooted in the northern valley. The success of the unstructured Zion churches since the 1970s in the central valley (Chikowa and Lumimba Parishes) has already been mentioned and compared with the plentiful Pentecostal churches of the 1990s; both have little structural organisation above the individual congregations, and both stress (in different ways) the healing ministry and the existence of spirits, witchcraft and demons.

In regards to the Catholic Church, a striking example of Christian initiatives happened in the 1970s, causing the conversion to Catholicism of large areas with Nabwalya. Missionaries coming from Chilonga had been coming to Nabwalya for decades, without seeing much success of their endeavors. Then a Catholic teacher took up the challenge of a last appointment before his retirement to Nabwalya; he considered it a vocation from God. He and his family (the Kaimbas) started to gather the neighbours together in their home for Sunday prayers. A number of non-Catholic also called them to help with prayers during burials. The initiative spread, and without the priests in Chilonga knowing about it, in one village after another, Catholic churches started to develop. Some years later, a delegation from Nabwalya presented itself on own initiative to the Chilonga parish council. By then they had created, by themselves, numerous prayer centres that are present until today.

Initiatives of the Zion churches (here in Masumba) that spread in the valley not through organized and hierarchical endeavours, but through personal charisms that centre around the gifts of prophecy ("prophita"), leadership ("busa"), discerning spirits and witchcraft ("searcher") and the gift of healing ("doctala")

11.

Conclusion:
questions for a pastoral approach

From a sociological viewpoint one can say that a Church is relevant if a number of people build up and shape their own identities in reference to that particular Church. This goes hand in hand with the initiatives that members are allowed to take: through own engagements, the level of identification increases. On the plateau this has taken place to a much stronger degree than in the valley. We may think for example of the many Church groups (*vipani*) with their distinctive uniforms; they are proud to be Catholic and want to be known as Catholics (or CCAP, or RCZ, respectively); members' social identity is constructed often in relation to Church membership. Such examples are rarer in the valley.

From a theological viewpoint, a Church's relevance depends on how far it helps people to discover God in their lives, and in how far the Good News of Christ lived by the Church is relevant for people. From this theological viewpoint, the Church is at the service of God's kingdom, which precedes the Church, goes beyond it, and rests on God's initiative more than on the initiative of the pastoral workers. This "kingdom centred view" makes pastoral work and pastoral initiatives meaningful also when it does not lead to fast conversion and strong identification with a particular Church.

This research was provoked by pastoral workers with the questions how to build better on people's experiences of God. It has identified some of the concerns where people strongly feel the presence or the absence of God: in relation to their ancestors, to witchcraft, to sickness, to death (*viwanda*) and the spiritual world (*mashawe*), to tradition (the *miyambo* – with special reference to the *chinamwali*), to the world of the animals, to political powerlessness, the selling of their land to outsiders by their own chiefs for selfish reasons, or the loss of control over the youth with an accompanying sense of disorientation. Openness, discussions and dialogue on these issues may provide the required "fertiliser" that allows churches to grow in the valley's soil.

This report has also identified some areas where the present Church structures are ill-adjusted to the valley. Pastoral workers look for ways

(1) how to help and encourage also the illiterate to participate in the church, those who are lost in long meetings, who cannot write reports, who cannot be there regularly, or who are unable to follow our literate minds and concepts;

(2) How to make the church and its structures (especially the catechumenate) meaningful for those in the valley who lead a very irregular life (like most of the men) and are often out. People in the valley do not believe in borders, nor in parish borders;

(3) How to reach fishermen and other groups of people absent from the church and build more on their own religious experiences;

(4) How to react to the injustices that eat up people's lives in the valley, also with reference to the wildlife lobby, and to other challenges of the changing valley, and how to help people to mobilise themselves.

The lack of finance has been a key-handicap that led to the pastoral neglect of the valley. The Catholic Church in the valley will not become self-reliant in the short run. Often a pastoral approach was based on the financial possibilities of the plateau. Saying this, the most important pastoral activities are not the most expensive ones. The priests whom I felt people remember most in the valley were those who went at times from house to house, just to greet people and ask how they were. And that is what people miss today in the Church. One old woman gave me this answer when I asked her where she prayed, and she answered with a big smile on her face, "*ine ndimapemphera kwa abambo cifukwa anandiyendera pa nyumba panga.* (I pray where the priest prays, because he came to visit me at my house!)" Priests and sisters with their silent presence at a funeral said often more than they could have done in a long church council meeting (that would have been poorly attended anyway). "Give us one real Christian to live here with us, and we will follow him," said a headman of Chasera. The demands of this call were summarised by a priest who worked many years in the valley:

> It is difficult to work in the valley. It is not an easy task. It is a vocation. If you do not have that vocation, then don't go to the valley. You will give up with the first rains. If you have the vocation, then you have no conditions, you can go tomorrow just with what you are wearing today; just leave what you are doing now, and the things you worry about today will be taken care of by somebody else tomorrow. But you, go to the valley, and you will see that living with the people and getting to know each other will make you happy, and this happiness comes from God. The word of God, when you really try to live it there in the valley, is very powerful and will find its own ways.[139]

* * *

Humble beginnings of Catholic prayer centres: Chikowa Parish, Mpamadzi & St Agnes, at the temporal prayer centres

Mtumba (Chikowa Parish), Catholic Church service.
Below: inside the small congregation of Mpamadzi Catholic Church

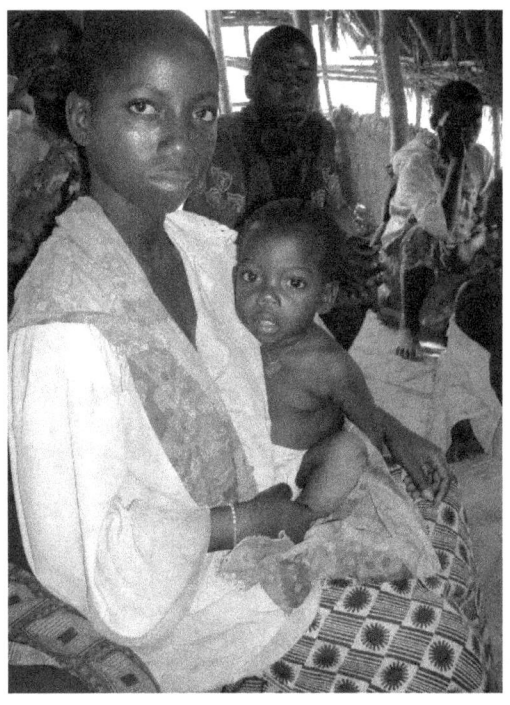

Saying good bye to Brother Vinod, who worked in Nyimba Parish. To the shock of people in Nyimba, he died in 2007, in a fatal car accident.

Chinsimbwe: an established Catholic church, people proud of their uniforms as signs of identity.

Learning how to walk in one's own pace: the challenge for the Christian Church in the Valley

Appendix I:
oral narratives of today

In what follows I give back a few narratives (folklore) that were narrated to me during meetings or interviews during the time of my research. They allow a glimpse into the *present* historical awareness of the story tellers. (Very different narratives have been recorded in the past). Note that the stories are contested; what I give back are views among other views (some of which I will give back in the endnotes).

THE KUNDA OF MAMBWE

Here I give back the account of Esner Njovu from Magezi at the occasion of the Malaila ceremony in October 2005:

> The Luba chief Chabala Makumba had many wives, among them *mukolo* Chanje, a *mwina Chulu* (the clan of the anthill, now the royal Kunda clan). He did not want male children and agreed with his wife that she should kill them all once they were born. She had only one daughter, Chiluya Manda. Then she gave birth to a boy, Mambwe. A slave girl convinced the mother not to kill him; she offered to care for the child while hiding him from the father: "This child will look after you in the future." When the boy was twelve years old, the mother brought him finally to the king and confessed the whole story. The king was very much impressed by the beauty and intelligence of the boy, who had not been given yet a name. The king named him Mambwe, and from then onwards the king stopped killing his male offspring. The next male children were Malama wa Chikuntho, Mambwe Kalindula and Mambwe Mucaca. Then they were sent out by their father to take their sister [so as to

start a royal line] to go and look together for their own country to rule. Chabala Makumba used to send his royal children of different mothers [future tribes] to the periphery so as to have protection from future enemies. Mambwe was given by his father a tail *(mucila)* which was a charm to change himself into a baobab tree, a stone or a guinea fowl. He was also given a stick with which he could cross the Luangwa, "like Moses". They took along also a large group of slaves. One such slave was Kalindawalo, a *mwina Mwansa*. They left him near the crossing of the Luangwa: *"ulinde amalo kuno."* Next they left Malama wa chikuntho. Next they left Kakumbi, a *mutenzi* (in-law) since he had married a daughter of Chiluya Manda; his task was to care for the *tuvimba* (ancestor shrines). Then he left somebody at Matula: Mambwe Kalindula who was Mnkhanya. Next they left Msoro who was also a *mutenzi* since he also had married a daughter of Chiluya. Next ku Mphata they left Mambwe Mucaca (Jumbe). Next Mambwe himself settled *kuli Chitontho* at Mazera to become *Mambwe wa ku Uluba.* Then came the *Mazitu* (Angoni). Mambwe escaped many times through his magic by changing himself into a guinea fowl, or a baobab tree, until the Ngoni caught his first wife, who revealed the secret: "you will find a very big *muuyu* (baobab) at Ulanda." The Angoni found the tree and pierced a needle into it; blood flowed out. So they speared the tree with a spear and Mambwe died; the body never came out of the tree and there is no grave. The Angoni rejoiced and called in their families to live in the country. But Mambwe had still an in-law who had married his niece. He was called Chibanda, a *mwina Mbawo,* and he went up the Angoni to invite them for a feast given for them as a sign of welcome and an invitation to rule them. They prepared plenty of beer and meat, and built many grass huts for the Angoni to sleep when they were drunk. At night, Mambwe's people ambushed the huts, which they burnt down with the enemies inside, except the officer in charge: they cut off one ear and sent him back to the Angoni to tell the story...

(**Note**: According to a narrative collected by Lane Poole – published in 1938 – Mambwe was killed by a Bisa headman Chalwe Cholola, whose wife had been raped by a Kunda in the group of Mambwe. Concerning the origin of chief Kalindawalo there exist many different narratives (of the *wene Mwanza* themselves, of the Chewa, the Kunda, etc.) and there exist also narratives of the "Chewa-Kunda deal" to seal each other's boundaries after the arrival of the Kunda. According to the narrative collected by Lane Poole, Kalindawalo was worried when he heard of the coming of the Kunda across the Luangwa, which made him sent some people down to settle in between as protection (the ancestor of chief Sanje and others.)

THE TAKEOVER OF KAMBWIRI (BISA)

The event has deeply marked Chewa/Bisa historical consciousness until today in the area of chief Mwanya, so more so since the Bisa royal family is fighting already for many decades to regain the chieftaincy. I was given different narratives by the Chewa and Bisa royal families,[140] especially in regards to the interpretations of the meaning of the takeover.

The takeover was grounded in the discontent of chief Mwase's sister Ntemba about the killing of her brother Mwanya and of all her male children. Mwase had them killed for fear they would take over his chieftaincy, and he refused the corpses to be buried – he had given orders for the corpses to be left for the birds to eat. [In some narratives, Mwanya and Ntemba were brother and sister – hence the affection for each other – while chief Mwase was their half-brother from another lineage – hence the jealousy. In other narratives all three were full brothers and sister.] Ntemba never came over the murder of her brother and her children and she contemplated for a long time to have them revenged. The Bisa trader Kambwiri used to pass through Mwase's headquarter on his journeys to Lake Malawi, and chief Mwase used to give him hospitality. On one such journey, Ntemba approached him and asked him to kill her brother Mwase if he was a man. Kambwiri refused, and Ntemba took off her *bukushi* (her strip of undercloth never to be seen by a man) with which she slapped him in the face [the most terrible sign of contempt]. Kambwiri left for the Lake [some say to Mbwani] for his business. On his way back, the same scene repeated itself. Ntemba promised Kambwiri "something he would like" in return for killing Mwase [according to the Bisa he was promised the country; according to a Chewa narratives he was promised sex, but not the country.] Again Kambwiri refused and left; this time, after being slapped again, he grabbed the *bukushi* from Ntemba and went with it. He went up to his uncle chief Kopa [or Kasense], showed him the *bukushi* and sought advice on what to do. His uncle took him to the bush, where they performed the poison ordeal on a chicken; the chicken died. On another chicken, he asked the opposite question, and the chicken survived the ordeal. Thus the uncle advised him to go ahead with Ntemba's plan: he would succeed. Kambwiri passed again through Chibendami on another journey and came back stocked with weapons. He approached Ntemba and told her that this very night the coup was to take place; Ntemba was to take into her quarters all the people she wanted to be spared. That night, Kambwiri's people started the slaughter of the Chewa, but Mwase could escape at first. [According to one narratives, Mwase had a magic through which he could transform himself into a bird (*nkwale*) and fly away to "Phiri Mwase" in Mpalabwe (Lukusuzi) where he went into hiding in the rocks.] Kambwiri's soldiers pursued him and forced an old man whom they found near the rocks to reveal the location of the chief; begging for his life he did so. Kambwiri's people cut off the head of Mwase and brought it to Kambwiri. [According to another narrative, Mwase was hiding in a rock within the *ilinga* itself, his fortified village, and he was caught and killed when he came out to empty his urinal.]

Seeing the corpse of Mwase, Kambwiri was upset since he had not intended to kill him. "Mwase was treating me well; why should I kill him? You were only supposed to capture him!" He asked Ntemba to confirm the identity of the body, which Ntemba did. Ntemba asked for the body of her brother to be left to the birds – as her own children had been on Mwase's orders, but Kambwiri insisted on a royal burial. Mwase accordingly was buried in Chibenda Minku, head and body together. Then Kambwiri and his people asked Ntemba for their reward. Ntemba had no sons left to rule, and she feared reprisal from her own family of the plateau. "They will not leave me!" So she gave Kambwiri the country and asked him to care for her and her relatives whom she had saved.

According to Bisa narratives, she gave the country to Kambwiri for good: *"tatwaitendeke ukwisa kuno"*- "we did not come here on our own account – we were asked by the Chewa themselves to come here and take over." According to the Chewa account, Ntembwa wanted only protection from Kambwiri, but she hoped her own male relatives or future children would eventually reign.

Kambwiri went back to Kopa [or Kasense] to narrate that he had succeeded. Kopa advised him to take a good number of people and go and settle in the new country. This then was the Bisa migration across the Luangwa. Ntemba had two daughters [or grand-daughters]: Chidoti and Ntemba, whom Kambwiri married to Bisa noblemen (his "sons"): to Saidi (a *mwina Mvula*) and to Mukwela (a *mwina Nswi*). [The present chief Mwanya and his royal family trace Ntemba II (younger sister of Chidoti) as their royal ancestral mother.

KAMBOMBO NARRATIVES[141]

> The first Kambombo, Chiweza "Goma", and the other Senga chiefs came from Luba country, from Mwata Yamwi. The reason for leaving their home country was protest against their father, the chief, who had sent them into his gardens for weeding. Chiweza and his people first settled among the Bisa of Chibesa Kunda, where Chiweza stayed for many years. Chiweza was given a wife by Chibesa Kunda;[142] by that time she was still a very young girl called Mwali, not yet able to bear children. Chiweza was a rich man. He was a trader and he had much cloth.[143] At some time Chiweza and his group left to find their own country. Their relative Chiwale had already gone ahead.[144] Before they reached the Luangwa, they left Lundu behind. At Mpyana Kunda they found people. Then they also left Mulopwe at his present place. Only the groups of Chiweza and his nephew Kamphata crossed the Luangwa. (Chikwa and Chifunda on the Eastern side of the Luangwa came in separate

migrations). When they had crossed and wandered around, they saw two mountains: Chiweza saw the Mphala Usenga, and Kamphata the Chiungwe. They separated, each one going to his mountain to found a country.

Chiweza's group consisted mainly of men; they had hardly any women with them. Chiweza came without any sister or aunt or niece. From the Luangwa, Chiweza's group first came to the Livumbu River, where Chiweza found [the Tumbuka] Chili. "Are you alone?" he asked Chili. "No, we are two of us. There is also Mpyana Kamimbe." From there, Chiweza went to Chimilila (the name means: we are only resting here, but we will go on), where he found Mungwalala, who told him: "*Nine Kazilondo mukhala pa wanthu.*" Then he went to Chama. Chama wanted to have Chiweza as his friend, not as his enemy, and he gave him his daughter Mulolwa in marriage. From Chama, Chiweza went up the hill Mphala Usenga, came down and settled. He called himself "Goma", because he had found his country ("*tagoma calo!*") His village was called Chipula Malume ("where men are grinding"); men were doing all the cores that were usually done by women, as they had no women with them. Men even did the grinding. To all the headmen or chiefs he had encountered, Chiweza gave a piece of black cloth which they wore around their shoulders to distinguish them from ordinary people. Thus the Tumbuka leaders were very happy with the arrival of the Senga. Chiweza was trading with the Portuguese.[145] The Tumbuka had no proper clothing, and they did not know what to do with elephants [that they could be used for trade]. When they killed an elephant, they just ate the meat and used the tusks to sit on them. They were very happy when the Senga took and sold their tusks and gave them some cloth. The name "Senga" comes from the fact that they were begging for land (*kusenga*). All leaders he encountered, Chiweza asked who their real leader was, and all leaders only gave their own names: Chili said: "it's me", Chama said: "it's me", and Mungulube said: "it's me." To all of them Chiweza replied: "nobody of you can surpass me."

As Mwali was not yet mature, Mulolwa, the second wife, was the first one to bear a child to Chiweza. The child was sick, and divination brought out that he was sick because he was born of the second wife. He should make this child his heir.[146] The child was named Kasolwe (*solwe-solwe* denoting the first- and only born, a royal title). When the child was born, Chiweza called Chama and the other headmen, and he asked them to give him the honour as their chief by rolling and clapping (*kulamba*).[147] All the leaders acknowledged Chiweza as their chief and did the *kulamba*. The first one to do so was Chama. Hence he was called "Mtaya calo" (meaning the one who threw the country away). The only one who did not do the *kulamba* on the occasion of the birth of Kasolwe was Mungwalala. He just turned round and went back to his village. The name of Mungwalala was Bengu. Chiweza sent soldiers after him, who killed him and cut off his head. Hence the name of the village Dumuka, meaning to cut the head. The village of Mungwalala was dispersed, and it took a very long time until people resettled and another Mungwalala was chosen (Kampuzunga, a son of Bengu).[148] Chiweza was recognized as leader, and the people were happy with him, because he gave them cloth and other things. Chiweza had also other children with Mulolwa, and when Mwali had grown to maturity he also had children with Mwali. When Chiweza died, he was buried at his settlement in Chipula Malume.

After Chiweza's death his nephew Kamphata was called to succeed. But Kamphata had established himself as chief Tembwe, and he was happy with his own country. As Chiweza had no other nephew, Kamphata judged that Chiweza's son Kasolwe should inherit the throne of Kambombo. While the chieftaincy of Tembwe and other Senga chieftaincies remained matrilineal in accordance to Luba custom, in Kambombo a son succeeds his father as chief. The Senga freely took over the custom of the Tumbuka whom they found. After the death of Kasolwe (2), his younger brother Katangalika (3) succeeded, who was born of the same mother. Then followed his brother

Mwimba (4), who was a son of Mwali. The chieftaincy thus passed to the line of Chiweza's first wife. Then followed Mtumba (5), the son of a sister to Kasolwe.[149] The line of Kasolwe was back in power. Then a son of Katangalika took over, Muzieba (6). Muzieba was succeeded by a son of Mwimba of the line of Mwali. He was called Kacila Fitanda (7), and he was afraid that Kasolwe's line would come back. He was known to be a very cruel chief who killed many of his brothers and relatives who might take over the chieftaincy. But the family came together and managed to kill Kacila. Until then, all the previous chiefs were buried in Soyo (except Chiweza, who was buried at his residence in Chipula Malume), but Kacila was buried on the other side, in Fipante. Senga chiefs are buried in the afternoon, so as not to pollute the country. At that time the chiefs were buried together with six life slaves and four elephant tusks. One slave was speared on top of the grave from mouth down to anus, and at his dying breath a bow and arrow was pressed into his outstretched arms; he was left with bow and arrow on the grave to deter witches.

A son of Muzieba, called Chiabe (8) succeeded Kacila as chief. Then followed his younger brother Chimbundu (9), who was killed in a fight with the Angoni (his head was chopped off and carried away). The Angoni (the *Mazitu*) had started to trouble the country already for some time. But the Senga had guns, while the Mazitu had only spears. The Senga trick was to dick game pits. When the Mazitu attacked, they would fake a retreat; the Angoni pursued, but fell into the pits in which they were then burnt to death. Kambombo also attacked the Angoni, and there is still a village in present Malawi called Kambombo where they fought. Kambombo's area was known for cotton, and when he went to war to attack Ngoni villages, his trick was to bind cotton pots on the feet of doves and set them alight. The doves would fly on the roofs of the Angoni and set their villages alight; the enemy had no time to look for weapons.

A son of Chiabe succeeded Chimbundu, called Munaka (10). Then followed Munaka's brothers Ituba (11) and Kavuluvulu

(12), then Ziabwata (13) who was according to some a son of Kacila, which is however refuted by others. Then followed Mutima Iwiri (14), a son of Munaka, then Kazika Alfeo, also called Chindila (15)[150], a grandson of Chiabe (the father being Muzayeka), then Nthowaimu (16), son of Kapembe, and then the present chief Kupula Jume (17), son of Ziabwata, grandson of Kacila.[151]

TEMBWE NARRATIVES[152]

While Kambombo's story is rather straight forward, with only few variations here and there, the narrative of chief Tembwe is much more complicated due to the fact that already for nearly hundred years two royal lines are competing for the throne, which flames up disputes of accession to the throne after the death of each office bearer. I start with the first part of the story, on which the contestants still seem to agree:

The first Tembwe was Kamphata, and the name Kamphata comes from the fish of the same name [a fish with poisonous stings said to emit electricity].[153] While his uncle Chiweza was still staying with chief Chibesa Kunda in Bisa land, Kamphata Zimba had come down to the valley to look out for a new country to live in, and when he had found it, he went back to fetch his uncle on the plateau. As there was a war going on between the Bisa, Kamphata and Chiweza were given a security officer by the Bisa chief,[154] called Chimunyero. They were also given a little girl called Mwali. Coming down to the Luangwa they came to the Msalongo River where they found Pendwe who was Zaongo. From there they went to Luzilukulu, then to Muzingwezingwe, and then up to Katyetye. Again, in Chibungwe they found people, and here Kamphata separated from Chiweza; Chiweza wanted to settle at the Chiphala Usenga, while Kamphata went to Kalimamtundu – in the shadow of trees – where there is a pond with water. When they separated, Chiweza took Mwali along with him, making her his wife, while Kamphata went with Chimunyero. When Chiweza died, Kamphata did not want to inherit the chieftaincy of

Kambombo; "I have my own country", he said. Kamphata had also taken a wife, called Chileka, who was from Mungwalala.[155] The early inhabitants found by Kamphata included Zaongo (Pendwe), Lumpimbwe (Katangalika) and Lundu.[156] Lumpimbwe and Lundu were Tumbuka, while Zaongo was a Bisa.

Here now the history, as narrated by chief Mafews Khunga:

Kamphata had only two children: a son called Chitimbe, and a daughter called Ndekazi. After the death of Kamphata, Chitimbe became chief, because there were no maternal nephews available yet. The name Chitimbe is a nickname, as he was cruel and tended to beat people when he had drunk beer. Ndekazi had three children: Msaya ♀ followed by twins: Mvwila ♂ and Chola. Msaya was however much older than the later twins, and she gave birth to a son called Ngalawa before her brothers were to be born. When Chitimbe died, Mvwila was only a small boy, while his nephew Ngalawa was already grown-up. The family appointed Mvwila as successor, but asked Ngalawa to guard the throne until Mvwila had come of age. But when Mvwila had grown up, Ngalawa was upset and did not intend to leave the throne; hence he nicknamed himself Kwinya (*"nakwinyirila!"*), and he is known by that name until today. Mvwila took over, but Kwinya prepared his own plans to regain the chieftaincy from him.

Mvwila rather than Kwinya is therefore the legitimate third Tembwe. This was in the time of the Angoni raids, and one day Mvwila's daughter was captured. She was called Mbile. Mvwila tried everything to get his daughter back, and finally he sent out his *nduna* Chimunyero to try his best to get her back. Chimunyero managed several times to enter the Ngoni camp masked as a food trader, and he managed to speak with Mbile. By then Mbile had made friendship with another Senga girl who had been captured from Chiwale; they had met in the Angoni camp and they both spoke the same language. This girl was called Mwandu. However, before Chimunyero could free

Mbile, the Angoni removed her to another camp as they had grown suspicious. Mwandu begged Chimunyero to take her out instead, and the two of them managed to escape together. Chimunyero did not know that Mwandu was pregnant. Mvwila however did not allow Mwandu to stay in his royal court; "you are not one of us." From then onwards, Mwandu was taken care of by an ivory trader who was residing in Tembwe's area; he was called Mung'andu (or Ching'andu), and he had risen to a prominent position in the chiefdom of Tembwe. Originally he was a Bemba[157] by tribe who had been working for many years with the Arabs, buying slaves and ivory and bringing them up to Bagamoyo. When he discovered that there was a lot of business in this trade, he decided to split off from the Arabs and to start his own trading empire. He came to Tembwe because he was looking for a base from where to buy elephants, and he had befriended the chief; Tembwe received him well, because Mung'andu gave him much respect and he rendered him useful services. Mung'andu now accepted Mwandu into his own family, and she gave birth to a daughter (whose father had been a Ngoni back in the camp) who was called Ching'andu, a line that was later to provide two chiefs to Tembwe.

Kwinya in the meantime took his opportunity to regain the throne, and he killed Mvwila by witchcraft. Kwinya regained the throne and became Tembwe IV, but after only a short time he himself was killed by witchcraft. As the Mvwila line then had no other children around who were big enough, they had to borrow a chief from the line of Ching'andu. Ching'andu had two children: Mbuweni ♂ and Ndeke ♀, and Mbuweni was made chief (Tembwe V).[158] Mvwila had three children: Mulilo ♂, Sanje ♀ and Mbara ♀. When Mulilo had grown up, he wanted to become chief, and as Mbuweni did not want to go, Mulilo's people killed him. But Mulilo himself reigned such a short time before he died, that he is not even counted in the line of the Tembwes. Again, there was no other male available in the line of Mvwila, and therefore Mbuweni's nephew gained the throne; he was called Chibere (Tembwe VI), and was a son of Ndeke.

Chibere was a compromise between the two families of Mbuweni and Mvwila, because he had married into the line of Mvwila, his wife being Muzongolwe.[159] After Chibere, a son of Mulilo's sister Sanje took over, Kamulibwe (Tiza Mulubwe), who became Tembwe VII and who ruled a long time until 1922, and was succeeded by Kambuwe (Tembwe VIII). He died in 1934, and another succession dispute broke out between the lines of Mvwila and Mbuweni, which the colonial government referred to Chasefu Mission for arbitration. The dispute was settled in favour of the Mvwila branch, and Chisasuni (Aaron Mande, Tembwe IX) was put on the throne. When he died in 1943, the Mvwila branch had the advantage of having a number of highly educated people in their ranks, as they had maintained a close connection with the Free Church of Scotland and supported formal schooling in Mission schools. Joseph Changwe, the brother of the late chief became Tembwe X and ruled until 1977. At his death yet another dispute broke out which took ten years to settle. By then also the Mbuweni branch had well educated and influential people in their ranks, and it took arbitration from Lusaka to settle in favour again of the Mvwila branch. Another Mvwila (Tembwe XI) reigned until his death in 1995, followed by Gibron Zimba (Tembwe XII, 1998-2002) and the present Tembwe XIII, Mafews Khunga.

For Mafews Khunga, Mwandu, the ancestress of his rival line, was not of royal blood but a slave girl. The family branch of Mbuweni, from the line of Mwandu, gives a different history:

> Kamphata had three children, the oldest one being his daughter Mwandu, followed by Chitimbe and Ndekazi.[160] The line of Mbuweni goes back to Mwandu, and the line of Mvwila to Ndekazi. Mwandu gave birth to her daughter Ching'andu and a son called Chikongela, who was lame and therefore unable to claim for himself the chieftaincy. Ching'andu gave birth to Kazilondo Mbuweni and his sister Ndeke. Meanwhile the grandson of Ndekazi, Mgalawa, son of Msaya, kept the throne for Nteye (Mvwila), who was the oldest of twins, the younger

one being Chola ♂. Chola like Chitimbe remained childless. Mgalawa (Kwinya) made war on Nteye and killed him. Then he made war also on his elder brother [second cousin] Kazilondo (Mbuweni), fearing him as a rival for the throne. This war between the two brothers took place at the pond of Lunguziwa. Kazilondo was hit by an arrow in his shoulder, but did not die since he had access to magic; he fled across the Luangwa to Fulaza at the Lundi River. Meanwhile Kwinya went back to Kasakanyanja and made himself chief. People, however, resented his harshness and poisoned him at the beer. (Kwinya used to drink his beer out of the skull of one of his victims, called Chimtolo.) As people did not want Kwinya's children to rule, they called back Kazilondo from Fulaza, who then took the name Mbuweni on the throne. He had married Nguli from the family of Msaya, and his wife betrayed him, as she wanted the chieftaincy to go back to her own line of Ndekazi. Kazilondo had a magic which made him invisible whenever enemies approached who wanted to kill him, but since he loved his wife, he confided the secret to her. Nguli went to the children of Kwinya and instructed them how they could kill her husband at the beer, and so they did. Nevertheless instead of the sons of Kwinya, Kazilondo's nephew Chibere took over as chief, and, in revenge for the death of his uncle, made war on the children of Kwinya: two of them were caught (one was called Chibwende) and Chibere ordered both their arms to be cut off, so that Kwinya's children scattered. Chibere left alive Kwinya's daughter Lekela ["the one left out"], but killed the sons on whom he could lay his hands. Kwinya's family eventually managed to kill Chibere at his village Nkhoka at Kabvumaupeta.[161] Chibere's mother Ndeke did not want to lose another child; that is why she refused to have any of her children inherit the throne. Kamulibwe of Mvwila's line then became chief, whom the British found on the throne, who reigned a very long time. At the succession dispute after his death, the British put a son of Mbuweni as a temporal regent (Chitimbe), who decided that the successor of Kamulibwe should be able to trace ancestry to both sides. Kambuwe therefore was chosen: Chibere at one time had had an affair with Ndekazi II (daughter of Mbara, daughter of Mvwila, daughter of Ndekazi I), and Kambuwe had been born out of that union. After Kambuwe's death, a new dispute broke out that was arbitrated by Chasefu mission, who settled it in favour of the brother of their worker Joseph Changwe (Aaron Chisasuni), at whose death around 1945 Joseph Changwe himself took over. Joseph was followed by his nephew Raban Nguluwe, who was followed by Gibson Zimba. [162]

For narratives of Chikwa Ng'uni and Chigunda Lungu see Lane Poole (1938), 24-27.

THE MWINE MUTONDO DRIVEN OUT BY KAZEMBE[163]

The first Mwine Mutondo was Chikuse, who came from Mozambique and Malawi, his mother being Awozi. On his journey (in Malawi) he met Gumba who was his relative. That was in Magodi. While Gumba stayed in Magodi, Chikuse came down to the Matizi River in the valley. From there he went to Nyimbwe (the country at the Lumezi River in the valley). That is where Chikuse died. The first village was at Chipopomo, near the village today called Kambwiri (the first mission of the CCAP in Kazembe's country). Chikuse was buried in Kaula Tsitsi, the name being derived from the shaving during the funeral. His younger brother Chikwekwe (his mother being Samanayo) took over the leadership. He left Chipopoma because of the death of his brother and went to Chidemba (Kampinda Mulodzi), and from there to Chiwembe. That was the time when Nguwa (the Chewa intruder Kazembe) arrived. Nguwa chased him away. This was possible, because Kazembe found that Chikwekwe was alone – most of his people had gone back to Gumba on the plateau to bring him into the valley; Gumba however refused to come, since he was already settled in Magodi at Chizingizi. Nguwa first had sent out spies: Guzani and Mankomba, who had come with Gontho and Kaliza Mimba. Nguwa by then was at the Matizi River. They went back to Nguwa to entice him to take over the country of Mwine Mutondo – "let us go now, because Chikwekwe is alone!" The Chewa did not want to kill Chikwekwe and his people; they came with sticks so as to drive them away from the country. Chikwekwe fled to Chidyake (Moto) on the other side of the river, where Bisa people were living under Sairi Chikuza. From here they crossed again the Luangwa to come to Mungwalala into the country of chief Chifunda (the country being called Chilenje). Before reaching Chifunda they slept at the Mutobozi River (Mutobozi wa Ansenga). Kazembe followed and reached the other branch of the river (Mutobozi wa Achewa). The river from now on would be the boundary. Both made their camps at their own side of the river; they saw each other but did not fight.

In the meantime the group that had gone to Gomba came back into the valley; when they found that their relatives were gone, many of them committed mass suicide in the Lumezi River, in a pond, together with all their animals that they were keeping. Others went on to seek their relatives. Eight women reached Chifunda. Since so many men had died in the mass suicide, they changed the law of inheritance from the patrilineal to the matrilineal side. They started to follow the matrilineal customs of the Senga of Chifunda.

From Mungwalala, Chikwekwe's people went to Mabuwa (a name indicating water holes), where Chikwekwe died. Chingaipe took over, who reached Chifunda. Chief Chifunda received them well, and he told Chingaipe: "you too are a chief, so we cannot stay together. Go and take the country at the Zewe River. They paid Chifunda ivory tusks of male elephants; the tusks of the females they kept, and since then the tusks of all male elephants would go to chief Chifunda as tribute. After Chingaipe followed Mwebe (his maternal nephew, since inheritance laws had changed), then Dodoli, then Chakanga, then Mulopwe, then Chikatabambo, then Munguza, then Matope, then Esaya Chirwa (+1955), then Chaswe Mwandila

(+1963), then Gibson Nyanje Zimba (+2002) and then the present Mwine Mutondo Witson Ng'uni (narrator of the story).

THE LUMPA WAR IN THE VALLEY (1964)

(The following narrative is a summary from meetings with village headmen and elders of different churches in Kambombo, Tembwe, Chikwa and Chifunda).

Towards the outbreak of the war, Lenshina's people had two fortified villages in the valley: Bindula (or Chaumbwa) in Kambombo and Mangwere in Chikwa (today's Doropa), which gathered communities also from other Senga chiefs who had not given permission to her people to settle in new and separate villages. In Chifunda, her supporters refused to build a fortified village; their leader (Newton Lungu) tried to avoid a war. Lenshina's followers cut through families: the one who was not with her was against her and was a *mulwani* (enemy). Lenshina toured the villages, and on one occasion mission educated CCAP members put forward some Bible verses to ask questions, but they were beaten up on that occasion by Lenshina supporters. Tensions were so high that people did not greet any longer those of the other side, nor give a cup of water to one who was thirsty, not even to a close relative. Preceding the war, one Lumpa member was killed in Chama, and a number of harassments too place. The final war however started with Lumpa attacks. The massacres in Chama started on Monday the 3rd of August 1964, when pupils were just back from holidays to commence school. It started in Kambombo at night, when Lenshina's group attacked the chief, but he managed to escape half naked to Kazembe; here he was picked up and saved by an Indian called Melek, who brought him in his car to Chama. They killed people in Kambombo, and then went on in the direction of Chama burning down first the village of Kazembe, but killing some people also in Chimbilima, Mungwalala, and Dungulungu. They were marching to Chama. In the villages around Chama people expected the attack and either left their villages or gathered at the school. Many school children fled into Malawi and slept in the bush. At Chama School a massacre occurred in which people of both sides died.[164] Lenshina's group attacked from a direction that people did not expect, but a certain Nowell Ng'uni defended people with a rifle, shooting heavily into Lenshina's group. Lenshina's group was large but disorganised and some were killed by their own people in the moments of confusion. From Chama, Lenshina's group retreated back to Chaumbwa, where they were making their own gunpowder for their muzzle loaders.

People all around Chama then got organised and planned their attack on Chaumbwa. They painted their foreheads and the back of their heads white as mark of recognition. A certain Chikonde entered the fortified village (*ilinga*) and put down his trousers, cursed people and said: "You have killed and all of you will be killed!" and left.[165] At some time someone of Chaumbwa shot at a certain Sudya Kumwenda of the attackers' camp and killed him. The attackers then threw petrol bottles on the roofs; as houses in the *ilinga* were built very close to each other, the whole village burnt down. The attackers then entered the village, and killed everybody: men, women and children. From Chaumbwa they went back to the villages and killed those Lumpa members who had not joined their fellow believers in the stockaded village. When the army marched in some days later they prevented further killings of Lumpa members.[166]

Also in Chikwa the war started with a Lumpa attack on the chief, whom a group of Lenshina's followers burnt to death in his house. Also a messenger and a headman (Malata) were killed. A number of villages were attacked.[167] The Lumpa attacks targeted chiefs and any person who owned a gun, seeking access to fire arms. Also old family scores were settled in the Lumpa war. Chief Chikwa was attacked and killed because he had rivals in the Lumpa camp who used the Lumpa war to get rid of their opponent. The army eventually came in, but the Lumpa members fled to the other side of the Luangwa.[168]

This report can be supplemented by Hudson (1999) and Mulenga (1998).[169] People did not speak to me about the massacres of Paishuko (the name means "where there is happiness", the map of Roberts places it near Chikwa) where UNIP supporters massacred an unfortified Lumpa village, that had seemingly not been involved in the violence of Chikwa. As in the case of Chama, the army moved in only after UNIPs attack. Hudson (1998, 48-50) then District Commissioner of Isoka, wrote that

> Examining the corpses littered around, the soldiers were horrified to find that most of the victims had been subjected to appalling tortures. According to an army officer, some of the women had been killed by grain mortar poles forced up their genitals. A senior police officer reported: "Many of the women and children had stakes thrust into anus or vagina or down their throats — this is how they were tortured to death" ... Many of the faces of the dead were contorted in extreme agony, but some were amazingly serene. Perhaps they had endured the torture because they were fortified by their faith and the prospect of a promised after life in heaven ... Even experienced army and police officers, accustomed to the sight of battle casualties and murder victims, were deeply shocked and angered by what they saw. The horror of Paishuko had a disastrous effect on their morale, with unfortunate results at Muyombe later on. After the dead had been photographed for possible court exhibit purposes, they were buried in a mass grave by policemen wearing gas masks. Nobody seems to have been brought to trial for these atrocious murders. In the absence of any survivors, there were no witnesses apart from those involved. Police enquiries would have come up against a powerful conspiracy of silence. Prosecutions might also have been politically inconvenient.[170]

Appendix II.
Population Statistics

Population (2000) of Eastern Province Districts reaching into the Luangwa valley (source: Statistical Office, census data of the 2000 census.)

Chama North	households	population
Chisunga	350	1,591
Kalinkhu	466	2,412
Kamphemba	1,604	8,459
Luangwa	1,263	6,263
Manthepa	555	2,855
Mazonde	205	1,139
Mbazi	447	2,074
Mphalansenga	388	1,898
Munchinga	958	4,763
Mwalala	490	2,755
Ndunda	898	4,355
total	**7,624**	**38,564**
Chama South		
Bazimu	1,243	6,392
Chibungwe	304	2,280
Chilenje	735	3,794
Chipala	134	712
Lumezi	741	4,198
Lunzi	1,126	6,090
Mabinga	948	5,374
Mapamba	764	3,536
Vilimukulu	778	3,950
total	**6,773**	**36,326**
Lumezi (x)		
Chamtonga	2,949	15,980

Chibande	1,444	6,132
Diwa	2,472	14,651
Kamimba	1,842	9,546
Kazembe	903	4,323
Lukusuzi	544	2,465
Lumimba	1,316	6,254
Wachitangati	1,071	5,247
total	**12,541**	**64,598**

Malambo

Chikowa	293	1,394
Chipapa	522	2,525
Jumbe	941	4,841
Kakumbi	1,119	5,549
Kasamanda	831	4,217
Malama	227	981
Mnkhanya	2,285	11,324
Mphomwa	175	1,031
Msoro	168	917
Ncheka	865	4,399
Ndima	1,184	5,862
Nsefu	964	4,336
total	**9,574**	**47,376**

Nyimba (x)

Chamilala	754	3,699
Chinambi	1,099	6,082
Chinsumbwe	271	1,388
Chiweza	1,152	6,424
Kaliwe	1,123	5,967
Katipa	348	1,750
Luangwa	423	2,390
Lwezi	1,429	7,490
Mombe	857	4,111
Ngozi	2,205	11,832
Nyimba	1,231	7,274
Vizimunda	2,307	12,018
total	**13,199**	**70,425**

Msanzala

Chasangu	2,258	11,473

Lusangazi	431	2,233
Mateyo Mzeka	1,544	7,485
Mawanda	1,631	7,686
Nyakwawise	1,655	8,862
Singozi	1,618	7,926
total	**9,137**	**45,665**

(x) only some parts of the district are located within the Luangwa valley

Appendix III.
Election results for the Luangwa Valley

Election results for the Luangwa Valley of Eastern Province (biggest parties only).
Compiled out of the following sources: www.elections.org.zm & www.osisa.org.
votes against votes cast; turnout: valid votes cast against number of registered voters.

Area	Party/pos.	1991 Presidential	1991 Parliamentary	1998 (x) Presidential	1996 Parliamentary	2001 Presidential	2001 Parliamentary	2006 Presidential
National	MMD	75.76%	74.01%	72.59%	60.88%	29.15%	28.02%	42.98%
	2nd	UNIP 24.24%	UNIP 24.99%	ZDC 12.75%	ZDC 13.79%	UPND 27.20%	UDA 23.77%	PF 29.37%
	3rd			NP 8.86%	NP 7.10%	FCC 13.17%	PF 15.58%	UDA 25.32%
	4th					UNIP 10.12%	10.59%	
	turnout	45.27%	45.40%	58.44%	58.7%	67.81%	53.46%	
Eastern Province Average	MMD	24.99%	22.14%	80.29%	58.90%	35.90%	34.49%	42.56%
	2nd	UNIP 70.40%	UNIP 69.70%	ZDC 18.43%	ZDC 23.16%	28.27%	26.18%	10.87%
	3rd			NP 8.45%	NP 6.13%	16.19%	16.97%	37.71%
	turnout	46.97%	47.02%	34.72%	95.32%	64.65%	64.09%	69.48%
Chama North	MMD	21.32%	20.94%	62.57%	65.07%	36.40%	49.42%	51.89%
	2nd	UNIP 76.33%	UNIP 78.34%	ZDC 22.74%	ZDC 30.26%	16.70%	36.74%	37.09%
	3rd			NP 3.81%		27.84%	4.99%	5.80%
	turnout	45.55%	58.92%	39.44%	99.99%	62.00%	57.16%	72.59%
Chama South	MMD	25.12%	22.61%	79.0%	81.06%	25.72%	32.78%	47.08%
	2nd	UNIP 72.54%	UNIP 74.42%	ZDC 10.20%		24.25%	24.33%	40.08%
	3rd			MDP 2.7%		25.09%	24.42%	10.80%
	turnout	43.25%	43.39%	50.48%		78.64%	79.50%	83.07%
Lumezi	MMD	29.87%	(xx)	75.59%	74.53%	43.15%	35.53%	45.27%
	2nd	UNIP 66.37%	67.49%	ZDC 10.52%	ZDC 16.13%	33.22%	29.84%	37.87%
	3rd			NP 8.31%	NP 8.16%	9.39%	14.22%	13.91%
	turnout	45.58%	45.68%	39.97%	50.91%	78.64%	79.50%	71.78%
Malambo	MMD	23.89%	22.27%	87.77%	68.41%	34.11%	26.17%	52.11%
	2nd	UNIP 73.30%	UNIP 73.38%	ZDC 14.03%	ZDC 13.06%	27.07%	33.22%	35.28%
	3rd			NP 7.01%	NP 11.22%	24.83%	18.18%	10.84%
	turnout	49.88%	57.24%	31.19%	37.27%	62.00%	60.88%	72.15%
Msanzala	MMD	32.31%	32.55%	74.52%	73.18%	34.13%	29.98%	49.57%
	2nd	UNIP 62.19%	UNIP 62.02%	ZDC 8.90%	ZDC 11.12%	22.10%	22.92%	33.14%
	3rd			NP 5.59%	NP 6.81%	21.72%	21.71%	7.42%
	turnout	48.95%	48.79%	37.82%	37.85%	76.09%	86.63%	86.60%
Nyimba	MMD	25.16%	25.54%	57.20%	51.05%	34.11%	47.39%	83.98%
	2nd	UNIP 71.35%	UNIP 69.96%	ZDC 12.84%	ZDC 9.99%	27.07%	20.00%	23.80%
	3rd			NP 10.32%	NP 11.77%	24.83%	32.60%	8.00%
	turnout	49.59%	42.90%	27.50%	27.89%	62.04%	47.25%	87.85%
Presidential Candidates	MMD	Frederick Chiluba		Frederick Chiluba		Levy Mwanawasa		Mwanawasa
	2nd	UNIP Kenneth Kaunda		ZDC Dean Mung'omba		UNIP Tilenji Kaunda		UDA HichHema
	3rd			NP Humphrey Mulemba		FCC Christon Tembo		PF Sata
	4th			MCP Chakombeka Chama				

(x): In 1998 UNIP boycotted the elections
(xx): an independent candidate won the second place

Endnotes

[1] Paraphrased from an interview with Fr. Lukas Gundi, May 2005, before he left Zambia to go back to his native Switzerland.

[2] Interview with Petros Chimukoko, Lumimba, June 2005.

[3] cf. http://en.wikipedia.org/wiki/Luangwa_River.

[4] Not all of Chama District is strictly within the Luangwa valley, but also its mountainous parts share with the valley a number of characteristics due to their physical isolation. This research focused on the lower parts of the Senga chiefs Tembwe and Kambombo which are near to the Luangwa River. For the purpose of extrapolating actual population figures from the census data of the year 2000, one should consider an annual population growth of two to three percent.

[5] Source: District Health Lundazi 2005.

[6] Chamilala: 3,700; Chinambi: 6,000; Luangwa: 2,400 (source: District Health Board). I have not obtained the figures for the other parts.

[7] Republic of Zambia 2003a and 2003b (2000 census report).

[8] This line of argument was put forward to me by Father François Richard, with a vast missionary experience in Chikowa Parish.

[9] Interview with Catholic teachers in Kalasa, November 2006.

[10] Interview with a Catholic aid worker and driver in the Luangwa Valley Project, Lumimba, September 2005.

[11] A woman in Mushalila, a village with very few *wene Mvula*. The core of the village is made up of other clans, many from Nyalugwe, but each lineage with its own story of origin.

[12] Interview with old men of Chitumbi.

[13] Astle (1999), 52, writing about a study conducted by Stier.

[14] Bradford Strickland's article on the Akunda, "My grandfather's gun was called 'field of children'" (2001) argues very pervasively how the forces of present politics are seen to have shaped the *njala* of today. Hunters exchanged meat with grain and all that was needed to raise the children, as the title of the article suggests. Once the gun was outlawed together with hunting, people's livelihood was impaired at its very core.

[15] Interview with hunters in Chasera.

[16] Chilonga Diary, 12th November 1900.

[17] "The Lwangwa Valley is fertile and teeming with game, but is so low in altitude and so hot and sultry as to be unfit for European settlement. In December the Valley is turned into a furnace, and the water springs and streams are completely dried up. At this time of year (December), the Lwangwa river, which must be overflowing its embankments and spreading a deep sheet of water all over the Valley at the height of the rainy season, is reduced to a mere trickle of water. The mountains of the Senga (between the Kibwa and the Lwangwa Valley) are salubrious, with plenty of water available everywhere, is very thinly populated." (Chilubula Diary, December 1900).

[18] Chilubula Diary, 9th June 1903.

[19] The traveller E.J. Glave as quoted in Astle (1999), 11.

[20] Hannecart, K. (1991), 57.

[21] Already Mwase wa Minga had been much involved in long distance trade; in fact Mwase's kingdom had been established as part of Mwase Kasungu's plan to build up his own trading empire (Langworthy 1970). Mwase Kasungu had left his brother Mwase wa Minga behind in the Luangwa Valley to control an important crossing of the Luangwa on the route to Mwata Kazembe. But while the Chewa tried to maintain their trading empire through their own traders (Langworthy 1970), Kambwiri was much closer linked to the Arabs.

[22] I use the terms Arabs and Swahili in this context interchangeably; the terms Swahili refer in this book not to a specific tribe or people, but to outside traders involved in the long distance ivory and slave trade, linked to the coast in Tanganyika and much influenced by important Arab trading dynasties.

[23] Ibid.

[24] Ibid. 598.

[25] Kambwiri Diary, June 1904.

[26] The Kunda chiefs Nsefu and Jumbe had even exchanged names with famous Muslim traders of the Lake during the time of their exile during the Angoni raids.

[27] In the chieftaincy Mwanya today there are mosques in Lukusuzye, Yakobe, Chasera and Mkasanga.

[28] William-Myers (1971), p57ff, suggests this point both with reference to the "Luangwa Pottery tradition" which reveals some ritual links to the Nguluwe clan, and to oral evidence from other clans that give historical seniority to the *wene Nguluwe*. He suggests (but not in a certain sense) that the beginning of the Luangwa pottery (a term derived from the works of Phillipson) dates into the 13th and 14th century, and that the introduction of this style into Unsenga, going along also with a revolution in iron forging, speaks of a certain organizational "new order" in which the *bena Ngulube* or *wene Nguluwe* may have played a dominant role.

[29] The earliest written sources referring to the Luangwa come from the Portuguese; Conçeicão in 1696 (writing about an expedition from Tete to the Luangwa and Kafue that eventually lead to the establishment of Feira and Zumbo in around 1700 and 1721) referred to the Mburuma chieftaincy reaching to the confluence of the Luangwa with the Zambezi. According to Lane Poole (1938), the Mburuma mentioned by the early Portuguese is not to be confused with the later Ambo Mboloma of the *bena* Nyendwa, but according to Williams-Myers he refers to the very Mboloma of the *bene Nyendwa*, who had extended his sphere of influence by then to the Zambezi valley and had become a threat to the Portuguese already by 1650. During the 18th century, the Portuguese tried to undermine the trade of Mburuma, with the consequence that Mburuma forced them to leave both Zumbo and Feira and retreat back to Tete (to return only in the 1860s). Williams-Myers (1971), 22ff.

[30] For example Lane Poole (1938), Whiteley (1951), Stefaniszyn (1964).

[31] Personal communication with chief Nyalugwe, September 2005.

[32] William-Myers (1971), 275.

[33] In other areas (for example Mozambique) men were said to have run away in fear and left their women and children behind to be captured just at the sight of a few Ngoni warriors with their shields and battle-cries. (Ibid.)

[34] Ibid. 261.

[35] Roberts (1976), 118ff, William-Myers (1971), 260ff.

[36] This happened in a double sense: children captured and incorporated during the first occupation of the Ngoni were grown up men at the time of the second occupation, and a number of Nsenga craftsmen incorporated during the second occupation rose up to high positions in the skill- and achievement oriented Ngoni society. The Nsenga chiefs Sandwe and the Kunda chief Malama, for example, were raided and subdued by the Ngoni-ized Nsenga Lukezo Mvula (William-Myers (1971), 284.)

[37] When Alfred Sharpe travelled at the end of the 19th century from Msoro to Chinsimbwe, he did not find a single village in between.

[38] See the interesting descriptions of Sandwe in William-Myers (1971), 294f.

[39] The Achikunda trader Nyalugwe for example was acknowledged as chief (and later even senior chief of the Nsenga), because other people of the area repeatedly ran away at the sight of any government official. Nyalugwe functioned as a kind of mediator between the British government and the frightened or mistrusting people around, until he was acknowledged as chief by the British. But tribal identity among his subjects is rather accidental: The chiefly family today considers itself to be Achikunda by tribe, but many of his subjects call themselves Nsenga in accordance with their surrounding neighbours and their own origins. A prominent clan in Nyalugwe are the *wene Tembo,* who spread also to the area of Mushalila (Chitumbi), where they call themselves Ambo (since they belong there to chief Luwembe), though they speak a different language and prefer to marry into Nyalugwe families. Whether they are Nsenga, Achikunda or Ambo is situational.

[40] Both aristocracies of Kunda and Ambo see each other as going back to a common ancestor, the Luba/Bisa chief Chabala Makumba. Mambwe (the *bena Chulu* cultural hero-ancestor of the Kunda), Kunda and Lungo (the ancestors of the *bena Nyendwa* and *bena Mpande* of the Ambo) are said to have been half-brothers, all of them being children of the Luba/Bisa chief Chabala Makumba. Chabala Makumba was said to have his male children killed which led to the migration from the Bangweulu area of his sons' lineages who were looking for land to satisfy their chiefly ambitions.

[41] The Nsenga chief Sandwe for example is said to be an offspring of the first Mambwe with a Nsenga woman.

[42] According to Lane Poole (1938, 50) the first written reference to the Kunda is found in an entry in the diary of Silva Porto in 1852. Twenty years earlier, the expedition of Monteiro passed seemingly through the heart of what is today Kunda land, without any reference to them. Poole concluded thereby that Kunda identity as a people originated between 1833 and 1852. The diaries

of Livingstone make no reference to the Kunda, which may be also due to the fact that he crossed further north of their territory.

[43] In other narratives, the name Awetwe refers instead to Kunda settlements in chief Nabwalya area where the term was said to be but another term for the Kunda in general. (Lane Poole, 1938)

[44] Lane Poole (1938), Whitely (1951), and the popular account published by the Anglican Church in Msoro called *Ifishilano*. See also the Mambwe narrative in the appendix.

[45] Striking is, however, that the Chewa immigrants in general do not emphasis the clan as much as do the Nsenga, Ambo, Kunda or Bisa.

[46] I was told on different occasions that the name Chibande or Chiwande comes from the Bisa verb *kubanda fyani* – to bend down grass by stepping over it so as to make a passage, referring to the first groups of people entering an empty land with no paths. It is acknowledged in most literature that the Chewa were the first to occupy the Chibande. Some Bisa families today, however, refer to groups of people from the West (meaning ancestors of the present Bisa) and also to Pygmies that would have preceded the Chewa. Since the Bisa have been fighting for the last 60 years to have their chieftaincy Kambwiri restored, it is difficult to evaluate the claim of earlier occupation. According to the Chewa tradition, recorded by Lane Poole (1938, 28), the name Chibande denotes a thorny shrub: when the children were playing in the grass, their feet were pierced by the thorns so that they shouted "Chibande, chibande", a term that became the nickname for the whole country. This story of Lane Poole corresponds with the name of the Chewa chief "Mwase wa minga" ("Mwase of the thorns"), a name he attained because of the thorny environment in the Chibande.

[47] Manoel himself was illiterate; the account comes from his later descriptions that were written down by others. Lane Poole (1938, 29)

[48] Ibid. 30.

[49] Lane Poole (1931), 134-138

[50] According to headman Mulamba (interview 13 July 2005) the Chewa had only one other village at that time, namely Ngongoma.

[51] Mothers were supposed to drop a *cinkula* backwards into the river and walk back to their homes without looking back; otherwise the whole village was polluted and at risk. Though the fear of *finkula* was not really limited to the Bisa (the Chewa and many other peoples feared them too), it became

known throughout the valley as a "Bisa custom", maybe because the Bisa made it a point to keep it against the British administration.

[52] Lundazi District Notebook Vol III, 43.

[53] Marks (1976), 17.

[54] The Bisa *bena Njoka* (or *bena Nzoka* or *bena Nsoka*) who are quite numerous in Mwanya area, trace their ancestor to Chongo, who had arrived in Nabwalya before the first *Ng'ona* chiefs, but he had not demarcated his country with *malongo* (broken clay pots left behind) as was the custom for claiming ownership over land. When Nabwalya came in and claimed ownership, Chongo committed suicide with one of his wives by drowning themselves in a pool, that is used until today by the *bena Njoka* for ritual purposes. According to the mythology, Chongo and his wife still appear today as two crocodiles, when the traditional *kupupa* (calling on the ancestors for blessings) is done along the pond.

[55] I was shown several letters written by Bisa headmen to the Republic of Zambia asking for a Bisa chief to be reinstalled together with Bisa ceremonies.

[56] At the time of the research, chief Mwanya, though not yet baptized, was closely associated with the Catholic Church. His two sisters were staunch Catholics, and a number of church councillors in Mwanya had some relationships with the palace.

[57] Much in contrast to the matrilineal peoples of the south, where polygamous unions are matrilocal (several wives of the same husband being scattered over several villages), among the Senga, all the wives stay together with the husband in the same household.

[58] The writings of Lane Poole have been very influential for shaping colonial ideas about tribal identities in Northern Rhodesia. While working for the chartered BSAC (arriving in Northern Rhodesia in 1913, he lived many years in the valley of (old) Petauke. Towards the end of his colonial cariere (from which he retired in 1939), he became Provincial Commissioner of Barotseland. In the District Notebooks, Lane Poole is acknowledged several times as *the* authority on Senga history; much of the colonial understanding of Senga history was strongly influenced by Lane Poole. Lane Poole arrived in his calculation at the year 1790, because he considered the arrival of the Senga to be contemporary with the arrival of the Tumbuka Mlowoka on the Nkamanga Plateau, and the date for that latter event had been proposed by his colleague Cullen Young. (See endnote 63 about the problems of associating the Tumbuka of Chama solely with Mlowoka.) The date 1790 is not

contradicted by the depth of generations from the first Kambombo to the present holder of office, nor by the arrival of the Angoni, said to have arrived on the scene sometime after the death of the first holder of office.

[59] See for example a letter of the District Commissioner of Isoka to Lundazi dated 09-02-1938 that refers to a summary of older entries regarding the "Senga tribe". The first time that the term "Senga" appears in written testimonies as referring to a specific people is (according to Lane Poole (1934), 20) as late as 1885. Around that time Mr. John Moir of Mandala (Free Church of Scotland) visited chiefs Kambombo and Chikwa. That Livingstone does not mention the Senga is not really a surprise, as he had crossed the Luangwa quite a bit south of Senga area. Nevertheless he placed Chibale on his map at the source of the Luangwa; the area is indicated as Bisa or as somehow lying in between the influences of Bisa and Mazitu (Ngoni). When John Moir visited the Senga, they had already a long and established history and identity as Senga.

[60] While references in written testimonies are lacking before 1885, the Senga have a firm place in the oral traditions of the neighbouring tribes, though there is also confusion because of the similarities of the names of the Senga and Nsenga. Bemba oral narratives go so far as to speak about the presence of the Senga in the time of Chiti, the first Chitimukulu who had come from Kola. The narrative speaks about a Senga chief Mwase on the Luangwa, whose beautiful wife Chiti seduced, on which occasion he was killed by a poisonous arrow in the subsequent fight with the Senga chief. References to the "Senga" in Bemba mythology dealing with the time of origin are usually interpreted by scholars to mean projections of the tribal affairs of the present (the time the myth was narrated) into a distant past. They tell us that the Senga were known to the Bemba at the time the story was narrated, but that does not lead to the conclusion that the Senga existed as a tribal entity at the time the Bemba journey was supposed to have taken place. Roberts (1970, 49) explains that "the fact that this latter part of the legend deals with recognisable peoples and places merely indicates that the myth has taken on a new purpose. It is now concerned to place the origin of the Bemba chiefdomship securely in relation to neighbouring peoples and chiefdomships. ... This route [of Chiti from the Luapula to the Luangwa and the Senga] approximates more or less to the furthest limits of Bemba activity throughout their pre-colonial history. The various people said to have been encountered on the way – Lala, Senga, Iwa and Fipa – were all subject to Bemba raiding, especially in the latter nineteenth century." The oral narrative shows that at least in the 19th century the separate tribal identity of the Senga was acknowledged by the neighbouring tribes.

[61] In 1910, the British counted 26 villages in chief Kambombo's area, with an average size of 30 huts each and a total of 572 male adults (Lundazi District Notebooks). By then the population had been enriched by further Tumbuka immigrants, for example the Tumbuka of Kanjumba, who were given land by Kambombo. From here one may guess how small the population was during the time of Chiweza. In 1933, the total male population of Kambombo was 626, corresponding to 757 women (many men were absent in the mines) and 1,158 children.

[62] According to Lane Poole, Chama was in the group of the incoming Bisa, but that contradicts strongly Chama's own point of view, as well as the narratives of other chiefs and headmen. A number of points in Lane Poole's account seem hastily written.

[63] Lane Poole concluded that the Tumbuka encountered by Chiweza had themselves only arrived shortly before Chiweza from Mlowoka by whom they had been allotted land. This view, however, is not easily reconciled with the fact that Lacerda encountered Tumbuka much further south, and that all the Senga chiefs found people living in the country they inherited; such a widespread and scattered Tumbuka presence can hardly be explained by reference to chief Mlowoka allocating land a few years before the arrival of Chiweza. Moreover, Mlowoka was himself a trader, while the Tumbukas encountered by Chiweza were said to be oblivious to the reality of long distant trade. Tumbuka presence in the valley seems much more ancient.

[64] The Senga are not the only case in which a Luba aristocracy set itself up over a patrilineal people, and one finds parallels a bit further north. The Namwanga dynasty, like the Senga, claims Bisa origin, and both adopted the patrilineal system of their subjects (Roberts, 1976, 91). The Iwa, just north of the Senga, claim to be an offshoot of the Namwanga. Roberts also suggested that the founder of the (patrilineal) Mambwe dynasty of Nsokolo was a fugitive (matrilineal) Bemba.

[65] For the Bemba records of raiding the Senga, see Roberts (1973), 49.

[66] The first Kazembe (of Kambombo) was Kalonga, grandchild of Kasolwe, followed by Muzomela (2), Chindambwani (3), Chimugatu (4), Kumakuma (5), Itenda (6), Chakokolapo (7), and Topa Nenge (8). According to the present group-headman Kazembe, even the name of the village goes back to a Luba name of the royal Senga family.

[67] According to the present Kapilingishya, this daughter of Kacila was called Chenda, and she was married to a royal man called Kasolwe with whom she had no children. If I understood the story well, after Kasolwe's death the

village split, since the childless Chenda had not been on good terms with her husband. She gave one part to her brother Masakamika, which became known as Kapilingishya, while another part went to Kapwanyanga. After Masakamika followed Tintinti (2), a son of Chenda, then Kadongo (3), the young brother of the latter. Then followed Chopusa (4) a paternal nephew. On his accession he enjoyed a pot of beer alone in his hut, an event that made other people upset who wanted to drink with him. When he heard that his people were grumbling, saying "the new headman is stupid", he called them all into his hut until it was packed. "You say that I am stupid? Know that from now on my village is called Kapilingishya!" After his death, his brother Chibapate (5) became headman "Mpapatila Bantu". Then followed his brother Luaniko (6), then his brother Kampani (7), then Robert Mwenera (8) ("*canenera – cang'wamina calo!*), and then the present Chabene Goma (9) who narrated this story to me. The first title holder of Chikhalanga was Chibisi, followed by Mulopwe (2), Mwesu or Mweru (3), Chitapankwa (4), Chigobi (5), Kalyalya (6), Kaimaima (7), and the present group-headman Anderson Goma (8).

[68] Interview with Gideon Botha and Traiwell Mkandawile. Ng'anjo Chibwato was a grandchild of Muzieba, the mother being Nguli. Another name was Kalu Sakati. Ng'anjo Chibwato had become very famous in Senga land because of his achievements in fighting the Angoni. He took by force the wife of a man called Musopa Kaleya, against the husband's will. She was called Nyanje, and before she got kidnapped, she had already one daughter with Musopa, called Kachima Kaleya. The father gave the daughter to the new husband. Nyanje herself was of royal origin; she was the daughter of chief Tembwe Mvwila, and because of the high status of Ng'anjo Chibwato, the chief agreed to her new marriage. Back in Kambombo, Ng'anjo Chibwato prepared beer and during the party made Nyanje his principle wife, giving her priority over all the others. (Altogether he had 14 wives). With Nyanje he had the following children: Kamutowa ♂, Mwini Kalambo ♂, Matekenya ♂ (an indication that at this time the Achikunda slave trader of the same name was well known in Senga country and that he had business deals with the Senga headmen) and Chidongo ♀. In this context Kachima Kaleya became very isolated: Chibwato now had many own children with her mother, and then many other children with the 13 other wives, and Kachima felt that she was not really a child of Chibwato. Therefore her brothers sat down together and decided to look for a place for her, away from Kambombo. At that time Kabvimba was chief in Tembwe. The brothers found a suitable place in Mundalanga, and they decided to ask chief Tembwe for that place. On the way to Tembwe they made halt at the present site of Ng'anjo Chibwato, which at that time was called Muzama. Muzama welcomed the men and persuaded

them to stay for the night; that was when the men told him about the purpose of their trip. They did not know that Muzama himself had cast an eye on Mundalanga, and while the brothers of Kachima were sleeping at his house, he himself left at night to reach chief Tembwe before his guests. When the brothers reached chief Tembwe the next day, they were told that Mundalanga had already been given to Muzama! The chief advised them to stay nearby, namely in Muzama's old site. That is how the old site of Muzama became the present site of Ng'anjo Chibwato. Of the children of Chibwato with Nyanje, only Kamutowa stayed with Kachima in Ng'anjo. He died in 1931. He had had three wives, who had all died by then, and he inherited still one more wife in *chokolo* (inheritance of a relative). In old age, Kamutowa nicknamed himself "Gwalawala" because his walking abilities were restricted to the area around his house. Lane Poole said that the oldest living headman he had interviewed was the headman Ng'anjo Chibwato, whom he considered very knowledgeable. Most likely, this was the same Kamutowa "Gwalawala". After the death of Kamutowa, a son of Chidongo called Rojala was made headman (another son of hers was already headman of Chiteke). In 1958, Jonathan Chisute inherited Ng'anjo up to 1994, when the present Gideon Botha inherited.

[69] Lane Poole (1936), 9

[70] Before that, Mperembe had made common cause with his brother Mpezeni, gone west, where they had come across the Bemba by whom they were beaten. While Mpezeni consoled himself by going up to the Bangweulu to fight there at least a few Bisa, Mperembe turned back to join his brother Mombera in Tumbuka country, and doing so he crossed the Luangwa.

[71] Lane Poole (1938), 26.

[72] Interviews with Lewison Banda, 19.06.2005 and 26.07.2006

[73] Saying this, the royal family includes still one ancestor into the royal line of chiefs, namely Kaimba, the uncle of Nguwa, whom they consider to be the first Kazembe. Kaimba did not come into the valley but died on the plateau. After Kaimba followed Nguwa (Kazembe II, buried at the Matizi), then his nephew Mkazi Ng'oma (III, buried at the Matizi), then his niece Chitete (IV) a woman who shifted the royal village to its present location, Chisalanda (V) her son (also called Mkazi Ng'oma), Kabimba Bungulu (VI) (also son of Chitete), Stephen Chitambo (VII, who reigned from 1955 until his death in 1990). Then followed Henri Phiri (+2002), a grandchild of Chitete.

[74] On the map – focusing on Swahili trade – the links of Mambwe are not indicated, nor are the Portuguese/ Achikunda links to the south.

[75] Note, however, that the Mwine Mutondo was a Tumbuka well acquainted with trade and different from the earlier scattered Tumbuka groups.

[76] Many priests felt ill at ease with the clan system, being afraid it would link them too closely to one particular family at the expense of others. Superiors warned the priests not to develop "particular relationships".

[77] 1940: Lundazi–Chama. 1943: Lundazi–Mbuzi road, linking up with Chitungulu and Nsefu. 1946/47: Lundazi–Kazembe.

[78] Zambia National Archives, District Notebooks, Ford Jameson Vol V, 19.

[79] District Notebook, Lundazi, Vol. II, 138.

[80] Ibid. Chipata Vol II, 526.

[81] See especially Astle (1999), White (2000).

[82] Chipata District Notebook Vol. I

[83] See Astle (1999).

[84] National Geographic, September 2005, 118.

[85] Banda Penias (former game guard), Chingozi (Chipalalila).

[86] Banda Penias, 18.6.05

[87] Meeting in the Catholic church of Kataba, 22.06.2005

[88] Ibid. 109.

[89] Meeting within the Catholic Church in Kazembe.

[90] http://www.zawa.org.zm/cbnrm.htm

[91] Of all hunting fees generated, 45% are supposed to flow to the CRBs, 5% directly to the chiefs, 40% to ZAWA and 10% to the Central Treasury. The concession fees however go almost exclusively to ZAWA (80%); the CRBs obtain only 15%, the chiefs 5%. (http://www.zawa.org.zm/cbnrm.htm, accessed January 2006)

[92] Mrs. Mutale in a meeting with the Catholic leaders in the Catholic Church in Chasera 13 July 2006.

[93] 16.07.2006 in a meeting in the Catholic church by church leaders.

[94] Interview with men in Kazembe in the Catholic Church.

[95] Incidentally, most of those who lived some time in Chipata had also lived some time in Lusaka, and they are therefore included in the 40%. Also the

elderly who had lived for years in Zimbabwe or South Africa usually have also lived some time in Lusaka or the Copperbelt and are therefore also included.

[96] Headteachers of Mushalila and Chikwasha schools.

[97] Marks (1976).

[98] District Notebook, Chipata, Volume V, 43ff. Entry of 1945.

[99] In one tragic incident I could witness how strong the expectation of a husband is for his wives to follow to his domicile. In Kambombo, a man committed suicide (he drank the chemicals for his cotton fields), because his third wife refused to settle in his village. When his sister came in and saw her brother had committed suicide, she took and drank the same chemicals, but she was later saved in hospital. The husband had taken it for granted that his third wife, whom he had just married, would come and live at his house, together with his other wives. She didn't.

[100] Group of first wives in Chikwa (meeting in Chilumba Catholic church).

[101] Group of first wives in Mwape (meeting in the Catholic church)

[102] Clarida (2003) describes the ambiguous situation where a person caught with game meat is handed over to wildlife authorities: on one hand the game guards understanding the motives of the poacher yet on the other hand failing to understand how someone can take such high risks for so little gain.

[103] Marks (1976), 128.

[104] Marks (1998), 134.

[105] Annual Reports 1954/55.

[106] The image of the UCZ in the northern valley has probably also to do with the war between UNIP and Lumpa (see later).

[107] Interview with Petro Chimukoko and Adrian Ng'uni, Lumimba, 15 June 2005. This is not an isolated opinion.

[108] Interview with Lewison Banda.

[109] Ambo and Bisa people referred to me a number of times to the Bemba proverb: *Akasabi ukulya akasabi kanankwe e kunona,* (a small fish needs to eat [=marry] its fellow small fish in order to prosper), meaning: marry close to your family, and you will prosper; else your belongings will diminish in endless disputes and will go to people outside the family.

[110] Verbatim, for the full flavour: "*Makolo wasu ezo pephelela ku cimuti ca msolo; monga akasowa mvula ezotetelela ku msolo mvula yeza lokwa. Ngati*

asowa nyama ezosenga kwa Nyamalenga nkhalamo yeza iŵela nakata nyama. Matenda akaŵela ezatetelela, munthu apola. A missioni akaŵele elesha no nena kuti: mucita monga mupephela mafano, pamene tinaleka kupephelela m'msolo. Makolo akale mulungu eze naye pafupi cifukwa ngati apepha mvula yeza lokwa: kufuma tyala ku cimuti na mvula ninshi yapona. Cifukwa mulungu eze naye pafupi, koma lelo cikanga cifukwa vutucita ni viipa veka. Tucita lini vinthu va bwino. Enzo ŵamwila ngako ŵanthu akale, cifukwa ezodziwa mulungu kuti nine wakufuna. Ndipo sanali kudziwa kuti pali munthu wina wake amene anafwila koma pamene tadziwa kuti Yesu atifwila mulungu e titalamuka. Kale akacita viipa mulungu ezo ŵazuzula no ŵapanika ni cifukwa cake zonse zinali bwino. Lomba vilusile cifukwa cakuti olo aye ku kawimba vula siyulokwa cifukwa macimo apaka. Ŵala ŵanthu akale mulungu enzomuyopa ndipo munthu oyumilile viipa ezomupaya. Ezomukhokometsa ku cimuti no mumwensha mwavi aŵa ŵanthu. Kale enze kuti munthu akacita cigololo ezo mukanzinga manja ni cifukwa cake ezoyopa. Amissioni akaŵela e tilesha vasu, aletsa miyambo yathu, koma yao miyambo aliye tipatsa."

[111] Interview with a group of young men in Ncheka/Chikowa, who don't pray in any church.

[112] A number of different approaches (often complementary) have helped to shed more life on female initiation. Richards (1956) showed how values and the hierarchical order (to a negotiated extent a chiefly order) was maintained through the rites, and Victor Turner (1969), how rituals transform people for another role in society. Mary Douglas (1966) had located female initiation rites in those types of societies where men can walk out of marriages rather easily, e.g. in matrilineal societies, but where the cash economy depends largely on access to men. One aspect of the argument is that women of the same family may put much pressure on a young bride to go a long way with her husband, not to give up when things are tough, but to please her husband even when she gets beaten. When a girl runs back home from her husband because she cannot bear it any longer, we may find her fellow women kin giving *her* a lesson (rather than her husband) after which she is sent back to him. At the same time, this commences a process of renegotiations also with the husband, so that conflicts can be aired and new grounds for the common life be found. Rasing (1995) looked at how female identity and power is constructed and negotiated in the rites.

[113] Name changed.

[114] The food he eats (*nsima* – hence the name of the sickness) does not pass through to the stomach but gets stuck, causing vomiting, coughing of blood

and death. In this case, the man coughed blood before he died, a condition traditional attributed to *nsima*.

[115] Gathered during a leadership seminar that I was allowed to attend at Msoro Anglican church in October 2006.

[116] Weller (1971), 37, in the words of Bishop Hine who visited Msoro a month after Rev. Kamungu's arrival.

[117] Ibid.

[118] Towards the west of Msoro, some teachers had actually preceded Kamungu and were included now into his jurisdiction. Kamungu himself was supervised by De la Pyrme in Ford Jameson, who was also responsible for selecting teachers.

[119] Ibid. 38.

[120] In Jumbe, I heard stories of Watchtowers being killed by people in conjunction with the authorities (police) in a process called "*kupereka cifuwa*" (to offer one's chest) in which armed men smashed the outstretched breasts with the guns. So far, however, I found no external evidence for this.

[121] Meebelo (1971), 133-185.

[122] This point has been made for many parts of Africa. See for example Gifford (1998).

[123] Minga Diary, 24th August 1924.

[124] District Notebooks, Lundazi Vol II, 153.

[125] District Notebooks, Chipata Vol. II, 155, 156.

[126] So for example in the Luapula (fieldwork notes of Kasamba Parish).

[127] Especially by Norman Long (1968) in his study on the Jehovah Witnesses in Serenje.

[128] Interview with Aisak Lungu, Chifunda, September 2006. Aisak Lungu had held at one time the position of a treasurer in the Lumpa Church in Chinsali.

[129] Oger 1960; 1991, Calmettes 1982; Hinfelaar 1994.

[130] Lenshina had her visions in 1953, the same year as the much opposed Federation came into being, an event that shattered trust in negotiations with the white regime. According to the subtle analysis and interpretation of Roberts (1970), the rise of Lumpa coincided with increasing frustrations in

politics: the ANC lost its grip on people, and people were increasingly looking outside politics for solutions to their problems. Lumpa's heights were around 1957/58, when political motivation was lowest. Also the prestige of the chief was equally low during the rise of Lumpa: their united appeals against Federation had been brushed away in a single stroke; at other times they were seen but as instruments and channels of the white regime. At their expense, Lenshina, at the height of her movement, resembled much a traditional Bemba chief (Calmettes 1978): she was treated as a *namfumu*, was surrounded by councillors, people brought tribute and worked on her fields, she re-enacted chiefly functions in the blessing of the seeds, and later she came to live in stockaded villages like the chiefs of old. Lumpa's decline thereafter coincided with the rise of UNIP; independence now came into reach especially after the release of Kaunda from prison in 1960, and politics became once more an option of focus. Most people left Lumpa long before the final war. The Lumpa war finally was intrinsically connected with the totalising tendencies in UNIP and Lumpa's own increasingly fatalistic and apocalyptic aspects. To be against UNIP came to mean to be against the Zambian nation. And to be not with Lenshina came to mean to be the enemy. While UNIP put pressure on the rural population to buy UNIP cards, Lenshina was burning them. Unscrupulous UNIP youths were given a free hand to burn down a number of Lumpa churches and beat up Lumpa members; Lumpa became more and more a kingdom within a kingdom, isolating itself into its own independent villages, which could defend themselves but that could and would also attack. While UNIP made it clear to Lumpa that there would be no place for it in an independent Zambia, Lumpa in turn made it clear that nobody belonging to UNIP could be saved; Lumpa attained more and more apocalyptic tendencies. In the meantime also the chiefs, who had been sidelined by Lumpa, recuperated themselves out of near oblivion through their alliances with UNIP, and in the valley much violence of Lumpa was incidentally directed against the chiefs (Kambombo was attacked and Chikwa killed).

[131] Concerning the Lumpa elite, a former treasurer of the movement (Newton Lungu, Chifunda) put it to me this way: "Things started to turn wrong when Lenshina's family came from the Copperbelt and wanted to take charge of things. When they came, I resigned as treasurer and came back to Chifunda. We were two treasurers from the valley and both of us felt that they would kill us, because they wanted to keep the money themselves." Newton Lungu then became leader of Lumpa in Chifunda. Elders in Chifunda praise him today for preventing the war in Chifunda. Why did he join Lumpa, I asked him. He had been sent by his headman to see what the church was all about – "we are hearing such wonderful things" – the headman told him – "go

and see what it is about." He stayed in Chinsali until the early 1960s and joined the movement.

The story that Lenshina had been bought by UNIP's enemies: Roy Welensky, Harry Nkumbula, Moise Tshombe in Katanga, is widespread in Chama, and also a certain "Bwana Ling" was often mentioned, who would have supplied her with weapons and with money to set up an independent kingdom. This was the official narrative of UNIP during the clashes and after.

[132] Narrated in Malama.

[133] David Gordon made this point in a conference on postcolonial politics in Lusaka, 2006, though he did not research in the Luangwa valley.

[134] Page 30.

[135] *The Times* (6.8.1964), quoted in Calmettes (1978). The article was written by Clairmonte.

[136] Interviews with village headmen and church leaders in Chama, Tembwe and Kambombo in September 2006.

[137] Hinfelaar (1994), 99, 79.

[138] Lumimba Council Minutes, 17th and 18th January 1958.

[139] Interview with Luigi Cassagrande.

[140] Chief Mwanya and his two sisters and brother-in-law, Paul Mwale on the Chewa side, and the Kambwiri "heir *in spe*", John Captain and his *bena Ng'ona* family, with a number of headmen on the Bisa side.

[141] The following narrative is a synthesis of individual narratives that I recorded from group-headman Mutanila (the 80 years old man was appointed by senior chief Kambombo to narrate the history to me; he is of the royal family), groupheadmen Chama, Kazembe, Mungwalala, Malama, Chikhalanga, Kapilingishya, headmen Iwiri, Muziebe, Njewa, and the leaders of the Catholic church councils (some of them themselves of the royal family). Where the narratives differed substantially, I indicate this in the following footnotes.

[142] According to group-headman Mutanila of the royal family. Others narrated that the young wife of Chiweza was given by the Bisa chief Kopa.

[143] Some say that he traded with traders of Lake Malawi.

[144] In Kambombo it is said that Chiwale came with Chiweza. But according to Mungwalala, Chiwale is related to Mungwala and Chiri, and that they had

come in the same Tumbuka migration from the East. "Chiweza found people in Chiwale", and they were Tumbuka.

[145] According to group-headman Mutanila.

[146] This part of the narrative comes from group headman Chikhalanga (in Kapilingisha), but was refuted by a number of other headmen on other occasions.

[147] Some say that Chama was tricked to do the *kulamba* (clapping for the chief rolling on the back, acknowledging his chiefly authority), saying it was a prescription of a *ng'anga* who said that otherwise the sickish child would not recover.

[148] According to the present Mungwalala, Saiwat Kumwenda (2005), Kampuzunga Kumwenda was succeeded by his younger brother Mukololo. Then followed Kaleya Kanjele Bende, a son of the wife of Kampuzunga from a previous marriage (Kampuzunga was not the father). Kaleya died in 1953. Then followed Zimba Madumera, son of Mutemwa Kumwenda, a *muzukulu* (grandchild) of Mukololo, who died in 1980 and was succeeded by Saiwat. The genealogy seems far too shallow. Bengu may not have been the Mungwalala encountered by Chiweza, as other narratives give the name of Juzi as the first Mungwalala.

[149] Though headman Njewa said that Mtumba was a brother of Mwimba of the same mother.

[150] According to Lundazi District Notebook, Kambombo Chimbalangandila started his reign in 1929, the year in which his predecessor (no name given) had died. We may identify Chimbalangandila with Chindila (Kazika Alpheo). According to the District Notebooks, he was deposed in 1947 for ivory offences (in that year most of the Senga chiefs were sacked) and succeeded by "Kambombo Mpundu" whom we may identify with Nthowaimu, though his predecessor still remained alive for quite some time. Chief Kambombo "Chimbalangandila" succeeded in 1929 and was deposed in 1947 after his conviction of ivory related offences.

[151] It may be useful to embellish the official genealogy of Kambombo with notes from the Lundazi District Notebooks and from Lane Poole; Lane Poole especially gave a very different genealogy of succession. According to him, Kamphata remained in Chipula-Balume until the death of Chiweza, and was denied succession to Kambombo's throne. It was only then that he looked for his own country in Tembwe. In oral history of today, both of Kambombo and Tembwe, Kamphata separated from his uncle before the latter settled in

Kambombo. The next difference comes with the wives of Chiweza. Poole asserted that Mulolwa was the head-wife of Chiweza, while Mwali was an inferior wife. He pointed at a succession dispute at the death of Chiweza between Kasolwe (son of Mulolwa) and Mwimba (son of Mwali). Today it is said that Mulolwa's status derived from the fact that she was older and thus the first wife to bear children, due to the tender age of Mwali.

[152] The following narrative is compiled from narratives given by (1) chief Mathew Khunga and a number of elderly women of his royal family whom he had gathered together, (2) group-headman Simon Kumwenda and his family, who was at the time of interviews a contender for the chiefdomship (by then Mathew Khunga had yet to be confirmed by the government), (3) a meeting attended by group-headman Lwambu, headmen Kamulibwe, Kamwendo, Kwinya, and a number of elderly royal women (Ndekazi, Chinka Mwase, Nyanje and Kwanangachi), (4) a meeting with headmen in Chitimbe attended by vice headman Chikwenda, group-headman Kabvivwanga, headmen Juma, Mphelo, Kambuwe and Chizovwa, (5) interview with group-headman Zaongo (Zakeo Ng'uni), (6) group-headman Ng'anjo Chibwato (Gideon Botha) and Traiwell Mkandawile in an interview.

[153] Incidentally, this fish is sought today by many as a powerful *cishimba* (*chizimba*), which is the activating and energising ingredient in the process of preparing many medicines.

[154] Some say that this Bisa chief was Kopa, but according to others it was Chibesa Kunda.

[155] According to chief Tembwe. Others say she was of unknown origin.

[156] Lumpimbwe is also called Katangalika, which gives rise to confusion as there are a number of villages called Katangalika in the areas of Kambombo and Tembwe. Lundu as well is not to be confused with Senga chief Lundu who was related to the group of Kambombo. It was group-headman Zaongo who was very clear about the insertion of Lundu, though the chief left Lundu out and included instead Buli. Most headmen however explained that Buli arrived only after Kamphata but was given a prominent *Induna* position due to his trading capacities and his role in settling a royal dispute (see later).

[157] According to Zaongo he was from Malawi.

[158] According to the present chief Khunga, the name Mbuweni comes from "Mbwa bene" – meaning "he is not ours", "he is from somewhere else" – and he sees in the name a proof of the non-royal origin of Mbuweni. His rival

contender for the chiefdomship in the time of the interview was from the line of Mbuweni.

[159] Again, according to the present chief Tembwe (Mathews Khunga), the name Chibere (meaning breast) comes from the fact that the chiefdomship belonged to the family of his wife (the breast), that Chibere was chief only because of the royal descend of his wife.

[160] This version is supported by the Lundazi District Notebooks, in which all genealogies include Mwandu as a daughter of Kamphata, either as the oldest or youngest daughter. According to Lane Poole, it was Mwandu's daughter, the mother of Mbuweni, who was ransomed from Angoni captivity for two elephant tusks; Mbuweni was born in Angoni captivity and was considered a stranger of unknown parentage.

[161] Some say he was killed by a group of Ngoni warriors who were hired by Kwinya's family.

[162] The succession disputes do not just concern the royal family. Lane Poole described some of the disputes as civil wars, which is confirmed by the narrative of the Kumwenda family. It means that across the chiefdomship, each claimant had his supporters who were ready to fight, which presupposes a strong identification of ordinary people with their chiefs, which is not necessarily the usual thing in the Luangwa valley. The northern valley attained a higher level of centralisation than the south. According to Lane Poole, chief Kamulibwe, who reigned roughly from 1870 to 1922, managed to bring his people together into very large stockades by means of which he could successfully defeat the Angoni aggressions, a fact for which he was highly esteemed. The same Kamulibwe submitted under the rule of BSAC and welcomed the Free Church of Scotland.

[163] Narrative of Witson Nguni, the present group headman Mwine Mutondo, 27.07.2006

[164] People today speak of about 30 people killed in Chama.

[165] Kampamba Mulenga wrote in his book that Chikonde entered the village completely naked and that he demanded the release of chief Kambombo's wife who was held hostage by Lumpa; after negotiations he could take her out.

[166] When I asked how many died in Chama during the final attack, I was usually given a figure of more than 100 but less than 200.

[167] People in Chikwa did not give me details in regards to the villages as in Kambombo. The governmental report speaks of 9 people killed.

[168] According to the official report they held out until the 10th of October but were eventually overcome; 60 Lumpa members were killed in the final countdown with the army.

[169] The book of Kampamba Mulenga, written from a Lumpa perspective, gives a number of details of what happened in Kambombo and Chikwa. I did not have his account when I interviewed people; it is much more detailed, and I found back a number of names that I had also heard of in my own interviews. Mulenga, however, seems to have problems with numbers in his book, and Mulenga's narrative furthermore portrays all events in the valley as a conflict between Lumpa and UNIP. People stressed in our meetings the other aspects of the conflict beyond the Lumpa-UNIP dispute. Lumpa had targeted people who had little to do with UNIP; when Lumpa needed guns, anybody with a gun became a target. People in Chikwa and Chama mentioned that the Lumpa conflict actually had been an occasion to settle old personal scores, and such personal rather than political scores took priority in the narration of the events to me.

References

NATIONAL ARCHIVE ZAMBIA (NAZ)

District Notebooks: Lundazi (Vol. I-IV); Ford Jameson (Vol. I-V); Petauke (Vol. I; Katete (Vol. I); Mpika (Vol. I-II);); Isoka (Vol. I-II); Serene (Vol. I-II)

ARCHIVES OF THE MISSIONARIES OF AFRICA, ZAMBIA

The following documents were accessed in the translations of Fr. Maurice Gruphat:

Annual Reports: Bangweolo & Nyasa Vicariates, Luangwa Mission Vicariate, Prefecture of Fort Jameson 1908-1945; 1946-1955; Fort Jameson Vicariate 1937-1955; 1954-1955
Quarterly Reports (Vol I-V)
Minutes of the local Council: Lumimba Mission 1949-1968
Mission Diaries: Lumimba (translated by Adrian Sawadogo); Chilubula (Vol. I-IV); Chilonga (Vol. I-V); Kacebere (Vol. I); Minga (Vol. I-IV)
Oger, L. 1960. *Religious Sects in Northern Rhodesia Lumpa Church: A Study of the Lenshina Movement 1955-1960.*
Oger, L. 1991. *Our Missionary Shadow: A Series of Historical Flashes at the Occasion of the Centenary Celebration of the Catholic Church in Zambia (1991) and Reflections on the Second Evangelisation 1992-1993.*
Oger, L. 1997. *Casting a Shadow over the Mission: Witchcraft – a largely ignored but likely approach to meeting Christ in the faith.* Translated by M. Gruffat.

PUBLISHED BOOKS AND ARTICLES:

Astle, W. L. 1999. *A History of Wildlife Conversation and Management in the mid-Luangwa Valley, Zambia.* Bristol: British Empire and Commonwealth Museum.

Binsbergen, W. van. 1981. *Religious Change in Zambia: Exploratory Studies.* London: Kegan Erik International.

Calmettes, J. L. 1982. *The Lumpa Sect, Rural Reconstruction, and Conflict.* M.Sc. (Econ) University of Wales.

Child, B. CBNRM Programme in Mambwe District under SLAMU (Summary)

Clarida, L. *Human Animal Conflict in the South Luangwa Valley of Eastern Zambia.* Excerpts from thesis

Comaroff, J. and J. 1993. *Modernity and Its Malcontents: Ritual Power in Postcolonial Africa.* Chicago, London: University of Chicago Press.

Douglas, Mary. 1966. *Purity and Danger: An analysis of the Concepts of Pollution and Taboo.* London: RKP.

Fields, K. E. 1982. Christian Missionaries as Anticolonial Militants. *Theory and Society* 11(1), 95-108.

Geschiere, P. 1997. *The Modernity of Witchcraft. Politics and the Occult in Postcolonial Africa.* Charlottesville: University Press of Virginia.

Gifford, P. 1998. *African Christianity: Its Public Role.* London: Horst & Company

Gibson , C.C. and Marks, S.A. (1995). Transforming rural hunters into conservationists: an assessment of community-based wildlife management programs in Africa. *World Development* 23(6), 941-957.

Gouldbury C. & Sheane H. 1911. *The Great Plateau of Northern Rhodesia: Being some Impressions of the Tanganika Plateau.* London: Edward Arnold.

Government Republic of Zambia (1965). *Report of the Commission of Inquiry into the former Lumpa Church.*

Hannecart, K. 1991. *"Intrepid Sowers": from Nyasa to Ford Jameson 1889-1946.* Missionaries of Africa, Rome.

Hinfelaar, H. F. 1994. *Bemba speaking women of Zambia in a century of religious change (1892-1992).* Leiden: E. J. Brill.

Hudson, J. (1999). *A Time to Mourn: A Personal Account of the 1964 Lumpa Church Revolt in Zambia.* Lusaka: Bookworld Publishers.

Isaacman, A. 1972. The Origin and Early History of the Chikunda of South Central Africa. *The Journal of African History* 13(3), 443-461.

Lancester, C. S. 1974. Ethic Identity, History, and "Tribe" in the Middle Zambezi Valley. *American Ethnologist* 1(4), 707-730.

Langworthy, H. W. 1969. *A History of Undi's Kingdom to 1890: Aspects of Chewa History in East Central Africa.* PhD Boston University Graduate School.

Langworthy, H. W. 1971. Swahili Influence in the Area between Lake Malawi and the Luangwa River. *African Historical Studies* 4(3), 575-602.

Lyons, A. 2000. An Effective Monitoring Framework for Community Based Natural Resource Management: A Case Study of the AMADA Program in Zambia. Thesis (MSc) University of Florida.

Marks, S. A. 1976. *Large Mammals and a Brave People: Subsistence Hunters in Zambia.* University of Washington Press, Seattle and London.

Marks, S. A. Back to the Future: Some Unintended Consequences of Zambia's Community-Based Wildlife Program (ADMADE). *Africa Today*

Marwick, M. G. 1963. History and Tradition in East Central Africa through the Eyes of the Northern Rhodesian Cewa. *The Journal of African History* 4(3), 375-390.

Matthews, T. I. 1981. Portuguese, Chikunda, and Peoples of the Gwembe Valley: The Impact of the 'Lower Zambezi Complex' on Southern Zambia. *The Journal of African History* 22(1), 23-41.

Mulenga Kampamba (1997). *Blood on their hands.*

Poole, E. H. L. (1938). *The Native Tribes of the Eastern Province of Northern Rhodesia: Notes on their Migrations and History.* Lusaka: Government Printer.

Poole, E.H.L. 1931. An Early Portuguese Settlement in Northern Rhodesia. *Journal of the Royal African Society* Vol. 30, No. 119 (Apr., 1931), 164-168.

Rasing, T. 1995. *Passing on the Rites of Passage: Girls' Initiation Rites in the Context of an Urban Roman Catholic Community on the Zambian Copperbelt.* African Studies Centre Research Series.

Republic of Zambia 2003a. *Zambia 2000 Census of Population and Housing: Summary Report.* Lusaka: Central Statistical Office.

Republic of Zambia 2003b. *Zambia 2000 Census of Population and Housing: Housing and Household Characteristics. Analytical Report.* Lusaka: Central Statistical Office.

Richards. A. 1980. *Chisungu: A girls' Initiation Ceremony among the Bemba of Northern Rhodesia.* London: Faber & Faber.

Roberts, A. (1970). *The Lumpa Church of Alice Lenshina.* London: Oxford University Press.

Singh, J. and H. van Houtum. 2002. Post-colonial nature conservation in Southern Africa: same emperors, new clothes? *GeoJournal* 58, 253-263.

Snelson, P. 1974. *Educational Development in Northern Rhodesia 1883-1945.* Lusaka: Kenneth Kaunda Foundation.

Stefaniszyn, B. 1964. *Social and Ritual Life of the Ambo of Northern Rhodesia.* London.

Strickland, B. 2001. "My Grandfather's Gun was Called *Field of Children*": Ecological History as Indictment Policy. *Africa Today*

Ter Haar, G. 1992. *Spirit of Africa: The Healing Ministry of Archbishop Milingo of Zambia.* London: Hurst & Co.

Turner, V. 1969. *The Ritual Process.* New York: Cornell University Press.

Vail, L. 1977. Ecology and History: The Example of Eastern Zambia. *Journal of Southern African Studies* 3(2), 129-155.

Wainwright, C. 1998. Success in Integrating Conservation and Development? A Study from Zambia. *World Development* 26(6), 933-944.

Weller, J. 1971. in Barret B. D. (Ed) *African Initiatives ion Religion.* Nairobi: East African Publishing.

White, L. 1995. Tsetse Visions: Narratives of Blood and Bugs in Colonial Northern Rhodesia, 1931-9. *The Journal of African History,* Vol. 36, No. 2, 219-245.

Wright, M. and P. Lary. 1971. Swahili Settlements in Northern Zambia and Malawi. *African Historical Studies* 4(3), 547-573.

INTERNET RESOURCES

www.zawa.org

www.elections.org.zm

www.osisa.org

www.freeweb.com

www.wikipedia.org

Index